THE PHILOSOPHY OF
SIMONE DE BEAUVOIR

SUNY Series, Feminist Philosophy
Jeffner Allen, editor

THE PHILOSOPHY OF SIMONE DE BEAUVOIR

GENDERED PHENOMENOLOGIES, EROTIC GENEROSITIES

DEBRA B. BERGOFFEN

STATE UNIVERSITY OF NEW YORK PRESS

Published by
State University of New York Press, Albany

For information, address State University of New York Press,
State University Plaza, Albany, NY 12246

Production by Marilyn P. Semerad
Marketing by Terry Abad Swierzowski

Cover painting by Ann Barbieri

Library of Congress Cataloging-in-Publication Data
Bergoffen, Debra B.
    The philosophy of Simone de Beauvoir : gendered phenomenologies,
erotic generosities / Debra B. Bergoffen.
       p.   cm. — (SUNY series, feminist philosophy)
    Includes bibliographical references (p.   ) and index.
    ISBN 0-7914-3151-7. — ISBN 0-7914-3152-5 (pbk.)
    1. Beauvoir, Simone de, 1908-   . 2. Philosophy, Modern—20th
century. 3. Feminist theory. 4. Sex role. I. Title. II. Series.
B2430.B344B47 1996
194—dc20
                                                      97-1516
                                                        CIP

For my parents
Lillian and Abraham Hantman
for lessons in love, generosity, and justice

For my children
and the enfolding bond

For the Casey Girl

and

For Bob
and the gift of a home in his heart

CONTENTS

Acknowledgments

The first draft of this manuscript was written during a study leave grant from George Mason University. Without that time this book would still be "in progress." While the university provided critical time for thinking and writing, two people in particular helped me use that time well. Peg Simons understood from the beginning and with more confidence than I, what I was up to and where it might lead. Her generosity, her enthusiasm and her friendship are present in the life of this text. Hazel Barnes offered another source of support. Her skepticism and challenges questioned my thinking without dismissing it. In taking the time and trouble to critique early papers and ongoing drafts of this manuscript, she alerted me to trouble spots and honed my reading of the text.

A book as long in the making as this one also owes much to conversations and correspondence with friends and colleagues. Phyliss Morris, Sonya Kruks, Bob Stone, Ron Aronson, Bill Mc Bride, Eleanor Holveck, Wayne Froman and Irving Karp pointed me to resources, exchanged ideas and helped me find my voice. Thanks are also due to Jeffner Allen whose original interest in the project helped it find a home and whose insistence that certain issues be addressed helped me avoid pitfalls.

I am especially grateful for the gifted assistance of Jennifer Mensch whose research assistance and help in formatting early drafts of the manuscript was invaluable. During the last stages of preparing the manuscript I was fortunate to have the help of Karen Misencik, whose talent, intelligence and attention to detail were critical to keeping things on schedule. Nancy Craig and Barbara Fraize are due medals of honor for computer trouble shooting.

Ann Barbieri's women have long been at home in my home—I thank her for creating a home for them on the cover of the book.

No account of my debts would be complete without the name Claire Moses. Claire's friendship is elemental—as basic to this book as learning how to read and write.

Parts of this book have appeared in earlier versions and essays. I wish to thank the following publishers for permission to reprint all or parts of the following articles: "Simone de Beauvoir: Cartesian Legacies," vol. 7 (1990), pp. 15–28, and "Toward a Feminist Ethics: First Steps," vol. 8 (1991), pp. 163–174 with the permission of *Simone de Beauvoir Studies;* "The Look as Bad Faith," vol. 36, no. 2 (Spring 1992), pp. 221–227 with the permission of *Philosophy Today;* "Casting Shadows: The Body in Descartes, Sartre, de Beauvoir and Lacan" vol. IV, no. 2–3 (1992), pp. 232–243, with the permission of *Bulletin de la Société Américaine de Philosophie de Langue Française;* "Out From Under: de Beauvoir's Philosophy of the Erotic," *Simone de Beauvoir: Contemporary Readings,* Ed. Margaret Simons, (1995) with the permission of the University of Pennsylvania Press; "From Husserl to Beauvoir: Gendering the Perceiving Subject" vol. 27, nos. 1&2 (January/April 1996), pp. 53–62, with the permission of *Metaphilosophy.*

Introduction

This book has had many lives. Most of them too ambitious. All of them concerned with properly situating Simone de Beauvoir within the philosophical tradition—with finding her philosophical place. This concern first seemed to require extensive philosophical groundwork going back to Descartes, perhaps further. Beginning this way, however, I found myself entangled in historical complexities that would not let go. Tracing the roots of Beauvoir's thought became more of a project in itself than a way of clearing a path to her.

Cut to the chase, I decided. Begin with Sartre. Situate her where she situated herself, within the frame of Sartre's existentialism. Another trap—particularly ironic in this case. An adequate analysis of Sartre showed signs of becoming interminable, another way of postponing Beauvoir.

And so it comes to this. A book about Simone de Beauvoir that situates her within the continental philosophical tradition by providing a sketch rather than a detailed account of the tradition itself. A book that situates Beauvoir within the frame of Sartre's existentialism by focusing on her existential perspective rather than the Sartrean frame. In short, a book about Beauvoir's philosophy. In this sense an irreverent book. For in calling Beauvoir a philosopher, I name her as she would not name herself. She called herself a writer. I do not take that name from her. But when she calls herself a writer in order not to call herself a philosopher—when she calls herself a writer in deference to Sartre the philosopher—my suspicions are aroused[1] I wonder about the hand she has dealt herself. So I take her cards and try a different play—one where she is a philosopher in her own right—on her own. In its irreverence, this book owes much to the tone of the times. It partakes of the renewed interest in Beauvoir that is part of the stock taking going on in feminist thought. More secure in our ability and right to speak in our own voices, we are more willing to recognize our debt to and distance from the woman who called herself an existentialist before she would call herself a feminist.

Among the various styles of writings available to us under the signature Simone de Beauvoir, some are unambiguously philosophical. They adopt the style of philosophical discourse; they situate themselves within the philosophical tradition; they present themselves as participating in the ongoing discussions of philosophy. These are the works that I am interested in here. In reading these works I focus both on Beauvoir's specific philosophical identity and on what I call her muted voice—what might be called the un-thought of Beauvoir's thinking. This voice speaks of joy, generosity, the gift, the erotic and the couple. Speaking on the margins of Beauvoir's texts, this voice marks out a space that I call erotic generosity. I argue that this space is the site of an ethic that warrants our attention.

Given my decision to read Beauvoir as a philosopher, and given Beauvoir's thought on the relationship between literature and philosophy, my decision to read only those works which are unambiguously philosophical may raise some eyebrows. Some explanation of my choice of texts may (or may not) bring these eyebrows down. The line between philosophy and literature is not neatly drawn. Neither is it firm. Plato, Nietzsche,

---

[1] See for example, Simone de Beauvoir, *After The War: Force of Circumstance I*, trans. Richard Howard (New York: Paragon House, 1992), p. 4; *Force of Circumstance II*, trans. Richard Howard (New York: Paragon House, 1992), p. 367; and Alice Schwarzer, *After The Second Sex: Conversations With Simone de Beauvoir*, (New York: Pantheon Books, 1984), p. 57.

Sartre and Beauvoir among others make this clear. For all its porousness, however, there is a boundary between literature and philosophy that is more than a matter of style. Beauvoir acknowledges this in her essay "Literature and Metaphysics." Though I am sympathetic to approaches that mine Beauvoir's literature for its philosophical import, I do not think that these approaches by themselves can establish Beauvoir as a philosopher. What makes Beauvoir a philosopher is not the fact that her literary writings are packed with philosophical ideas (in this she is like Milan Kundera) but the fact that she chose to write philosophical works and to develop her ideas philosophically. In other words, I think that the best way to make the case that Beauvoir is a philosopher is to focus on those writings where she works with concepts, develops arguments, and establishes the relationship between her ideas and other philosophical positions.

As the project of this book is twofold, to recognize Beauvoir as a philosopher, and to attend to her muted (as distinct from her dominant) philosophical voice, I have focused on those philosophical texts where her muted voice is clearest. In several instances I have attended to texts that have largely been ignored. My hope is that my reading of Beauvoir will be sufficiently compelling to convince people that Beauvoir is a philosopher to be reckoned with and that her philosophical texts, neglected and otherwise, deserve careful attention.

As a philosopher, Beauvoir works within the continental, phenomenological, existential tradition. Influenced by the thought of Descartes, Hegel, Marx, Husserl, Merleau-Ponty, and Sartre, Beauvoir takes up specific legacies and takes part in the philosophical debates of her time. As an independent voice in a three-way conversation with Sartre and Merleau-Ponty, Beauvoir introduces the concepts of joy, the erotic, generosity and the gift. Appealing to these concepts, Beauvoir challenges the tradition to rethink its understanding of the subject and intersubjectivity. She formulates an ethic that exposes the limits and dangers of theories of liberation that appeal solely to an ethic of transcendence and the project.

[handwritten in left margin: Reemo defenair]

As I see it, the driving force in Beauvoir's thought is the idea of ambiguity. This idea is not *ex nihilo*. It has its roots. Specifically, the idea of ambiguity is Beauvoir's way of framing the answer to the challenge of Cartesian dualism. It is her way of acknowledging the body; her unique contribution to the phenomenological-existential tradition's insistence that as humans we are situated subjects whose first, primordial and most crucial situation is the body.

At first, in *Pyrrhus et Cinéas*, Beauvoir's commitment to embodiment is ambiguous. Though she never repeats the Cartesian error of segregating the subject from the body, in *Pyrrhus et Cinéas*, Beauvoir's focus on the transcending activities of consciousness almost blinds her to the ways in which these activities are limited and conditioned by the complexities of the embodied subject's situation. It is in *Pyrrhus et Cinéas* that Beauvoir's debts to Hegel and Sartre are greatest. Though she never explicitly repudiates these debts, Beauvoir's subsequent philosophical writings challenge them; for the barely heard muted voice of *Pyrrhus et Cinéas* becomes, in *The Ethics of Ambiguity*, *The Second Sex*, "Must We Burn Sade?" and *The Coming of Age* an insistent note that cannot be ignored.

In listening for and attending to what I call Beauvoir's muted voice, I am reading Beauvoir according to her principles of good literature. I am suggesting that as an author she adopted these principles in her philosophical as well as in her literary writings and that as her readers we should be looking out for the ways these principles are at work in her texts. In short, I am suggesting that good philosophy, like good literature, is nuanced and that reading for the nuances is important for understanding the sense of the text. Reflecting on *The Mandarins*, Beauvoir tells us that she rejects novels that have a message because:

> ... thesis novels always impose a certain truth that eclipse all others and calls a halt to the perpetual dance of conflicting points of view ... [2]

---

[2] *Force I*, p. 270.

Further, when discussing Anne and Henri of *The Mandarins*, Beauvoir tells us that:

> I attempted to establish between them a sort of counterpoint, each reinforcing, diversifying, destroying the other.[3]

Though I do not see Beauvoir's muted voice destroying her other voices, I do see it offering a counterpoint to her dominant voice. I also see it as important for identifying her place in the philosophical tradition and for assessing her role in contemporary feminist discussions; for, once this voice is heard, we discover the inadequacies of attaching the labels existentialist, Marxist, or humanist to the thought of Simone de Beauvoir.

In the pages that follow I take three approaches to Beauvoir's muted voice. First, I situate it. Second, I track it. Third, I consider its place in contemporary philosophical and feminist discussions and look to its future. Situating Beauvoir within the philosophical tradition is the business of the first chapter. Though in no way a complete or adequate account of the traditions that ground Beauvoir's thought, this chapter examines these traditions to establish Beauvoir's allegiance to phenomenology and affinity with Merleau-Ponty. It indicates that this allegiance and affinity play a critical role in the way Beauvoir approaches the myth of femininity and that Beauvoir's attention to the erotic as a philosophical category can be traced to her phenomenological roots. This chapter begins to make the case that the import of the category of the erotic is substantial and that ignoring it renders our account of the philosophical scene inadequate. Attending to the category of the erotic, we see the ways in which phenomenology and existentialism, in their insistence that we attend to the particulars of lived, concrete experience, provided an opening for the birth of Beauvoir's feminist theory. From this perspective, Beauvoir's category of the erotic may be seen as fulfilling the

---

[3] *Ibid.*, p. 265.

phenomenological-existential promise to account for the human subject as a finite, embodied, desiring being.

Tracking the birth and development of Beauvoir's category of the erotic is the business of chapters two through five. Each of these chapters takes up a single text and listens for its muted voices. These chapters read Beauvoir as drawing out the ethical implications of the phenomenological thesis of intentionality and as pursuing the moral dimensions of the existential idea of freedom. They trace the ways in which, Beauvoir develops the ideas of risk, reciprocity, and ambiguous subjectivity and track the ways in which Beauvoir links these ideas to the drama of the erotic event. These chapters argue that in attending to the philosophical importance of the erotic event, Beauvoir transforms the meanings of subjectivity, recognition, and community.

Most of Beauvoir's readers identify her work with a single paradigm of recognition and intersubjectivity. I identify two. The first paradigm, present from the very beginning of Beauvoir's thinking and dominant throughout the course of her philosophical reflections, is modeled on Hegel's account of the master-slave dialectic. It aligns reciprocity with violence. As I see it, this Hegelian model of recognition represents Beauvoir's first but not final word. There is, in the muted voice of Beauvoir's texts, another model of recognition at work—an erotic one. Here reciprocity and violence are decoupled. Here the conditions of the possibility of the moral relationship are not grounded in our willingness to inflict or suffer death, but in our willingness to assume the risks of our ambiguous subjectivity—the risks of finitude, vulnerability, and the bond.

This other model of recognition is part of Beauvoir's ambiguous legacy to us. Sounding as her minor key, its meanings are not fully developed and its implications are less than clear. In chapter six I think through some of the philosophical and feminist implications of this ambiguous legacy. Following some of the leads of Beauvoir's category of the erotic, I develop the idea that Beauvoir's muted voice provides us with the beginnings of a feminist ethic that is not only for women. I call this ethic feminist because it attends to the value that Beauvoir, in the early pages of *The Second Sex*, tells us women have recognized and protected throughout the history of patriarchy—the value of the bond. I say that it is not only for women because, although within patriarchy only women recognize and protect this value, the possibility of a non-patriarchal society resides in the hope that the value of the bond will be recognized by both men and women and will become, for both sexes, the source of a new vision of reciprocity, sexuality, love, and the couple. family!

Listening to Beauvoir's muted voice, I discover that Beauvoir's place in contemporary feminist thought is other than that of the respected mother whose relevance is purely historical. I also discover the truth of one of Beauvoir's earliest insights: that we have no way of anticipating how our projects will be assumed by others and no way of controlling the directions our thought may take. For as I examine the current feminist field I find a strong affinity between Beauvoir's erotic ethic of generosity and Irigaray's account of the maternal body. Though I do not wish to push this affinity between Beauvoir and Irigaray too far, I think it important to examine it.

Beauvoir sees more than one way out of patriarchy. There are economic, social, political and erotic routes. All will be needed to absolve women of their status as woman, the inessential other. The route opened by Beauvoir that I explore here is the route of the erotic. Beauvoir does not tell us as much about this route as she might have, but what she says points to the beginnings of a feminist erotic ethic—an ethic that figures our desire for recognition according to the paradigms of generosity and the gift. Within the parameters of this ethic, the possibilities of the erotic speak to the intersubjective possibilities of the ambiguity of our condition; for following this ethic we are given the chance to live the immanence of our transcendence in/through the touch of generosity. This

touch forfeits the strategies of domination for the joys of discovering the other who offers me a home in their otherness.
This touch frees the meaning of the bond from its patriarchal
baggage.

The point of this reading of Beauvoir is not to make her
something she is not—a philosopher for all seasons or a theorist
for all feminists. The point is to see her for more of what she
is—a complex thinker whose work, philosophical, feminist
and otherwise, cannot be neatly categorized as existential,
Marxist, liberal, or humanist in order to be easily assimilated or
casually dismissed.

CHAPTER 1

The Erotic as a
Philosophical Category

Simone de Beauvoir: author; that is how she wished to be known. Belatedly she accepted the title feminist. She never took up the name philosopher. Declining to call herself a philosopher, Beauvoir earned a degree in philosophy, taught philosophy, wrote what she referred to as metaphysical novels and left us with a group of writings, *Pyrrhus et Cinéas, The Ethics of Ambiguity, The Second Sex,* "Must We Burn Sade?,"and *The Coming of Age,* that can only be classified as philosophical. Knowing, perhaps, that we would take note of these things and take to calling her a philosopher, Beauvoir warned us away. Her philosophical works, she said, were not original; they merely echoed Sartre's thought.

Having read her letters, we know that Beauvoir is not a trustworthy narrator when it comes to self-portraits. Having read her philosophical works, I find that she is not a reliable source when it comes to assessing her philosophical voice(s). Reading her rather than taking her at her word, I find Simone de Beauvoir taking up the legacies of the continental tradition as she enters a three way conversation with Sartre and Merleau-Ponty.

As I track the trajectory of Beauvoir's philosophical works, I discover both a consistency and a development in her thought. From *Pyrrhus et Cinéas* to *The Coming of Age,* the philosophical focus is ethical, the method is phenomenological and the commitments are existential. Between *Pyrrhus et*

Cinéas and *The Coming of Age*, however, Beauvoir's attention is more and more drawn to the specifics of the historical, concrete situation and her thesis of ambiguity becomes more complex. It attends more to the body, the flesh, and the other; it establishes the erotic as a philosophical category; it redeploys the meanings of risk, the gift, generosity, and joy to create an ethic of erotic generosities.

In part, the developing complexity of Simone de Beauvoir's philosophy reflects the insistent presence of what I call Beauvoir's muted voice; for beginning with *Pyrrhus et Cinéas* and continuing through *The Coming of Age*, Beauvoir's dominant "existential" voice is infected/rendered ambiguous by a voice that challenges the idea of the autonomous subject and the ethic of the project. Though it speaks in measured tones and appears on the margins of the text, this muted voice is not, I think, marginal. Listening to/for it is crucial for understanding Beauvoir's place in the philosophical and feminist fields and critical for understanding her legacy to philosophy and feminism.

Attentive to Beauvoir's two voices, this reading brings Beauvoir's muted voice into relief as it tracks the ethical tensions produced when Beauvoir's muted and dominant voices intersect. Tracing the development of Beauvoir's muted voice I discover that though it is wrong to read her merely as echo of Sartre, it is also a mistake to read her without reference to Sartre. More surprising (perhaps) I discover that Beauvoir cannot be read without reference to Husserl and Hegel, and that she should not be read without reference to Merleau-Ponty and the Marquis de Sade.

The next chapters of this book explore the soundings of Beauvoir's muted voice and the intersections of Beauvoir's two voices by closely reading Beauvoir's philosophical texts. This chapter sets the scene of that reading by identifying the basic categories of Beauvoir's thought and by sketching the philosophical horizon that frames/sustains Beauvoir's reflections.

Cartesian Roots

As a phenomenologist, Beauvoir's roots are Cartesian. Agreeing with Descartes that the individual subject is the proper philosophical point of departure, Beauvoir, like Sartre and Merleau-Ponty, follows Husserl to retrieve the lived body for philosophy. Where Husserl, Sartre, and Merleau-Ponty save us from Cartesian dualism and solipsism by appealing to the experiences of perceiving subjects, Beauvoir saves us by appealing to the possibilities of the erotic subject. For Beauvoir, retrieving the lived body for philosophy means more than retrieving the full meaning of perceptual experience—it requires according philosophical significance to the lived erotic.

Beauvoir's Cartesian roots set the challenge of her ethical thinking. Descartes' epistemological question: How do I as this instance of consciousness escape solipsism? becomes for Beauvoir the ethical question: How do I as this individual subject recognize the failure of egoism? In the process of answering this question, Beauvoir restores the body to consciousness and consciousness to the body in ways which go beyond the phenomenological challenge to Descartes' dualism. With Beauvoir, twining consciousness and body means more than recognizing the legitimate meanings of perceptual experience. It involves retrieving the erotic dimensions of the lived body.

Descartes' dualism degrades all bodies. Bodies, according to Descartes, are the source of perceptual confusions, mistaken thinking and self-misunderstanding. Today, we have little trouble recognizing the unhappy implications of this extreme dualism: the alienation of self and world, the loss of perceptual richness,[1] the distortion of subjectivity.[2] We have, however, had great trouble disentangling ourselves from the legacy of

---

[1] See for example Marjorie Green, *Descartes* (Minneapolis: University of Minnesota Press, 1985).
[2] See for example Susan Bordo, *The Flight To Objectivity* (Albany: State University of New York Press, 1987).

Cartesian thought: the idea that perception is the fundamental
activity through which we encounter the world and the other.

It is not immediately obvious that focusing on perception
ties us to the Cartesian tradition. It sounds counterintuitive.
It sounds less counterintuitive, however, when we recall that
Descartes referred to perceptions of the mind as well as perceptions of the senses and allowed that the former but not the
latter could be trusted to be truthful (e.g., the wax example). If
Descartes rejects sense perception, shouldn't embracing it eject
us from his trajectory? At first, in the hands of Husserl, it
seems to. For in Husserl's phenomenology, it is through perception that the body is retrieved for subjectivity and it is
through perceptual consciousness that the embodied other is
recognized as a subject within a world that is not exclusively
mine.

Husserl

Husserl's *Cartesian Meditations* present the epoché as the
methodological heir of Descartes' radical doubt. Countering
Descartes' degradation of the body and its perceptions,
Husserl calls on us to ground our philosophical investigations
in the phenomenological givenness of embodied perceptual
experience. He moves the body from side to center stage. The
phenomenological route to philosophical truth is not grounded
in a doubt that severs consciousness from its body but in a
bracketing of the prejudices of the natural attitude which blind
us to the fullness of experience. It is as embodied perceivers
that we experience the world and it is as embodied perceivers
that we discover the presence of the other and the necessary
relationship that exists between us.

The world, Husserl reminds us, is always experienced by
us from some place or other. As we can never be in more than
one place at once, and as there is no privileged place, we each
need the perspective of the other (the view from the other
side) to complement and fill out the meaning of the world as
seen from our particular place. The possibility of trading

places is a crucial ingredient of world constitution. Thus, according to Husserl, perceptual experience reveals the necessary embodiment of the subject and the necessary intersubjectivity of the world.[3] The other's experiences of the world are imbedded in and necessary to mine.

Two things emerge from Husserl's reworking of Descartes' *Meditations*. First, by appealing to the phenomenological clarity of bodily perceptual experience rather than to the natural light of reason's clear and distinct ideas, Husserl counters Descartes' degradation of the body and its perceptions. Second, by attending to the essential embodiment of perceptual experience, Husserl challenges idealist and empiricist accounts of experience. The subjective point of departure is aligned with the idea of transcendence in immanence such that the subject/object dichotomy is dissolved as the distinction between the subject and its other is preserved. At least, this is Husserl's claim.

What should be noted, however, is that the embodied subject discovered by Husserl is a one dimensional being. It is a perceiver modeled on the ideal of the scientist. Each embodied subject is said to have its own habits and style but these appear to be irrelevant to the activities of world constitution. The phenomenologically discovered embodied other, though different from me, is interchangeable with me. Philosophically, that is, as perceivers, our differences are a matter of indifference. Complementarity rules. Conflict is absent.

That embodied subjects are sexually desiring embodiments goes unnoticed. That bodies in the lived world of everyday experience cannot easily exchange places, that our experience is vertically and hierarchically positioned as well as horizontally and spatially situated goes unsaid. That as often as not we experience and respond to each other violently is passed over in silence. Reflecting on this silence, we begin to

(handwritten margin note: It's empirical, not experience)

---

[3] For more on this see Elizabeth A. Behnke, "Edmund Husserl's Contribution to the Phenomenology of the Body in *Ideen II*," *Study Project in the Phenomenology of the Body Newsletter*, 2:2 (Fall 1989), pp. 15–18.

notice that a phenomenology grounded in the category of perception may elude Descartes' dualism without eluding the Cartesian bias that the subject is first and foremost a knowing subject. We begin to notice that affirming the body within the context of the Cartesian project of truth may not get us to the realities of the lived body and may not alert us to the full complexities of subjective embodiment and the self-world-other relationship. Husserl's epistemological other may (or may not) solve the problem of solipsism; it does not, however, speak to the question of the ethical other.

Merleau-Ponty—Sartre—Beauvoir

When historians of philosophy decipher the influence of phenomenology on French thought, they take note of the ways in which Sartre and Merleau-Ponty take up Husserl's challenge to Descartes and rework Husserl's concepts of the epoché, intentionality, and the transcendental ego. They recognize the dialogue/dispute between Sartre and Merleau-Ponty as crucial to the French philosophical scene. They do not notice Beauvoir's place in this conversation. We cannot, however, fully understand the legacy of Husserl's phenomenology without attending to Beauvoir's role in the French appropriations of Husserl.

The contrast between Sartre's and Merleau-Ponty's relation to Husserl can be marked in several ways. First, where Sartre defined himself chiefly in relation to the early Husserl of the *Ideas* of 1913, Merleau-Ponty took Husserl's later, unpublished works as his point of departure.[4] Second, where Sartre took up Husserl's theory of consciousness, Merleau-Ponty directed his attention to Husserl's "wild flowering world and mind."[5] Third, where Sartre, taking up Husserl's idea of philosophy as a science and pursuing Husserl's search

---

[4] Margaret Whitford, *Merleau-Ponty's Critique of Sartre's Philosophy* (Lexington, Kentucky: French Forum, 1982), p. 13.
[5] Maurice Merleau-Ponty, *Signs*, trans. Richard C. McCleary (Evanston: Northwestern University Press, 1964), p. 181.

for certitude identified consciousness with the project of lucidity, Merleau-Ponty, attending to the implications of Husserl's attack on the subject-object split, pursued the thought of ambiguity. Fourth, where Sartre, concerned with moral and political questions introduced Hegelian desire into Husserl's intersubjective world, Merleau-Ponty, staying closer to Husserl's epistemological concerns, only marginally attended to the question of the ethical other.[6]

Beauvoir publicly inserted herself into the Sartre-Merleau-Ponty debate in her essay "Merleau-Ponty and Pseudo-Sartreanism." Maintaining her position as the non-philosopher whose only philosophical voice is Sartre's, Beauvoir identified Sartre as Husserl's rightful heir. She accused Merleau-Ponty of distortion and plagiary. According to Beauvoir, the Sartre Merleau-Ponty attacks is a pseudo-Sartre. The ideas that Merleau-Ponty claims for himself are really Sartre's.

Reading Beauvoir's essay "Merleau-Ponty and Pseudo-Sartreanism" we are led to identify Beauvoir with Sartre. (That of course is what she wanted us to do.) Reading this essay, however, we discover that the Sartre portrayed there is not a familiar Sartre. According to Beauvoir, Merleau-Ponty is guilty of substituting a caricature of Sartre for the real thing. Merleau-Ponty, Beauvoir says, misreads Sartre to produce a pseudo-Sartre. According to Beauvoir, the ideas presented by Merleau-Ponty as his own are really Sartre's and the ideas presented by Merleau-Ponty as Sartre's are misrepresentations. Thus when Merleau-Ponty claims that his ideas (which are actually Sartre's) refute Sartre's (which are actually not Sartre's) he demonstrates the superiority of Sartre's thought. If the plot of this essay sounds convoluted, its message is not: Merleau-Ponty is a disengaged Sartrean—a philosopher who refuses to take up the political implications of the ideas of ambiguity and situated existence.

Michael Yeo, "Perceiving/Reading the Other: Ethical Dimensions," *Merleau-Ponty: Hermeneutics and Postmodernism*, ed. Thomas W. Busch and Shaun Gallagher (Albany, N.Y.: State University of New York Press, 1992), pp. 41–42.

If readers of the "Pseudo-Sartreanism" essay have trouble accepting Beauvoir's claim that reading Sartre as a philosopher of the subject, and reading 'the look' as his paradigm of intersubjectivity amounts to a deliberate distortion of Sartre's thought; if they have trouble identifying the real Sartre with the philosopher who insisted that everything comes from the situation; if they do not recognize Sartre as a philosopher who rejects the idea of pure freedom/consciousness; they can perhaps be forgiven for finding Beauvoir's attack on Merleau-Ponty little more than a woman's defense of her beleaguered man. If, however, we give up the idea that Beauvoir is Sartre's woman, we may see what Sonya Kruks sees: that the idea of situated freedom (attributed to Sartre in the "Pseudo-Sartreanism" essay) is Beauvoir's idea, and that this idea is as indebted to Merleau-Ponty's thought of ambiguity as it is to Sartre's idea of engagement.[7]

Read from this perspective, "Pseudo-Sartreanism," like *The Ethics of Ambiguity*, uses Sartre as a cover. Here, it is Beauvoir, not Merleau-Ponty, who might be accused of pseudo-Sartreanism. Her strategy, however, differs from the one she attributes to Merleau-Ponty. Rather than appropriating Sartre's thought for herself, she camouflages her voice in his. I leave it to her biographers to analyze her motives. My interest is in deciphering Beauvoir's philosophical voices. Given this interest, the "Pseudo-Sartreanism" essay is of interest because it provides an entry into Beauvoir's thought and some clues to the Beauvoir, Sartre, Merleau-Ponty relationship. For if we find it difficult to follow Beauvoir in reading the look out of Sartre's philosophy and if we are reluctant to agree with Beauvoir's claims regarding Sartre's emphasis on the situation, we discover that Beauvoir's unique reading of Sartre shows us the difference between Sartre and Beauvoir and reveals the affinities between Beauvoir and Merleau-Ponty.

---

[7] Sonia Kruks, "Simone de Beauvoir: Teaching Sartre About Freedom," *Feminist Interpretations of Simone de Beauvoir,* ed. Margaret A. Simons (University Park, PA: Pennsylvania State University Press, 1995), pp. 79–96.

Reading Beauvoir's review of Merleau-Ponty's *Phenomenology of Perception* provides other clues. Written in 1945, Beauvoir's "La Phénoménologie de La Perception de Maurice Merleau-Ponty" compares the thought of Sartre and Merleau-Ponty without appearing to pass judgment. Here Beauvoir, presenting us with a more familiar Sartre, contrasts Merleau-Ponty's embodied subject with Sartre's "naked" *pour-soi*. She notes that Merleau-Ponty's temporally and spatially lived body make for an opacity of the subject and a relationship between consciousness and the world that precludes Sartre's thought of consciousness as an absolutely free negating activity and rejects Sartre's account of the *pour-soi-en-soi* opposition.

Given that her essay is a review of Merleau-Ponty's work not Sartre's, we expect Beauvoir to attend more to Merleau-Ponty's thought than Sartre's. But comparing this review to the later "Pseudo-Sartreanism" essay which also purports to be a review of Merleau-Ponty's work, several things are striking. Not only does this earlier essay give Sartre the minor role of the philosopher whose work is at odds with Merleau-Ponty, it also positions Sartre as a philosopher of extremes. Indeed, if we read Beauvoir's description of the abyss that separates Sartre's *pour-soi* and *en-soi*, we are tempted to suspect Beauvoir of accusing Sartre of reintroducing the subject-object cut which it was the merit of phenomenology to heal.

In this 1945 essay it is Merleau-Ponty, not Sartre, who is the philosopher of the concrete. Here it is Merleau-Ponty, not Sartre, who in attending to the realities of embodiment discovers the limits of freedom. Here it is Merleau-Ponty, not Sartre, who gives consciousness the ability to transform itself from a hole in being into a hollow within the fold of being. Here it is Merleau-Ponty's, not Sartre's, thought that has important implications for the problems of the human condition, especially the problem of sexuality and language.

The Sartre Beauvoir embraces in "Pseudo-Sartreanism" sounds very much like the Merleau-Ponty she approves of in the earlier 1945 essay. Perhaps Sartre and Merleau-Ponty have exchanged positions. Perhaps Beauvoir has transposed their names. Perhaps ... perhaps ... perhaps. Beyond the perhapses there is this: Beauvoir's constant affirmation of consciousness as embodied and permeated by a situation not of its making but for which it is somehow responsible; Beauvoir's consistent rejection of the concept of lucidity for the ideas of opacity/ambiguity; Beauvoir's continuous demand that epistemological investigations be linked to ethical considerations.

One of the striking things about this review of Merleau-Ponty's *Phenomenology of Perception* is the way it begins and ends by linking morality and epistemology. Beauvoir introduces us to phenomenology by situating it within its cultural, historical, and intellectual horizon. This horizon is dominated by the idea of a universal moral law and the concept of scientific objectivity. Both have the same effect: a negation of subjectivity and a divorce of subject and world. Modern morality requires that we subordinate our unique sense of rightness to prescriptions of moral duty. Modern science requires that we substitute a cold world of independent objects for the lived world of objects at hand. Beauvoir insists that modern science and morality are contested by our lived experiences of personal uniqueness and world intimacy. According to Beauvoir, the merit of phenomenology is that it pays attention to this contest and restores us to the lived/living world. Epistemologically, phenomenology allows me to rediscover the world as my home. Ethically it gives me the right to say "*Je suis la.*"

The unique merit of Merleau-Ponty's phenomenology, according to Beauvoir, is its account of the lived body. Here Beauvoir pays special attention to Merleau-Ponty's discussion of the illusions of amputees and is interested in the case of the man who could live but not represent his body. What interests her most is Merleau-Ponty's account of the difference between the body as a way of inhabiting and having a world and the body as an object in the world; for according to Merleau-Ponty, the body as an object is a secondary reality. It is superimposed on the body as lived and can therefore be severed from it. The body as lived, however, is primordial. It cannot be taken from me—it is the way I express and realize my existence.

This 1945 essay is one of the few places where Beauvoir's affinity for phenomenology as distinct from existentialism is apparent. As one of the places where we see Beauvoir's ethical concerns expressed without reference to Sartre, it allows us to see *The Ethics of Ambiguity* as other than the ethics called for by *Being and Nothingness* and lets us read *The Second Sex* as other than an existential feminism. Given Beauvoir's insistence on the relationship between phenomenology and ethics; given her claim that Merleau-Ponty's analyses of the lived body provide a fruitful ground for an analysis of sexuality, language, and the general human condition; and given her interest in the relationship between the lived and represented body, we are prepared to attend to the phenomenological ground of *The Ethics of Ambiguity's* discussion of intentionality. We are prepared to read *The Second Sex's* discussion of woman's body and its distinction between sex and gender as a rethinking of and challenge to Merleau-Ponty's ideas regarding the relationship between the lived and represented body. On the one hand, *The Second Sex* might be said to reject the idea that the represented body is superimposed on the lived body, if by superimposed we mean artificially appended. On the other hand, the liberating moment of *The Second Sex* may be said to be grounded in the hope that as superimposed, woman's represented body can be jettisoned as women's lived bodies are allowed to speak.

Reading Beauvoir's review of Merleau-Ponty's *Phenomenology of Perception*, the "Pseudo-Sartreanism" essay and *The Ethics of Ambiguity*, together, we appreciate the way Beauvoir insists on linking epistemological analyses to ethical issues. We are also tempted to see her as the Hegelian synthesizer of Sartre's and Merleau-Ponty's dialectical oppositions. Whether we assign Beauvoir the role of harmonizer or equate her thought with Sartre's, however, we make the same mistake. We give Beauvoir the role of the philosopher by making her a *woman* philosopher—a philosopher who stands by her man or a philosopher who brings peace to the quarreling men. If, taking our cue from both of these reviews, we attend to Beauvoir's undecidability regarding Sartre and Merleau-Ponty, and if we ask about her relationship to Husserl and Hegel before ascertaining her relationship to Sartre and Merleau-Ponty, then we are in a position to discover Beauvoir the philosopher—an independent voice in a three way conversation.

Merleau-Ponty

As Merleau-Ponty traces the development of Husserl's thought, he sees Husserl redefining the activity of constitution from "the project to gain intellectual possession of the world" to "the means of unveiling a back side of things we have not constituted."[8] Taking up the image of the hands that touch each other of *Ideas II,* Merleau-Ponty introduces the idea of the flesh and explores the carnal realities of the lived body. Like Husserl, Merleau-Ponty finds our subjective and intersubjective lives inexorably twined; and like Husserl, Merleau-Ponty refers our experience of the other to "the thickness" of things, and to the experience of the body. Things, Merleau-Ponty says, "… have the right to many other witnesses besides me;"[9] "… the fully objective thing is based on the experience of others and the latter upon the experience of the body."[10]

As the experience of feeling and being felt, of hands touching each other, captures the ambiguity of embodiment, the experience of the handshake, the double touching of self and other that blurs the subject-object and noesis-noema distinction, captures the intersubjectivity of our givenness to each other. With Merleau-Ponty as with Husserl, embodied perceiving entangles us in the world with the other and gives us a world of reciprocal intersubjectivity.

---

[8] *Signs,* p. 180.
[9] *Ibid.,* p. 170.
[10] *Ibid.,* p. 176.

Rejecting Hegel's fight to the death struggles of subjects that claim a monopoly on Being, Merleau-Ponty develops the notions of the flesh and reversibility; the one blurring the boundary between my body and the world; the other puncturing the barriers between myself and the other; both pointing to an always immanent but never realized coincidence that speaks the "ultimate truth" of the intertwining.[11] Thinking the flesh and reversibility, Merleau-Ponty comes to the thoughts of sexuality and the erotic.[12] The perceiving subject is sexed; perception has an erotic structure. Sexual life, Merleau-Ponty tells us, expresses an original intentionality that endows experience with vitality and fruitfulness. Calling on the name of Freud, Merleau-Ponty refuses to assign sexuality a peripheral role in human life. Insisting that sexuality permeates our existence and that the flesh, reversibility, and ambiguity of the body is preeminently experienced in sexual experience, Merleau Ponty writes:

> the importance we attach to the body and the contradictions of love are therefore related to a more general drama which arises from the metaphysical structure of my body which is both an object for others and a subject for myself ... sexual experience ... [is] an opportunity ... [for] acquainting oneself with the human lot in its most general aspects of autonomy and dependence.[13]

Even here, however, Merleau-Ponty holds the thought of difference at bay. Sexuality is treated as a generalized human phenomenon. Reading Merleau-Ponty we are barely aware of sex/gender differences. The idea of reversibility informs the idea of sexuality. Though Merleau-Ponty's subjectivity is carnal, it does not articulate the tensions of desire or live the temptations of possession and submission. If with Merleau-Ponty we

[11] Maurice Merleau-Ponty, *The Visible and the Invisible*, trans. Alphonso Lingis (Evanston: The Northwestern University Press, 1968), pp. 135–149.
[12] Maurice Merleau-Ponty, *Phenomenology of Perception*, trans. Colin Smith (London: Routledge & Kegan Paul, 1965), pp. 154–173.
[13] *Ibid.*, p. 167.

are more than scientist-perceiving subjects, we are still subjects of the same[14]—hence the unproblematic nature of our inter-subjectivity—hence our reciprocity.

Sartre

Sartre, reading Husserl with Hegel, challenges Husserl's and Merleau-Ponty's thesis of reciprocity. Bringing Hegelian desire into the phenomenological scene, Sartre transforms the meaning of trading places. Husserl's and Merleau-Ponty's shared world becomes Sartre's contested world. Now perceptual world constitution is contaminated by conflict. No longer ideal scientist/perceivers who see each other as completing their finite experiences; no longer confronted by objects whose thickness speak of their right to many perceivers; no longer subjects who approach each other with open hands; Sartre's embodied subjects, refusing their finitude and their ambiguity, insist on the absolute truthfulness of their existential place. The other as cohort perceiver is replaced by the other as menacing threat. The object as requiring the gaze of the other to fill it out, is replaced by an object that cannot support more than one look. The embodied subject recognizes the subjectivity of the embodied other in order to repress and exploit it. The other, like me, is the one for whom the world exists. But though it may be true that perceptually the world gives itself to me as the world of the "we," existentially I find this mode of givenness unacceptable. I want the world to be mine. I will accept you as a character in my script but not as a coauthor. In the name of my subjectivity I will refuse to recognize you as anything other than an object in my world. I use your perceivability and embodiment against you. I reduce you to a bodily quasi-object. As meaning giving subjects in an intersubjective world where we are each vulnerable to the power of the other

---

[14] Emanuel Levinas, *Outside the Subject*, trans. Michael B. Smith (California: Stanford University Press, 1994), p. 101.

to define us, trading places becomes a matter of not getting caught at the keyhole.

As Sartre works through the phenomenological implications of Hegelian desire, the other is transformed from the one who reveals unseen dimensions of the world and the fullness of its/my ambiguity, to the one who invades my sense of ownness. I discover that there are some desires that can only be lived with, for, and/or against the other. I discover the other as the one who threatens my desire; the one who shows me my desire; the one who takes my desire from me; the one whose desire I wish to be.

Sartre's analyses of shame, pride, and the caress make it clear that solipsism is untenable, not only because I cannot experience the world as a world without invoking the presence of the other, but also because I cannot fully experience myself outside of the other's presence. For Merleau-Ponty this means that I and the other enfold each other as we reveal the ambiguities of selfness and otherness, for Sartre this means that the other has the power to define me. If Sartre's descriptions of bad faith insist that I am free to evade this power and am therefore responsible for succumbing to it, his portrayal of the look makes it clear that neither evasive action nor the determination to be free can eject me from the field of the threat of the other.

Between *Nausea* and Sartre's later writings the sense of this threat changes. In *Nausea* it is not the other as subject who threatens my place in the world, but the otherness of existence that threatens my sense of the world. Here Sartre, like Merleau-Ponty, seems to be picking up on Husserl's allusion to wild being. Relying on the sense of touch rather than the sense of sight, Sartre introduces us to a root of a chestnut tree as it intrudes upon Roquentin's neatly fixed subject-object world. Forced by the agitations of the strangeness of existence to live the epoché and bracket his everyday attitudes, Roquentin discovers the ambiguities of his existence. He does not, however, react to this discovery with pleasure.

Nauseated, Roquentin flees the ambiguities of existence for the clarity of the negress jazz singer's music.[15]

Like Roquentin, Sartre will prefer lucidity to ambiguity. He does not share Merleau-Ponty's marvel or taste for ambiguity. This is not to say that he will ignore the ambiguity of the human condition, but rather to indicate that he will approach this ambiguity as a contest between freedom and facticity rather than as an intertwining of the possibilities of our situated existence. From now on, it is the otherness of the other subject rather than the strangeness of existence that will elicit his interest.

In *Being and Nothingness* consciousness dominates facticity. The accounts of bad faith make it clear that our choices constitute the situation. I choose the meaning of my facticity. I am always free to usurp the look of the other. In the studies of Genet and Flaubert, Sartre reassesses the relationship between freedom and facticity. Here the subject subjected to the power of the situation is not accused of bad faith. The situation, now seen as setting the conditions of our (free) choices, is never, however, given the power to divest the subject of its freedom.

If freedom and facticity become more permeable as Sartre's thought unfolds, the idea of reciprocity never finds a comfortable home in Sartre's work. The characters in *No Exit* search for it; the group in fusion appeals to it; the caress longs for it. But Estelle, Inez and Garcin prefer the ploys of the look and bad faith to the risks of recognition; the group in fusion resorts to the blood oath of terror; and the caress is either relegated to the role of foreplay or sacrificed to the erotics of sadism or masochism.

The body, dismissed by Descartes, retrieved by Husserl, and rendered ambiguous and fleshed by Merleau-Ponty, becomes with Sartre an enactment of and a threat to my subjectivity. It is as embodied that I am a subject, but it is because

---

[15] For more on this see, Debra Bergoffen,"Sartre: From Touch to Truth," *Alaska Quarterly Review*, Vol. 3, No. 1&2 (1984), pp. 123–133.

I am an embodied subject that I can be perceived as an object, and it is because I can be perceived as an object that I can become a thing in a world controlled by the other. Something lost. Something gained. Having recognized the entailment of subjectivity, the body, and desire, we have lost the clarity of the body-subject relationship. The body is now not only that through which I am a lived subject, it is also that by which my subjectivity may be taken from me.

The desire that Sartre interjects into the embodied subject is Hegelian desire, a desire seeking recognition but rooted in the demands of the fight to the death and destined for the oppressions of the master-slave relationship. Like Husserl's embodied subjects who are diverse but not other, and like Merleau-Ponty's ambiguous subjects whose reciprocity lies in their shared flesh, Sartre's desiring subjects live the desire of the same. Each desires the same thing, to be recognized as the source of the meaning of the world, to have power over others/all; and each lives this desire in the same way, the look.

Though Sartre like Merleau-Ponty addresses the question of sex, the effect of sexuality on lived embodiment goes largely unnoticed in his accounts of imperialist desire and bad faith. In the description of the man and the woman in the cafe for example, Sartre describes a sexual encounter without deciphering the relationship between the sex/gender status of his characters and the meanings of their interactions.

Beauvoir

Surveying the scene in the cafe, Beauvoir will decipher what Sartre passes over in silence: it is the woman, not the man who objectifies her body; it is the man not the woman who looks. He objectifies her as the target of his desire. She, not he, is said to be guilty of bad faith. Reflecting on this scene, Beauvoir has some questions for Sartre. Is it an accident that this first example of bad faith is a heterosexual affair? Is this bad faith dynamic dependent on the encoded sexuality of its characters?

Pursuing these questions Beauvoir discovers the concept of gender. The concept was revolutionary. It was not, however, born *ex nihilo*. Had we been paying attention to Beauvoir's philosophical voice, and had we seen her as participating in the French appropriation of Husserl, we might not have been so ill prepared for *The Second Sex*. It might not have taken us so long to situate it within the phenomenological-existential as well as the feminist traditions. For had we not been duped into hearing Beauvoir as an echo of Sartre and instead seen Beauvoir as a party to a three way conversation concerning the meanings of embodiment, the flesh, ambiguity, and the other, we might have noticed the relationship between Beauvoir and Merleau-Ponty. We might, for example, have noted that a book that claimed to provide us with the ethics called for by *Being and Nothingness* was titled *The Ethics of Ambiguity* and that ambiguity was a word/concept prevalent in Merleau-Ponty's but not Sartre's vocabulary. More importantly, we might have noted the ways in which *The Ethics of Ambiguity*, attentive to Husserl's concept of intentionality, reworks the relationship between noesis and noema and transforms the phenomenological knowing/perceiving subject into an existential subject caught up in the contest between the moods of joy and anxiety. We might have seen how the line from *The Ethics of Ambiguity* to *The Second Sex* pursues Husserl's notion of the life world to transform the phenomenological concept of horizon into the existential idea of the historical situation which permeates our freedom. Focused on the way Beauvoir, like Merleau-Ponty and Sartre, was grappling with the legacy of Descartes, Husserl, and Hegel, we would have seen the ways in which Beauvoir took up this legacy, took stock of the debates between Sartre and Merleau-Ponty, and marked out a path that took up Sartre's moral concerns without ignoring Merleau-Ponty's insights regarding ambiguity, the flesh, and the erotic.

It was by confronting the question of the ethical other, insisting on the fundamental reality of desire, and remaining

attentive to the social/historical implications of the phenomenological critique of the subject-object dichotomy, that
Beauvoir explored the relationship between the situation and
embodied desire, and discovered the concept of gender. In
introducing the concept of gender and examining the processes
of gendering, Beauvoir may be seen as participating in the
phenomenological-existentialist project of historicizing the
embodied subject. Subjective embodiment, Beauvoir notes, is
always sexed and gendered. Further, given current historical
conditions, our bodies are sexed and gendered according to
the categories of patriarchy—categories which pervert the
meanings of desire and subjectivity and which undermine the
conditions of the possibility of reciprocity.

Exploring the perversions of sexuality inherent in patriarchy's sex-gender codes, Beauvoir discovers that the imperialist perceiving subject described by Sartre's "look" is also an
erotically embodied subject. As embedded in an erotic perceiving body, consciousness must now be scrutinized for the
ways in which its perceiving/knowing activities are sexed,
and for the ways in which its erotic desires situate it in the
world. Beyond discovering the difference between sex and
patriarchal gender, Beauvoir discovers that erotic experience
disrupts (or at least has the power to disrupt) the perversions
of subjectivity perpetuated by patriarchy. She explores the
ways in which attending to these erotic disruptions refigure
our understanding of the existential-phenomenological subject
and direct us to an ethic of the erotic.

If we trace Beauvoir's philosophical development, we see
that the specifics of Beauvoir's attention to the erotic, especially her concepts of erotic risk and generosity, are grounded in
her unique interpretation of intentionality. At first, in the early
work *The Ethics of Ambiguity*, Beauvoir treads the path of
Husserl, Sartre and Merleau-Ponty. She attends to the question
of intentionality without attending to the question of the sexed
body. Indeed, though it is always clear that Beauvoir's intentional subject is embodied, Beauvoir does not, in *The Ethics of*

Ambiguity, directly attend to the question of embodiment. For that, we have to wait for *The Second Sex.* Taken jointly, however, *The Ethics of Ambiguity* and *The Second Sex* provide us with a unique vision of intentionality that takes up Merleau-Ponty's thesis of ambiguity and mood of marvel, and Sartre's analysis of the desire of the look, as it redeploys the phenomenological attention to embodiment from an attention to the movement and desire of the same to an analysis of the contesting desires of intentionality and to a critique of a patriarchal system that reifies the play of desire of intentionality by categorizing the otherness of sexual difference as the otherness of the subject and its inessential other.

In introducing the concept of gender and examining the processes of gendering, Beauvoir does more than politicize the dynamics of the look and bad faith, she discovers new meanings of embodiment. She discovers that though the body's perceivability marks it as a source of alienation, its vulnerability marks it as the source of subjective affirmation; for it is in recognizing my vulnerability and assuming it that I discover the link between risking the lived body and my subjective and intersubjective possibilities. Further, in identifying the erotic body as crucial to the dialectic of risk, recognition, and subjectivity, Beauvoir challenges phenomenology's vision of the subject. As embedded in an erotic perceiving body, consciousness must now be scrutinized for the ways in which its erotic desires situate it in the world.

Beauvoir's turn to the erotic directly challenges Descartes' notion of the body as a machine. Her challenge, however, goes beyond the phenomenological insistence on the concept of the lived body. It treads moral ground. Descartes sets moral and metaphysical investigations apart from each other. Beauvoir finds them essentially connected.

Beauvoir links the issues of morality and the body in her discussions of boredom and repetition. She raises the issue of boredom/repetition in three contexts: (1) her analysis of Sade's writings which, she says, degrade the erotic; (2) her analysis of marriage which, she says, in its current patriarchal

Arendt?

condition degrades the couple;[16] and (3) her analysis of the situation of the worker whose life, she says, is degrading insofar
as it is a "pure repetition of mechanical gestures."[17] Each of
these analyses may be read as a condemnation of the effects of
Cartesian dualism. In each case, the degradation is effected by
reducing the body to a machine; and in each case the repetitious
regime imposed on the body is morally offensive because it
cuts the body off from the lived meanings of its subjectivity.

From Beauvoir's point of view, to treat the body as a
machine is to oppress the lived body. Envisioning the body as
a mechanism inaugurates a certain callousness which becomes
the support of institutions that ignore the intentional realities
of the body. This callousness, this willed ignorance, sets the
stage for oppression. Like the myths of femininity, which cut
women off from the possibilities of their subjectivity and render
them amenable to patriarchal powers, Descartes' dualism cuts
the body off from the intentionalities of disclosure and renders
it available for exploitation. As an extended thing, the machine
body cannot be said to be violated when it is enveloped in
repetitious regimes. So long as Cartesian dualism prevails,
degradations of the body will either go unnoticed or, when
they are noticed, will be deemed irrelevant to the subject
(soul) and will be dismissed as morally irrelevant.

Beauvoir's attention to the erotic body acts as a counterweight to Cartesian dualism not only because it, like the
phenomenological lived body, infuses the body with subjectivity,
but also because it, unlike the lived phenomenological body,
affirms the value of the disturbances of the body. According to
the usual explanations, Descartes' severance of body and soul
is grounded in his artificial skepticism. Drew Leder tells a

[16] Simone de Beauvoir, *The Second Sex,* trans. H. M. Parshley (New York: Vintage Books, 1974), p. 496.
Simone de Beauvoir, *Le Deuxieme Sexe* (Paris: Gallimard, 1949), vol. II, p. 48.
[17] Simone de Beauvoir, *The Ethics of Ambiguity,* trans. Bernard Frechtman (New York: Philosophical Library, 1948), p. 83.
Simone de Beauvoir, *Pour une Morale de l'Ambiguite* (Paris: Gallimard, 1944), p. 120.

different story. According to Leder, Descartes could separate mind and body, could claim that he was mind not body, and could get us to support these claims (or at least get us to take his claims seriously enough to try to refute them) because the structure of bodily disappearance makes the notion of immaterial reason both possible and plausible.[18]

Given Leder's account of the lived body as a self-effacing and "dys-appearing" reality, that is, as something that hides itself when all goes well and calls itself to our attention when it dysfunctions as in illness, pain, fatigue,[19] we see that Descartes'dualism draws on the lived experience of the body and transforms a psychological defense mechanism (I am not that body that threatens me) into a metaphysical system. When instead of facilitating our thought processes it disrupts them and distracts thought from its aims, when it announces my vulnerability, the body is called other. Descartes answers the finite body's announcement of my perishability with proofs of God's existence and the soul's immortality.[20]

Leder credits Husserl with undermining Descartes' dualism by making the invisible body visible. Thanks to Husserl, the body now appears in its enabling as well as in its disabling moments. We are able to balance our experience of the body as that threatening, thing-like other with experiences of the body as my way of being in and toward the world. Leder does not see that Beauvoir's philosophy of the erotic takes us beyond Husserl's correction. Beauvoir's account of the lived body does more than balance our view of the body as disruptive of self and world with an affirmation of the body as constitutive of self and world, it confers value on the disruptive possibilities of the body. More than insisting that we give up the Cartesian defense against finitude, Beauvoir insists that we attend to the revelatory meanings of the body's erotic disruptive powers. In leaving Beauvoir out of his account of contemporary philoso-

[18] Drew Leder, *The Absent Body* (Chicago: University of Chicago Press, 1990), p. 127.
[19] *Ibid.*, p. 93.
[20] *Ibid.*, p. 139.

phy's rescue of the body, Leder misses an important part of the story. The history of philosophy is again depicted as a conversation among men, the disturbances of the erotic are ignored and feminism is seen as a thinking that happens outside the philosophical scene.[21]

Being included in a narrative that claims to account for philosophy's development does not, however, necessarily bode well for Beauvoir. Where Leder sees the movement from Descartes to contemporary thought as retrieving the body from its invisibility, Martin Jay discovers another development —a movement that challenges the privileging of sight. Leder tells his story without reference to Beauvoir; Jay mentions her. But being mentioned does not amount to being attended to. Jay either assumes that Beauvoir and Sartre speak in the same voice or accepts uncritically familiar criticisms of Beauvoir's thought.

Interested in detailing the story of recent French thought regarding vision and visuality, Jay notes that French intellectuals were interested in redressing the cultural losses that resulted from privileging sight. Their scrutiny of vision was not, therefore, simply an attack on the priority traditionally accorded the visual. It was a way of calling attention to the philosophically significant meanings/values of the other senses.[22] Jay calls this movement in French thought the denigration of vision. He gives Sartre and Merleau-Ponty leading roles in his story. Beauvoir is allowed a minor appearance. Instead of being seen as pushing Sartre's and Merleau-Ponty's challenges to vision, however, she is seen as countering their innovations. Paying scant attention to Beauvoir's theory of ambiguity; paying no attention to her discussion of the erotic; Jay accepts the idea that Beauvoir's feminism urges women to become (more like) men, and misses Beauvoir's point—that

---

[21] For more on this issue see: Margaret A. Simons, "Sexism and the Philosophical Canon: On Reading Beauvoir's *Second Sex*," *Journal of the History of Ideas*, Vol. 51 (July/Sept. 1990), pp. 487–504.

[22] Martin Jay, *Downcast Eyes: The Denigration of Vision in Twentieth-Century French Thought* (Berkeley: University of California Press), pp. 588–590.

under patriarchy neither men nor women confront the ambiguity of their condition because within patriarchy each sex is given a gender specific bad faith role. Man (or at least some men) gets to play the fantastic bad faith role of the absolute, transcendent subject. Woman gets to play the derogatory bad faith role of the immanent (almost) object. In attacking the bad faith of patriarchy, Beauvoir is not advocating a role reversal; she is demanding a dismantling of these roles altogether. The immoralities of patriarchy are not redressed if woman assumes the bad faith position of the one who looks. The immoralities of patriarchy will only be erased if/when both sexes accept the ambiguity of their condition and reject the imperialistic desires of the gaze.

In asking how our vision grounded desires might be undermined, Beauvoir discovers the erotic and the revelatory powers of touch. In turning to the erotic, Beauvoir challenges the mirror economies of sight and the look. For if sight serves the illusions of autonomy and self-identity and empowers the desires of the imperialist other, the erotic touch shatters these illusions and undermines these desires. The sensuous touch discovers the polymorphous body. It discovers the ambiguity of the human condition. With this touch, I discover that I am a transcending subjectivity immersed in the passivity of the flesh. Through this touch I discover the other's subjectivity neither as threatening nor as something that I can control/dominate. I discover that though

> ... the magic of eroticism spontaneously evaporates rather rapidly, the miracle is that to each lover it entrusts for the moment and in the flesh, a being whose existence reaches out in unlimited transcendence; the possession of this being is no doubt impossible, but at least contact is made in an especially privileged and poignant way ...[23]

Beauvoir calls patriarchy perverse. She identifies its fundamental perversion as the negation of women's subjectivity. In

---

[23] *The Second Sex*, p. 498/*Le Deuxieme Sex*, vol. II, p. 50.

detailing the everyday strategies of this negation (the con-
struction of the female psyche, the coding of the woman's
body, the myths of femininity) Beauvoir teaches us about the
power of images and about the ways in which the look objectifies, reifies, and alienates women from their human condition.
In turning to the erotic and attending to tactile sensuality,
Beauvoir discovers that where vision bifurcates the immanence and transcendence of subjectivity, touch senses their
intersection. She discovers that where sight presents my body
to the other as a discrete object available for domination, touch
blurs the boundaries between self and other. In this blurring I
discover that any exploitation of the other touches me.
Touching and being touched, I experience the intersubjectivity
of my subjectivity.

As concretizing the meanings of subjectivity, as reassessing
the meaning of the disruptive body, and as interrogating the
sense of sight in order to reassess the experience of touch,
Beauvoir may be seen as participating in a progressive philosophical development. From an ethical perspective, however,
we are not so much in the presence of a linear movement of
thought as we are confronted by the circling and recircling of
the questions of the other and reciprocity. In rejecting
Descartes' proofs for the existence of God and appealing to a
phenomenology of perception to free us from solipsism,
Husserl transforms our relationship to the world and the
other. Instead of finding myself immediately related to God
and only in mediated relationships to the world and the other,
I now find myself immediately in touch with the world and
reciprocally related to the other. Sartre disrupts Husserl's formula for reciprocity. He shows us the ways in which perception, infused as it must be by desire, undermines the reciprocity of the world of the "we." Beauvoir questions Sartre's portrayal of desire. She shows us that the reciprocity of the world
of the "we" remains threatened so long as we privilege the
perceptual-objectifying claims of the gaze. By introducing the
category of the erotic, however, and revealing the erotic meanings of the body as flesh, Beauvoir re-marks the dynamic of

desire. This re-marking takes up Merleau-Ponty's idea of the fold and creates an opening for a phenomenology of reciprocity—a differential return to Husserl's world of the "we."

In retrieving the erotic body for the conscious subject, Beauvoir straddles two traditions, the existential-phenomenological tradition and the feminist one. What is new for phenomenology—the idea that the body is sexed—is old news for feminists. In Beauvoir's hands, however, the existential-phenomenological perspective offers new insights for the feminist understanding of the sexed body. Her notions of desire and subjectivity also bring a new voice on the scene—an unexpected and to date a marginalized voice—the voice of the Marquis de Sade; for Sade too claimed to be a philosopher of the erotic whose task it was to unmask the hypocracies of patriarchy.

Sade

Noting that Beauvoir closes *The Second Sex* with an appeal to the liberating possibilities of the erotic and its generosities, and that her essay "Must We Burn Sade?" was written shortly after *The Second Sex*, my suspicions are aroused. I wonder about the relationship between the eighteenth century libertine and the twentieth century feminist. Pursuing the suspicion that Beauvoir's interest in Sade is more than casual, I discover that Beauvoir's Sade essay is crucial for fleshing out Beauvoir's muted voice and for piecing together the phenomenological-existential and feminist strains of her thought. It also serves to remind me that Beauvoir's turn to the erotic is not a return to romanticism but an acknowledgment of the limits of economic power. The dominant voice of *The Second Sex* urges women to pursue economic independence. The muted voice urges us all to retrieve the erotics of generosity. The Sade essay is Beauvoir's way of alerting us to the dangers and difficulties involved in this retrieval.

Beauvoir tells us two things about her reaction to Sade: first, that of all his works she found *Justine* the most intriguing; second, that she had trouble writing the Sade essay.[24] Although Beauvoir does not tell us what intrigued and troubled her, we can make some educated guesses. First there is the issue of the harem. The image of the harem appears early and often in Beauvoir's work. Long before the question of woman catches Beauvoir's attention, the image of the woman in the harem disturbs her. In her account of her visit to Tunisa, Beauvoir recalls:

> that strange village where ten thousand people live under ground. The market place was a seething mass: nothing but men ... chattering and happy; the dark blue-eyed women some young and beautiful, but all sad looking were to be found at the bottom of the many shafts which opened onto the caves ... Down in these dark smoky caverns I saw crowds of half naked children, a toothless old woman, two dirty looking middle aged women and a pretty girl covered with jewelry who was weaving a carpet. As I came back up into the light I passed the master of the house returning from market, resplendently healthy ... I pitied my sex.[25]

Though this experience may not be an experience of a harem, when Beauvoir refers to the harem it is this condition of women that she intends to call to mind. Today we are alerted to the dangers of bringing Western eyes to non-Western realities. Beauvoir did not seem to suspect that she might not fully understand what she saw. She focused on the healthy looking men who moved freely in the sun and the women living in the dark. She saw injustice and exploitation. Given this experience and the role of the image of the harem in her thought, Beauvoir was prepared to see Sade's harems as more than figments of a perverted imagination. She was prepared to explore the truths of Sade's parodies.

Reading *Justine*, Beauvoir cannot have failed to appreciate Sade's skill at demystifying the image of woman. She also must have appreciated the way in which he denaturalized the incest taboo and exposed the relationship between the mar-

---

[24] Simone de Beauvoir, *Letters to Sartre,* trans. Quinton Hoare (New York: Arcade Publishing, 1990), p. 486.
[25] *Force I,* p. 58.

riage—motherhood institution and patriarchal power. Though Sade created private enclaves for his libertines' theatrics, he made it clear that family life is neither intimate nor private. Power politics is the name of the game wherever the game between the sexes is played.

In publicizing the dirty secrets of family life, Sade exposes the link between erotic pleasure and political power. In their seclusion, the libertine castle, monastery and/or bedroom only appear to be private places. In fact they are places where privacy is forbidden. The point of removing the libertine site from its social setting is not, as Sade often suggests, to secure it from the social gaze, but rather to establish the total congruence of the public and the private—to reveal the sham of the so-called public-private distinction. The orgy is neither an intimate nor a private affair. It is a public display of political and sexual power, and it is as public display of this power that it triggers and satisfies the libertine's erotic desires. This parody of patriarchy hits the mark.

However intrigued Beauvoir may have been with Sade's exposé of patriarchy, she cannot enlist him as a reliable ally. As an existentialist, Beauvoir cannot accept the libertine's essentialism. Neither can she accept his notion of freedom, tied as it is to the idea of a preordained project—the pursuit of pleasure. And, as she makes abundantly clear in "Must We Burn Sade?," she will not reduce the erotic to an ego centered hedonism or deprive it of its crucial element—the risking of the self before the other. Sade's excesses do not, on Beauvoir's reading of them, approach the domain of the excess: the festival, the generous, and the gift. As ordered, calculated, and ultimately dispassionate displays of sexual power, they remain within the realm of reason and the economy of exchange.

Beginning where Beauvoir begins, with the solitary individual, Sade argues that eroticism only seems to connect us to others. According to Sade it is as erotic-desiring beings that we desire pleasure, and pleasure, he insists, is a solitary experience. Sade's challenge to Beauvoir is crucial. Like Beauvoir,

Sade links the question of ethics to the issue of the erotic body. Like Beauvoir, Sade insists on the subjective point of departure; and like Beauvoir's subject, Sade's subject is an embodied, sexed, desiring being. But unlike Beauvoir, who argues that the category of the erotic provides the ground for an ethic of sensuous generosities, Sade argues that erotic desire precludes the possibility of reciprocity. According to Sade, we are, as isolated desiring subjects, insulated from any claims the other may make on us. As erotic, the embodied subject pursues only its own pleasure.

Sade's challenges to Beauvoir's existentialism, feminism, and category of the erotic cannot be easily dismissed. They constitute a genuine disturbance. Sade and Beauvoir identify patriarchy with the issue of the body. In attending to the body, both are confronted with the question of biology. From Sade's point of view, Beauvoir's account of the relationship between the biologically given body and the subjectively lived body is naive. From his perspective, Beauvoir's analysis of the effects of women's weaker, birthing body on the dialectic of violence misses the ways in which violence is linked to violation and transgression; it fails to see the ways in which the ambiguity of her bodied sexuality makes woman the perfect object of the excesses of desire.

To fully understand Beauvoir's concept of ambiguity we need the name of Sade. While Merleau-Ponty gives us the phenomenological sources/resources of/for this concept; and while Sartre points to its existential and political possibilities, Sade alerts us to its bodily-erotic implications. Had Beauvoir explored the sounding of her muted voice more directly she might have attended to the relationship between the phenomenological/existential, and libertine understandings of ambiguity. As things are, she left us the legacy of hints and the task of exploring them.

We understand why Beauvoir did not dismiss Sade as a ranting perverse pornographer, given the affinity between his libertine harems and her images of the harem and given his

[handwritten annotations in top margin: "clear, intentionality for often, now not what is for pleasure, yet"]

exposé of patriarchy's gender codes. Once we attend to Beauvoir's description of intentionality, other affinities between the feminist and the libertine appear. We see that Sade's descriptions of the libertine desiring subject recall Beauvoir's descriptions of the intentional subject who, seduced by the desire to be, insists on being the absolute meaning of the world.

Following Beauvoir's lead and reading Sade against *The Second Sex*, we must consider whether we have adequately understood patriarchal desire if we only understand it in terms of domination. Reading between Sade and *The Second Sex* we are alerted to the link between violence, the affirmation of subjectivity, and violation. We are given another way of listening for the limits of an ethic of the project and are alerted to the dangers of an ethic of the erotic. We are reminded that there is, in addition to Beauvoir's excess of generosity, an excess of transgression, and that the desires of this excess may have more to do with women's exploitation than we have suspected.

Reading Sade and Beauvoir we are reminded that in the eighteenth century, French dictionaries defined the erotic as that which concerned love and as that which carried connotations of delirium and excess.[26] Beauvoir argues for remembering the link between the erotic and the delirium of spontaneous generosity. Sade argues for the link between the erotic and delirium of transgression. Beauvoir links delirium and the erotic to an ethics of uncalculated reciprocity. Sade argues against any such link.

In tracking Beauvoir's relationship to the existential-phenomenological tradition, we find her challenging it to account for the lived body as erotic. In examining Beauvoir's relationship to Sade, we find her being offered a counter challenge: to demonstrate that the erotic, given its lived excessiveness, its

---

[26] Lynn Hunt, *Eroticism and the Body Politic* (Baltimore: The Johns Hopkins University Press, 1991), p. 3.

transgressive desires, and its destabilizing effects, can become the basis of an ethic of generosity and the ground of a politics of reciprocity.

We cannot say that Beauvoir took up this challenge directly, for within the context of Beauvoir's philosophy the erotic speaks in muted tones. But if we read Beauvoir within the full complexity of her horizon and link her name with the names Descartes, Husserl, Hegel, Merleau-Ponty, Sartre, and Sade, we discover the crucial place of the category of the erotic in Beauvoir's thought. We see that though this category draws on the phenomenological idea of ambiguity to align the idea of desire with the ideas of otherness and reciprocity, it carries ambiguities of its own. Sade reminds us that the disruptive powers of the erotic are not always or necessarily liberating. He shows us the underside of Merleau-Ponty's wild being.

The erotic and its attendant excesses may, as Beauvoir suggests, propel us toward the other in generosities that transcend the order of exchange. Attending to Sade, however, we see that the erotic may also lure us toward the other in a mood of transgression that sanctions violence and violation. Without the name of Sade, we might be tempted to see Beauvoir's ethic of erotic generosities as a purely phenomenological affair—a way of moving from the epistemological to the ethical other and a way of aligning the ethical otherness of the phenomenon of ambiguity with the demands of reciprocity. Given the name of Sade, we see that the disruptive forces of the erotic can as easily annihilate as recognize the ethical other and that generosity, though spontaneous, must also be desired.

Accepting the idea that Beauvoir is a philosopher with a voice of her own depends on a close reading of contemporary French philosophy that sees Beauvoir as part of a three way conversation with Sartre and Merleau-Ponty rather than as Sartre's, the ventriloquist's, dummy. It depends on accepting the idea that the category of the erotic is crucial to Beauvoir's thought. It also requires a close reading of Beauvoir's philosophical writings. This chapter offers a point of departure (and only a point of departure) for the close reading of contemporary French thought. The next chapters offer a close reading of Beauvoir's philosophical texts. They flesh out the task of this book: to discern the sounds of Beauvoir's muted voice and the implications of her category of the erotic.

CHAPTER 2

The Necessity of Violence,
The Gift of Generosity
Pyrrhus et Cinéas

In *The Force of Circumstance I*, Simone de Beauvoir speaks of her pleasure in writing *Pyrrhus et Cinéas* and of being pleased by the reactions it provoked. Beauvoir attributes her decision to return to philosophy and to write *The Ethics of Ambiguity* to these pleasures. She does not, however, give *Pyrrhus et Cinéas* high intellectual marks; for she attributes its positive reception more to a postwar populace starved for ideology and literature, than to the merits of the work itself.[1] Bob Stone suggests other reasons for the essay's warm reception. He notes that as an ethics concerned with the question of violence, *Pyrrhus et Cinéas* reflected the realities of life in occupied France, and that Beauvoir's justification of violence in the name of freedom resonated with the French in 1947.[2]

The fate of *Pyrrhus et Cinéas* is curious. It has never been translated into English. Barely mentioned, I suspect that it is hardly, if ever read. Yet if one were intent on making the case that there is little in Beauvoir's thought that cannot already be found in Sartre's, this would be the place to make it. Though *Pyrrhus et Cinéas* is an ethics and therefore dominated by the question of the other, its point of departure is the subject as transcendence and freedom. The subject posing the ethical question is a Cartesian-Sartrean ambiguity: a consciousness

---

[1] *Force I*, p. 13.
[2] Suggested in correspondence of January 28, 1994.

that finds itself alone despite its existence among others; a freedom whose appeals and projects open it to and link it with the other; a freedom without guarantee that its projects will succeed or that its appeals will be heard.[3] Though Sartre's concepts of bad faith and the look are not named, they are present throughout the text. More significantly, the idea of the project and the concept of absolute freedom are essential to the ways in which Beauvoir works through the issues of relationship, responsibility, and violence. Like Sartre's *Being and Nothingness*, Beauvoir's *Pyrrhus et Cinéas* insists that freedom, though situated and often thwarted, is never negated. Further, pursuing Sartre's notion of the project, Beauvoir argues that it and it alone is the basis of our relationship to the other.

If much of the content of *Pyrrhus et Cinéas* is Sartrean, the style and mood are not. And this is the first sign that however close Beauvoir gets to Sartre, she is never his clone. If *Pyrrhus et Cinéas* had set the tone for existentialism, existentialism would never have gotten the reputation (deserved or not) of being a philosophy of angst and despair. However hard-headed its realism, *Pyrrhus et Cinéas* is decidedly optimistic.

Once we take Beauvoir seriously as a philosopher, we realize that *Pyrrhus et Cinéas* is a wrongly neglected work.[4] Attending to it alerts us to the continuities and breaks in Beauvoir's thought. We are able to track the course of Beauvoir's thinking and situate it within the existential-phenomenological and feminist traditions as we see how some ideas are rethought e.g. the relationship between transcendence/freedom and the situation; how some ideas move from the bare edges of Beauvoir's work to positions of importance, e.g. the idea of generosity; and how some concepts are philosophically rooted, e.g. the ideas of risk, struggle and violence.

---

[3] For an analysis of Sartre's Cartesian inclinations see Wilfred Desan, *The Tragic Finale: An Essay on the Philosophy of Jean-Paul Sartre* (New York: Harper Torchbooks, 1960).

[4] An exception to this neglect is Bob Stone's "Simone de Beauvoir and the Existential Basis of Socialism," *Social Text*, 17 (1987), pp. 123–142.

The Human Condition

Pyrrhus et Cinéas begins with an imaginary conversation between Pyrrhus, the king of Epirus, born in 318 BCE and Cinéas, his advisor. They are discussing Pyrrhus' plan to conquer the world. Of course this can't all be done at once. It must be a cumulative project, one finite action followed by another. But finally the conquest will be completed. "Well," Cinéas asks, "what will you do then?" "Why," the king replies, "I'll rest." Cinéas protests. "If all you are going to do when you are finished is rest, why begin at all—just rest now." Not bad advice given the human costs of ambitious sovereigns. But this is not Beauvoir's point. The issue for her is not the morality of military conquest but the viability of the idea that all action is futile.

Beauvoir uses this imagined conversation between Pyrrhus and Cinéas as Descartes used his method of doubt. Where Descartes appealed to the skepticism of his First Meditation to establish the necessity of the thinking subject, Beauvoir uses Cinéas' cynicism to establish the necessity of action. Further, as Descartes used the experience of doubting to establish the certainty of consciousness, Beauvoir uses the experience of futility to establish the inevitability of human transcendence and its attendant desires.

Between Cinéas and Beauvoir there is this point of agreement: none of our goals represents a satisfying end; once we finish one project we move on to another. The issue between them concerns what to make of this phenomenon. Cinéas, applying criteria of rationality, decides that all of our actions are futile. That we act for certain purposes which once realized fail to be sustainable as ends, indicates to him that no act is fulfilling and that all action is foolish. His argument is not that I often fail to successfully conclude a project, but that all projects are by definition unsuccessful. The problem is not that I fail the exam that I try to pass, but that in passing the exam my project remains unconcluded. There is the course to pass, the degree to earn, the profession to succeed in—and then?

Given the inevitability of this perpetual motion which, according to Cinéas, gets us nowhere; and given the further complication that there is no way to ultimately guarantee the justness of the goal guiding all this activity, why begin? Action, Cinéas concludes, is perverse.

Beauvoir agrees rationally this makes no sense. But she also disagrees—reason is not the appropriate judge. We cannot, Beauvoir argues, call a givenness of the human condition a perversion. However reason may measure our inevitable disposition to act, it cannot stop us from acting, and it is here, in this unavoidable and inevitable spontaneity that we find the truth of our being.[5] What is perverse from the point of view of reason, is necessary from the point of view of the human condition. The necessary requires our attention.

Cinéas' question is wrongly put. It is not a matter of deciding whether or not to act. This decision is not ours to make. As human beings, we are a spontaneous activity. We are compelled to pursue the desires of transcendence. The question concerns the meaning of this transcending spontaneity.

Rather than discard Cinéas' critique of our action as futile, Beauvoir preserves his idea of failure. Recognizing the ways in which we are defined and limited by our failures becomes essential to Beauvoir's existential critique. To be a human being is to be a failed thing. As human I cannot enclose myself within myself. I am always and necessarily incomplete and beyond myself. As a not-thing, I am, Beauvoir says, a spontaneity that loves, wants, and acts. I am, in a word, a transcendence.[6]

In identifying human finitude with transcendence, Beauvoir situates herself within the existential tradition. In analyzing the way in which I, as transcending desire, find myself among, allied with, and/or opposed to others, Beauvoir shows the point at which existentialism departs from its Cartesian roots. Unlike Descartes' solitary subject who could appeal to God to establish a universal design for nature

---

[5] Simone de Beauvoir, *Pyrrhus et Cinéas* (Paris: Gallimard, 1944), p. 11.
[6] *Ibid.*, p. 16.

and history and a common human community, Beauvoir's singular subject confronts the task of creating a meaningful human world. Dismissing the ideas of God, Nature, and Progress as bad faith myths, Beauvoir rejects the idea of a pre-given order of Being.[7] Contingency, not necessity, marks the world.

As a free subject in a contingent world living alongside others, but not in an original community with them, I have existential desires and ethical tasks. Existentially I want to project myself into the world and leave my mark on it. Ethically I am obliged to recognize the other's existential status. I must refrain from self-projections and refuse projects which compromise, ignore, or negate the other's freedom.

The phenomenology of the embodied subject complicates the situation. As a lived subject I experience my presence in the world as a bodied self-surpassing activity. The other, however, has no access to my lived embodied experience. To the other I am a presence in the world—a represented bodied freedom at best, an objectified bodied other at worst. In *Pyrrhus et Cinéas*, Beauvoir pursues the ethical dilemmas posed by the ambiguities of the lived and represented subject more influenced by Sartre's idea of consciousness than by Merleau-Ponty's idea of embodiment. While Beauvoir will speak of the body as our original lived situation and focus on the situated conditions of freedom in her later work, here she tends to align the body with the represented subject. The consequence of this alignment is an ethics that considers the morality of violence from the perspective of power and distinguishes between the power of violence to violate the represented subject and the possibility of violence touching the subject's lived freedom.

The ambiguity of the human condition, however, is not limited to the relationship between the lived and represented subject and its other. It intrudes on the lived subject itself. I am a stranger to myself as well as to the other. Otherness is not

---

[7] *Ibid.*, pp. 36–60.

always imposed on me from without. In experiencing myself as a self-surpassing activity toward an open future, I become unknown to myself.[8]

Though Beauvoir takes note of the way in which I am and must be a stranger to myself, she does not pursue the implications of this strangeness and ambiguity. Her focus in *Pyrrhus et Cinéas* is on the ways in which we are alien to each other. Here she is interested in analyzing the implications of this alienation for the ethics of the project. She takes up a twofold task: one, to create an ethic that respects the other's strangeness; and two, to prevent the idea of the other's strangeness from sliding into the idea of our necessary estrangement (the look). Maintaining the tension between the strange and the estranged, Beauvoir insists on the difference between acting with the other and acting for the other. While I must act with others, I cannot claim to act for them. However devoted I may claim to be to the other; however certain I may be that I know the other; however sincere I may be in my desire to do what is good for the other, I can never, Beauvoir insists, substitute myself for the other. The other's desire, project, and good always transcend me.[9] In claiming to act for/as the other, I claim an impossible intimacy. Beauvoir is quite clear on this point. There is nothing to justify this claim. As the one who transcends me, the other is forever a stranger.

Being barred from acting for the other does not, however, bar me from acting with the other. As Beauvoir sees it, the necessary failure of acting for the other entails the moral imperative to act with the other. In establishing the distance between myself and the other, Beauvoir also builds bridges across the divide. Her concept of the other as obstacle and her notion of the appeal keep her idea of separated subjects from collapsing into the idea of the isolated or oppositional subject. Rejecting the ontology of the "we" and the enemy, Beauvoir appeals to

[8] *Ibid.*, p. 56.
[9] *Ibid.*, p. 77.

the ontology of the obstacle. As unknown to me in your transcendence, you are present to me as an other—an obstacle. As other-obstacle you are both in my way and open to my appeal. In appealing to you to become my ally, I recognize the distance between us and I bridge it. In responding to my appeal, you demonstrate that though there is no pre-given human bond, "we" relationships are possible. The ontology of transcendence positions the other as an obstacle. The presence of the other as obstacle necessitates the appeal. The appeal is the condition of the possibility of a human community.

To insist on action/transcendence as the truth of humanity is to insist on the distinction between the given and givenness. The given is that which is produced by my acts and the acts of others. As project, the given is sustained by freedom. No givenness, however, no state of affairs, nothing divine or natural grounds freedom. Nothing constrains freedom to preserve the given. As that which transcends the given, my acts and those of others may either produce links and continuities or create breaks and discontinuities. Nothing favors the link over the break. Each of our actions is better understood as a new beginning than as an extension of what already is. Whether this new beginning will carry the past forward or repudiate it is essentially undecidable. All links are contingent. They depend on my desire and/or the desire of the other.

Our situation as finite, contingent, particular subjects is this: we live among others whose projects, like ours, are individual but not isolated. The other is always in sight. As my original obstacle, possible ally, and potential enemy, I can never ignore you. Once I understand that my project is inherently contingent and can therefore only be sustained if you pick it up as yours, you become important to me. I must make you my ally. In recognizing you as the other who transcends me, I understand that you are an obstacle to my project not only because you may oppose it but also because you are free to ignore it or to take it up in ways that are foreign to me. Thus, I must struggle against your indifference and your reinventions as well as against your outright oppositions. In my appeal I try to transform your freedom to bypass and/or oppose my project into a desire to endorse it.

Because there is no givenness, no God, no temporal continuity, no human essence to ground or guarantee the fulfillment of my vision, I cannot pursue my project without at the same time appealing to others to recognize the value of my actions and to preserve their meaning. As Beauvoir sees it, in embarking on my project I also take on the task of creating a public to whom I can appeal. This public is essential to my project. It is through the project that I am linked to/with others and it is through these others that I, as my project, am linked to the future.[10]

The intentionality of the project moves toward universality and eternity. My project is inclusive. I appeal to all to adopt it as their own. I appeal to the future to guarantee its perpetuity. I look to the project to establish the necessity of my singularity. I seek, through identifying myself with my project, to transcend my finitude, but this is impossible.

As I can neither control the other nor predict the future, my projects are contaminated with uncertainties. There is the uncertainty of the other—an uncertainty that Beauvoir likens to the worlds of Kafka where verdicts and closures are forever deferred.[11] There is the unpredictability of the future. These undecidabilities are inevitably linked. The unpredictability of the future is the uncertainty of the other, and in this sense there is little difference between the present and the future. For though I cannot in the future, as I can in the present, appeal directly to the other, I cannot either in the present or in the future control the course of my project. Once proposed by me, it is in the hands of the other. As my project, I am always at risk. As finite desire I may aspire to eternity, but as reflective finitude I discover that the meaning of my transcendence is its undecidability. I am an openness to infinity whose desire to be

[10] *Ibid.*, pp. 109–110.
[11] *Ibid.*, p. 118.

immortal is at the mercy of others.[12] The Epilogue to *The Force of Circumstance II* poignantly expresses this point. Explaining her interest in young people, Beauvoir writes:

> I am interested in them: the future is in their hands and if in their schemes I recognize my own, then I feel that my life will be prolonged after I am in my grave.[13]

Given this insistence on the absence of givenness and this focus on the uncertainties and risks of our actions, we might be led to believe that the premises of finitude, transcendence, and contingency bar Beauvoir from advocating the necessity of certain concrete projects. We would be wrong. Appealing to the only given available to her, the fact that we must appeal to the other, Beauvoir identifies certain conditions as conditions of the possibility of the appeal: health, knowledge, leisure, and freedom.[14] As the success of any project depends on the success of its appeal, and as appeals cannot, Beauvoir says, be heard when we are constantly fighting illness, ignorance, and misery, the first project (the meta-project) must be to establish the conditions of the possibility of the appeal. Any project which rejects these conditions or which in its execution would negate them must, Beauvoir says, be opposed.

In her initial analysis, the appeal emerges as the condition of an existential ethic because it creates a relationship between transcending subjectivities that negotiates their distance and preserves their otherness. As Beauvoir continues to examine the appeal, she discovers that it is conditioned and that its conditions establish the parameters of the ethical project. In developing the category of the appeal, Beauvoir brings the idea of necessity to her ethics of contingency; establishes the moral boundaries of freedom; and explicates the moral implications of the ambiguities of the lived and represented existential subject.

---

[12] *Ibid.*, p. 119.
[13] *Force II*, p. 376.
[14] *Pyrrhus et Cinéas*, p. 115.

In appealing to you I recognize you both as the lived freedom that escapes me and as the represented freedom who
appears in the world as the ego and its projects. The appeal is
a uniquely moral attitude. Standing between the
command/demand and indifference, it recognizes the limits
of our intersubjectivity as it affirms the value of the "we." In
pursuing the idea of the appeal, Beauvoir is saved from the
mistake of forgetting the body and equating freedom with
consciousness; for as she examines the meaning of the appeal,
Beauvoir discovers that the appeal itself is conditioned by the
material situation. She discovers that the ontology of consciousness calls for, but cannot call forth the appeal. The
appeal can be sounded and heard only in certain situations.

This discovery of the necessary situatedness of freedom is
a crucial mark of Beauvoir's thought. In *Pyrrhus et Cinéas* the
idea of freedom as fundamentally situated and embodied,
such that it can in certain situations and embodiments be
undermined entirely, struggles with the idea of freedom as
fundamentally inalienable. Here the implications of embodiment, though sighted, are not yet securely in place. As
Beauvoir continues to pursue the implications of ambiguity,
however, the idea of absolute freedom loses its appeal.
Ultimately the materialities of freedom cited in *Pyrrhus et
Cinéas* take center stage in Beauvoir's thought.

Violence

When the other is either an indifferent other who does not
hear my appeal, or a sympathetic other who would pursue
my project differently, the struggle of freedoms against each
other is fairly benign. When the other confronts me as an
opposing freedom, however, the stakes are raised. Now the
meaning of struggle and obstacle takes on an edge. Now I am
confronting a threatening rather than a merely separate freedom. Now the struggle takes on a different face—the face of
danger, risk and violence. Confronted by the other's dangerous freedom, I discover that it is only through risking myself

against the other that my project stands any chance of success.[15] In this risk and risking we enter the domain of violence.

There is something scandalous about Beauvoir's discussion of violence. Though she will ultimately identify it as a mark of our failure, Beauvoir refuses to call violence evil. This refusal refers back to the analyses of transcendence, the situation of the other, and the conditions of the appeal.

According to Beauvoir, two conditions are necessary to establish relations with others. First, I must be able to make my appeal. Second, I must have access to others who are free *"pour moi"*, that is, others who will respond to my call.[16] The first condition requires a certain material situation, health, etc., as well as the right to speak. The second condition can only be produced on the grounds of the first. Everything then depends on the first condition. Without the possibility of appeal, I am cut off from the other and my project is condemned to the void. Given this danger I am justified, Beauvoir says, in violating the freedom of those who would silence me. I am justified in treating them as objects.[17] Further, when the appeal to the other's freedom produces an enemy rather than an ally, when persuasion fails, I have no choice, Beauvoir says, but to resort to violence.[18]

At first it seems that violence might be avoidable. It seems that we might at least hope for a world in which the appeal always produced allies and persuasion succeeded. A utopian hope perhaps, but a hope nonetheless. Beauvoir offers no such hope. There will never be consensus. We will never persuade everyone to our cause. There will always be an other who opposes us. We are, she says, condemned to violence.[19] Her analysis of this condemnation is tortuous.

Beauvoir begins by justifying violence on two counts. The first depends on the distinction between the represented sub-

---

[15] *Ibid.*, p. 105.
[16] *Ibid.*, p. 113.
[17] *Ibid.*
[18] *Ibid.*, p. 116.
[19] *Ibid.*, p. 117.

ject's facticity and the lived subject's transcendence. The second depends on the necessity of allies. The first argument insists that the freedom of lived subjectivity cannot under any circumstances be negated. The second makes the case that violation of another's freedom is under certain circumstances permitted. According to Beauvoir's first argument, as my relationship to/with the other is limited to a relationship with their represented facticity, I can never touch their lived subjectivity. However violent I may be, I can never harm the other as lived subject. My blows only touch the other's ego representations.

This position on violence is tied to what might be called Beauvoir's Sartrean line on freedom. Though Beauvoir argues that we are always in a situation, she insists that we never coincide with it. As lived transcendence I am always beyond my represented facticity. Though the situation may create obstacles, the situation as obstacle is never fundamental. Nothing constitutes an obstacle to my transcendence.[20]

Lest we underestimate the extreme to which Beauvoir is willing to push this dichotomy between the freedom that I am and the situation which would constrain me, Beauvoir provides us with the example of the executioner. According to Beauvoir, not even the executioner has the power to destroy our freedom. We carry our death within us, Beauvoir writes, the executioner does not bring it to us. Continuing this line of thought, Beauvoir asks whether we really can know when the best time to die might be; more dramatically, she asks whether the Athenians really killed Socrates.[21]

To justify this analysis and to avoid the accusation that she is being too abstract in not taking the power of the situation into account, Beauvoir appeals to the authority of Descartes. Though she is not ignorant of the situation's power, she argues that we must distinguish between power and freedom. The violence of the situation falls within the domain of power. The other exercises power in torturing me, but this power is

---

[20] *Ibid.*, p. 80.
[21] *Ibid.*, p. 85.

limited by my freedom. As transcendence, my subjectivity is beyond any threat of violence.[22]

According to Beauvoir, my violence accomplishes its task as it misses its mark. Through violence I curtail the other's power to oppose my project. In curtailing the other's power, however, I do not, it seems, curtail their freedom. Thus though I may, from the perspective of their represented facticity, be said to harm the other, I cannot, from the perspective of their lived freedom, be said to have done evil. Evil, it seems, refers to a violation of lived subjectivity, and such violations in this analysis are impossible.

As freedom, the other is always beyond my power. In resorting to violence, I cease treating the other as a freedom and reduce them to an object in order to remove them as an obstacle to my project. My violence is directed to the other's facticity. Because it is not directed at and cannot touch the other as freedom, it cannot be called evil. Because it is necessary to destroy this threat to my project, it can be justified.

A strange argument. Does Beauvoir really wish to claim that it is as object that the other threatens me? Apparently not, for though she appeals to our need of allies to justify violence, she uses this same appeal to undermine the legitimacy of violence.

We cannot, Beauvoir says, accept the use of violence lightly.[23] If I always resorted to violence I would be alone in the world. More importantly, in oppressing one person, Beauvoir says, I make all humanity appear as a pure thing, and this negation of transcendence is the mark of a failure for which there is no compensation.[24] Thus, though Beauvoir will not condemn violence as evil, she will not accept it as moral. Violence is the mark of our failure.

Until now the failures of finitude provided Beauvoir with moral parameters: the parameter of the appeal that recognizes and reaches across to the other's transcendence; the parameter

---

[22] *Ibid.*, p. 86.
[23] *Ibid.*, p. 117.
[24] *Ibid.*

of the material conditions of the appeal. These parameters legitimate the ethic of the project. The failure of finitude disclosed by violence reveals the weakness of an ethic grounded in the appeal and the project; for it shows that this ethic can neither always bridge the distance between us nor always let this distance be.

Responsibility

Concerned that her hard line on freedom and her arguments for violence sometimes seem to imply that our conduct toward the other is a matter of indifference and sometimes seem to commit her to an ethical egoism, Beauvoir attempts to clarify her position and to distinguish it from what she calls bourgeois humanism.[25] Admitting that her clarifications may appear paradoxical, Beauvoir insists that they are unavoidable. They reflect the paradox of our condition.

Beauvoir approaches paradoxes as puzzles to be understood rather than solved. *Pyrrhus et Cinéas* opens by introducing us to the paradoxes of action and finitude, and goes on to explore the paradoxes of the situated transcendent subject. The tensions between the requirements of the appeal and the justifications of violence reflect these paradoxes. In developing the moral concept of the appeal and its conditions, Beauvoir imbeds the subject in the situation. In justifying violence, Beauvoir isolates the free subject from its situation. Ultimately, however, the justification of violence privileges the situation; for it rests on the idea that creating the conditions of the appeal justify the negation of the enemy's freedom.

Understanding that maintaining the tensions of a paradox is more difficult than affirming one or another part of the paradox, Beauvoir understands that she will be misunderstood. She turns to the idea of responsibility to show us other ways of approaching the relationship between transcending

---

[25] For an example of the bourgeois humanism to which Beauvoir is opposed see for example the works of Ayn Rand.

and situated subjectivity in the hope of helping us appreciate the tensions of the ethical paradox and the difficulties of avoiding them.

Beauvoir's concept of responsibility appeals to the phenomenology of world constitution. Having rejected the morality of acting for the other, Beauvoir cannot make us responsible for the other in the usual sense. I am morally obliged to recognize you as ultimately responsible for yourself. Recognizing that I cannot choose for you and that, given the argument that protects your freedom from my violence, my choices do not touch you, I also see that my choice is part of your situation. In one sense the conditions of poverty may be seen as given: not enough food; no place to sleep; no access to education. In another sense they may be seen as constituted: the fruits of sin; the results of laziness; the realities of exploitation. Whether or not I am responsible for the material conditions of poverty, I am responsible for constituting the meaning of poverty. My constituted meaning becomes part of the way the world is experienced. I am therefore responsible for whether or not the meaning of the world contains the meaning of freedom and the possibility of liberation. Where the phenomenology of perceptual constitution sees the other as giving me the object in its multiple fullness, Beauvoir's phenomenological concept of responsibility calls on me to enhance the meaning of the world and thereby multiply the other's possibilities.[26]

In constituting the world, I am responsible for the ways in which it situates the other. Still I cannot be said to be responsible for the other's choices and the situation cannot be said to determine them. However much I am responsible for giving your situation meaning, I am never responsible for what you make of it. Insisting on the inalienability of our freedom, Beauvoir insists that we are wholly responsible for our decisions and actions. According to Beauvoir, the slave who obeys chooses to obey, and the woman who complains to her hus-

---

[26] *Pyrrhus et Cinéas*, pp. 89–90.

band that she sacrificed her youth to him forgets that this sacrifice was her choice.[27]

Then the master is not responsible for the exploitation of the slave? Beauvoir will not allow this conclusion. Though the slave is ultimately responsible for and morally unjustified in accepting the condition of slavery, the master is responsible for creating it. The slave's moral violation may be categorized as bad faith. The master is guilty of violating the conditions of the appeal.

In Beauvoir's analyses of the appeal, represented and lived freedom, violence, and responsibility are grounded in the concept of the project. The other appears as an obstacle who may become an ally or enemy when I consider the other as a freedom who may or may not work with me. If we see each other as allies working toward a common end, we appeal to each other's freedom to carry out our common task. If we see each other as enemies working toward different ends, we undermine the other's work in the name of our own. In either case the relationship is mediated by the project.

Given the perspective of the project, whether I validate or violate your subjectivity is decided by whether or not your work supports mine. As allies who take up each other's values and validate each other's freedom we are useful to/for each other. As enemies who refuse each other's values and negate each other's freedom we war against each other because we cannot be useful to each other. In either case, the idea of the moral community—the possibility of the "we"—refers to the project in two senses. One, it refers to a community of allies who work for a common project because they have responded to each other's appeals. Two, it refers to those who are committed to the project of realizing the material conditions of the appeal.

---

[27] *Ibid.*, p. 72.

Generosity

Pyrrhus et Cinéas opens with the question: Why act? Beauvoir identifies this as an ontological issue and answers it with the ontology of transcendence, freedom, and spontaneity. We act because of who we are. For Beauvoir the question Why act? is a screen. Her real interest is in another question: How should I act? She uses the discussion of the ontology of freedom to establish the need for an ethics of freedom. As we look at the role Cinéas plays in Beauvoir's shift from ontology to ethics, we note that though Beauvoir's ontology is grounded in her critique of Cinéas' cynicism, her ethics takes up his notion of action as project. Cinéas attacks the idea of action as project for its essential incompleteness. Beauvoir uses the incompleteness of action as project to establish the necessity of the appeal.

As Beauvoir delves into the complex and often competing requirements of the ethic of the project; as she finds herself acknowledging the irresolvable paradoxes of this ethic; as she attributes these paradoxes to the paradoxes of the human condition, she makes an unexpected move. She speaks of freedom in the context of generosity and the gift. Introduced as an aside and taking up no more than two pages, this turn to generosity is crucial on two counts. First, it provides an alternative to the paradigm of the project; second, it shows that the other's transcending freedom creates a moral impasse only when/if I see it in terms of my project and try to capture it for my ends. Though Beauvoir does not use her discussion of generosity to critique her ethic of the project, it has the effect of underscoring its difficulties. Attending to the discussion of generosity, and especially to its conclusion, where the gift is identified as the paradigmatic moral act, we see that the paradoxes of the human condition do not necessarily ensnare us in moral dilemmas. It is not so much the human condition as the paradigm of the project that leads to the difficulties of Beauvoir's analyses of freedom, the appeal, and violence.

So long as intersubjectivity is seen through the prism of the project, the other appears to me as either an obstacle, ally, or enemy. If I adopt the lens of generosity, however, these relationships disappear. The distinctive mark of generosity is that the other no longer appears to me as a freedom to be harnessed for my goals and I no longer experience my freedom as teleologically conditioned. Instead of representing freedom as necessarily oriented toward something known and knowable, I see the other's freedom and represent my own as a transcendence that escapes calculation.

Citing the example of maternal love, Beauvoir characterizes the generous act as an act done for nothing.[28] It is neither for herself nor for her child that the generous mother cares for her daughter or son. It is not for herself, because the mother gains nothing from her care. This child cannot be construed as the mother's project. The generous mother knows that no human being can be another's project. It is not for her child, because the generous mother knows that her care cannot make the child one thing or another. This care can only give the child's transcendence its point of departure. This act, done for nothing, is done in recognition of the duality of our condition. As facticity, the child needs its mother's care. As transcendence, the child needs the kind of caring that allows it to explore its possibilities. It needs the kind of caring that does not demand allegiance.

Beauvoir does not limit the possibility of generosity to the mother-child relationship. She also speaks of the generous man.[29] Unlike the generous mother who acts for nothing, the generous man wants something—to be recognized in his freedom. But unlike the ally who ties recognition of freedom to allegience to the project, the generous man asks only that his act be acknowledged in its spontaneity. He asks that his act not be reduced to some sort of facticity; that it not be construed as either determined or self-interested.

---

[28] *Ibid.*, p. 83.
[29] *Ibid.*

In a sense, the generous man asks more of us than the ally. Allies call on me to align my freedom with their projects and therefore do not, strictly speaking, ask me to acknowledge their freedom *per se*. The generous man, by asking nothing of me, by not calling on me to be his ally, asks me to recognize the otherness of his freedom. By not needing me, the generous man shows me that as transcending spontaneities neither he nor I are useful to each other. Without being of use to each other, we cannot be construed as objects for each other. Having no purpose beyond itself, the generous man's act is a gift. It is a pure expression of freedom. In receiving this gift, I acknowledge the generous man in his transcendence and I recognize the full meaning of the otherness of transcendence—spontaneity without/beyond goal, purpose, or end.

It is difficult, Beauvoir says, to receive a generously given gift.[30] Fearing that they have been viewed as objects by a strange freedom, receivers of gifts, wanting only to believe in their own freedom, attempt to transform the giving of the gift into an economic exchange. They try to pay the giver back. The attempt is an insult. It may also be bad faith, for in refusing the gift, I insist on containing freedom within the limits of the project—on saving it from its excess. In refusing the gift, I refuse the otherness of the other and myself. To give the generous man what he wants, recognition of his freedom by acknowledging that his generosity is for nothing, is also, for me, an act of self-recognition and a confontation with otherness.

Moving the generous relationship from the situation of the mother and child to the situation of the generous man, Beauvoir concludes her discussion of generosity by telling us that a lucid generosity ought to guide our acts. When our acts are generously guided, she says, we assume our choices without imposing them on others. As generous, we leave it to the other to take up our choices in their own way.[31]

---

[30] *Ibid.*
[31] *Ibid.*, p. 84.

As a model of action, generosity returns to and unsettles the ethic of the project. It unsettles it insofar as its paradigm of abundance and excess challenges the teleology of the project. It returns to it insofar as its refusal to impose itself on the freedom of the other provides a model for the appeal.

Within *Pyrrhus et Cinéas* this model is the sound of Beauvoir's muted voice. It has nowhere to go and no ground to stand on because it speaks to the possibility of an unmediated intersubjective relationship, and within *Pyrrhus et Cinéas* this possibility is foreclosed. As Beauvoir begins to explore the possibilities of unmediated relationships, however, and especially as she develops the idea of the erotic, the thought of generosity is retrieved. Within *The Second Sex*, for example, the possibilities of generosity and the gift are linked to the idea of the erotic as the unique site of our encounter with the immanence and transcendence of the other.

Here, as in Beauvoir's later works, the tensions between the intersubjectivity of generosity and the project are not worked through. The discussion that turns to generosity returns to the project. Beauvoir again speaks of our relationship to each other in terms of use and need. Coming from the discussion of generosity, however, we are struck by the way the meaning of transcendence changes when it is moved from the context of generosity to the paradigm of the project. From the perspective of generosity, transcendence is understood as spontaneity. It is an affirmation of freedom as gratuitous. From the perspective of the project, however, transcendence is linked to the ideas of the future and universality. It is seen as the way in which I project myself into the world. Between the transcendence of generosity and the transcendence of the project two different desires are at work. The desires of generosity affirm finitude and transcendence in themselves. The desires of the project aim to transcend the singularity and finitude of the subject by affirming the values, objects, etc., constituted by the transcendent act. Where the desires of generosity recognize the impossibility of transcending finitude, the desires of the project are caught up in the impossibility of transcending the human condition.

Given my finitude and contingency, the things, ideas, and values that I call mine must be taken up by the other if they are to endure. Hence my dependence on the other. Without confirmation of the other, I am confined to the gratuity of the present. Given my transcending subjectivity, however, those acts through which I represent myself are not me. Though mine, they do not and cannot capture my lived subjectivity.

The acts through which I exist for the other can never, Beauvoir says, be assembled into a whole called me.[32] Thus though I appeal to the other to validate my freedom by taking up my values, ideas, etc., I cannot appeal to the other to know or accept me as I am; for the other, I only exist as ego-appearance.

Attending to the question of my relationship with the other, Beauvoir does not pursue the ways in which this discontinuity between spontaneity and the object it produces applies to my relationship to myself. She does not explore how there may be more obstacles to my project and freedom than the projects and freedoms of others. Had she explored the relationship between generosity and the project, Beauvoir might have pursued the thought that my transcendence, insofar as it cannot be contained by any project, and my project, insofar as I identify myself with it, may be obstacles to each other.

Beauvoir's ontology of finitude and difference precludes the giveness of the "we." Her existential notion of choice/choosing precludes the giveness of either historical continuity or progress. Like Descartes, Beauvoir will have to find a way to bridge the gap between the discrete moment and the historical flow. She will have to discover a way to link the singular individual with the collectivity of the "we." Turning to Descartes,

---

[32] *Ibid.*, p. 98.

Beauvoir reworks his analysis of time to support her discussions of the "we," history, and intersubjectivity.

With Descartes, temporal continuity is ensured by divine power, for this is what it takes, according to Descartes, to link the discrete moments of time. With Beauvoir, there is no divine power to establish or maintain temporal continuity. We are caught in a temporal flow of discrete moments. Given that the only continuities that exist are those created by finite, singular freedoms, and that these continuities are inherently unstable (vulnerable as they are to being undone by any new choice), there can be no justification for the ideas of historical progress, a common humanity, or a unified singular life. Further, given that we can always negate our commitments and that we are engaged in multiple projects, we cannot claim that we are either defined by any one of our acts or that all of our actions constitute a whole. In this godless Cartesian world, singularity prevails. The singularity of the other is unknowable. The singular self is not a unity. The discrete moment cannot be incorporated into an historical continuity. The project is necessarily limited. Humanity is always plural.

Learning from Descartes that the ontology of singular subjects and atomic moments can be transcended, but barred from following Descartes in his appeal to God, Beauvoir turns to the constituting powers and desires of freedom to save us from a disjointed, fragmented universe and introduces us to the concept of joy. By all accounts the reference to joy is unnecessary. The ontology of transcendence is sufficient for Beauvoir's argument. As unnecessary, however, this reference to joy is crucial; it is part of the signature of Beauvoir's thought. For Beauvoir, freedom/transcendence must be aligned with joy. Attacking the Stoics for their isolated and indifferent sense of freedom, Beauvoir makes it clear that our transcendence must be understood in terms of desire and that joy is the characteristic desire of freedom. Our joys, she writes, are rooted in a past which they transcend in their movement toward a future ensemble.[33]

---

[33] *Ibid.*, pp. 21–32.

Like the analysis of generosity, this discussion of joy, temporality and transcendence stops short. It is not taken up again in *Pyrrhus et Cinéas*. Like the idea of generosity, however, it finds its way back into Beauvoir's thought. And unlike the ideas of generosity and the gift, which despite their recurring presence in Beauvoir's work never make it to center stage, the idea of joy finds a place in Beauvoir's dominant voice. It is also radically rethought. In *Pyrrhus et Cinéas*, joy is aligned with the project desires of continuity. In *The Ethics of Ambiguity*, joy will be identified with spontaneity.

In *Pyrrhus et Cinéas* Beauvoir merely notes the project and generosity facets of transcendence. She does not attend to the ways in which these two trajectories of freedom are at odds with each other. She does not seem to see that the desire to perpetuate my project is at odds with the non-teleological desires of spontaneity. When she returns to the question of transcendence in The *Ethics of Ambiguity*, however, this doubling activity of transcendence will be considered from the perspective of the tension between the desire to be the object created by freedom and desires of the spontaneity of freedom. Moved from the problem of the question of the other to the question of consciousness, the Janus-face of transcendence will become the source of the unique structure of intentionality which informs *The Ethics of Ambiguity's* concept of ambiguity.

The idea of transcendence, insofar as it determines the meaning of the other and establishes the parameters of intersubjectivity, also becomes more nuanced as Beauvoir attends to the phenomenon of intimacy. Within *Pyrrhus et Cinéas*, the Other is positioned as an inaccessible freedom who either becomes my ally or enemy. Within *Pyrrhus et Cinéas*, the me-other relationship must ultimately fail; for whether you become my ally or enemy, I can never get what I want from you—your freedom. After *Pyrrhus et Cinéas*, however Beauvoir rethinks the question of intersubjective desire. In bringing the themes of generosity and intimacy together and in exploring the meanings of the gift, she figures the other as an uncanny freedom rather than as an inaccessible transcendence. She refers to the other as the one who can be touched but not cap-tured—the one whose strange freedom calls to me as it eludes me. The question of the other becomes less a matter of catching them in their transcendence (an impossibility) and more a matter of acknowledging their otherness.

Breaks and Continuities

Beauvoir would have us believe that the question of woman was far from her mind until Sartre put it there. Like the issues of generosity, otherness and joy, however, women are present in *Pyrrhus et Cinéas*. Not yet a concept to be ana-lyzed, women are concrete realities that appear at crucial moments.

Beyond the already cited example of maternal love, Beauvoir cites the examples of the old woman and the wife to clarify her philosophical positions. To illustrate the point that all submissions to authority are chosen, Beauvoir tells us about an old woman who refused to acquiesce to a priest's demands. Responding to the priest's expectations that she serve him, the old woman, belying her humble and powerless status and challenging the idea that piety requires submission to authority, tells the priest to serve himself.[34] To show us the limits of our responsibilities regarding the other, Beauvoir tells us that giving birth to a criminal does not make a mother responsible for the criminal.[35] To expose the deceptions of devotion, Beauvoir notes that more women than men seek refuge from the demands of freedom by becoming devoted to another person[36] and cites the instance of the wife (but not the husband) as the example of the one who accords the other absolute value in order to invalidly anchor her existence.[37]

---

[34] *Ibid.*, p. 38.
[35] *Ibid.*, p. 69.
[36] *Ibid.*, p. 70.
[37] *Ibid.*, pp. 70–71.

What is especially interesting in *Pyrrhus et Cinéas* is the way in which the situation of the woman, the wife, and the slave are juxtaposed. Though there is no attempt to link the woman to the slave, and though, given Beauvoir's hard line on freedom, there can be no analysis of the ways in which the situations of the woman and the slave conspire to negate their freedom, we are nevertheless given a definition of the happy slave that applies to the wife and that is preserved, if not cited, in Beauvoir's later analyses of the woman-slave relationship in *The Second Sex*.

As Beauvoir describes it, the happiness of the happy slave is a matter of existential, not material satisfaction. It has all the markings of bad faith—the refusal to acknowledge oneself as contingent, unanchored, self-responsible, and free. Happy slaves, according to Beauvoir, are happy because they see their existence as justified in the needs and necessity of the master. Having not yet formulated her ideas of mystification and ideology, Beauvoir tells us in *Pyrrhus et Cinéas* that happy slaves abdicate their freedom in order to feel essential and that it is in claiming to become essential to a necessary other that slaves find their happiness.[38] The wife's happiness is found in this same willed and willful delusion. The slave calls the necessary other master, the wife calls him husband.

Reading *Pyrrhus et Cinéas* we are struck by its difference from Beauvoir's later work. *Pyrrhus et Cinéas* delineates an ethics of the finite subject, absolute freedom and the project. All abdications of freedom are tracked down, exposed and condemned. The Stoic, the believer, the happy slave, the devoted wife are each accused of trying to evade their human condition. No excuses are accepted for these refusals of transcendence. Nothing less than a total commitment to the philosophy of the project is allowed; for it is with the project that I am, insofar as I can be, defined; it is in the project that I dis-

---

[38] *Ibid.*, p. 70.

cover my joy; and it is through the project that I am related to the other. Given this preeminence of the project, transcendence becomes an irremediable obstacle to intimacy and an apology for violence. As inherently elusive, the other is always beyond our reach. Though we can extend ourselves toward others in generosity, we can neither touch them with love nor destroy them through murder.

It is possible to read Beauvoir's later philosophy as a response to the failures of *Pyrrhus et Cinéas*. It is possible to see Beauvoir's discussions of the erotic in *The Ethics of Ambiguity, The Second Sex,* "Must We Burn Sade?" and *The Coming of Age* as a response to the impossibilities of intimacy of *Pyrrhus et Cinéas*. It is possible to see Beauvoir's thought, from *The Ethics of Ambiguity* on, as haunted by the question of intimacy. It is also possible to see Beauvoir's revisions of the subject-situation relationship as a reaction against the impossible discussions of evil in *Pyrrhus et Cinéas*. It would be a mistake, however, to push this focus on discontinuities too far. As the place where Beauvoir's philosophical thought begins, *Pyrrhus et Cinéas* is also the place from which it develops.

As focused on the project, *Pyrrhus et Cinéas* also attends to the failure of the project. According to Beauvoir, the heart of this failure lies in the essence of transcendence. As products of singular spontaneities who never come to rest, our projects are always finite, contingent, and incomplete. Refusing either to evade this crucial facet of our existence or to defer to it in despair, Beauvoir characterizes it as our joy and makes it the foundation of an ethics of a finite subject whose otherness to itself and others becomes the source of its relationships and responsibilities.

This response to failure is repeated throughout Beauvoir's work. The failures of finitude always become the ground of an affirmation. Whether the question is that of *Pyrrhus et Cinéas* —what is our relationship to the other?—or that of *The Ethics of Ambiguity*—what are the moral implications of intentionality —or that of *The Second Sex*—how are we to understand the condition of women?—it is ever, for Beauvoir, a matter of rethinking the meaning of failure. Considering that, for Beauvoir, failure is the mark of finitude, this effort of rethinking is crucial; for in the end it concerns the pervasive question of Beauvoir's thought: How shall we live the contingencies of our existence?

CHAPTER 3

Contesting Intentional Anxieties:
The Ethics of Ambiguity

Beauvoir wrote *The Ethics of Ambiguity* with an eye toward her relationship with existentialism, especially Sartre. Presenting herself as Sartre's other voice, Beauvoir presents *The Ethics of Ambiguity* as an extension of the thinking of *Being and Nothingness*. It is, Beauvoir tells us, the ethics that complements and is called for by Sartre's ontology.

I read *The Ethics of Ambiguity* looking in two directions, backward toward its philosophical influences, and forward toward *The Second Sex*. Reading forward, I remember that this writer who refuses to call herself a philosopher is an untrustworthy narrator when it comes to exposing *her* philosophical ventures. Accepting her declared debt to Sartre, I look for its limits. Refusing to read her under his thumb, I look for the marks of her independence.

Reading backward, I find Beauvoir's account of her reliance on Sartre less than reliable. Her philosophical affinity to Sartre is not as clear as she leads us to believe. It is certainly less than it was in *Pyrrhus et Cinéas*.[1] Much more than an answer to Sartre's critics, much more than Sartre's echo, *The Ethics of Ambiguity* is a complex reworking of competing strains within the continental tradition. Beauvoir names many of her non-Sartrean sources: Hegel, Husserl, Marx, Heidegger,

---

[1] For an account of the Beauvoir-Sartre intellectual relationship that refutes Beauvoir's account and sees Sartre as the debtor, see Kate Fullbrook and Edward Fullbrook, *Simone de Beauvoir and Jean-Paul Sartre: The Remaking of a Twentieth Century Legend* (New York: Basic Books, 1994).

Kierkegaard, Bataille. She leaves out the name Merleau-Ponty. All are present in her delineation of the ambiguities of the human condition.

The Ethics of Ambiguity takes up the phenomenological, dialectical, Marxist, and existentialist ideas circulating in the French intellectual scene of the 1940s. Without adopting any of these ideas completely or rejecting any of them totally, Beauvoir resituates them. What emerges is a unique ethical vision. Its uniqueness does not lie in its insistence on the ambiguity of the human condition/situation, or even in its move to simultaneously affirm the absolute value of the particular individual (the "I") and the unconditional value of the bond (the "we"). It lies rather in the way it insists on affirming the joy of existence and the moral value of generosity.

Perhaps insists is too strong. The main lines of the text seem Sartrean. There appears to be little that is new. But if we pause to pursue certain nuances, we notice one little thing—a somewhat altered description of intentionality. This one little thing reverberates in the unexpected appearance of words like love. It reverberates in the return to *Pyrrhus and Cinéas'* themes of generosity and joy. It leads to a tension between the Sartrean existential line Beauvoir claims to be defending and another way of thinking. It directs us to the text's other voices. Picking up on these voices we discover Beauvoir the philosopher. Read as a multi-voiced text whose ethics is grounded in a phenomenology that speaks of contesting intentional desires, *The Ethics of Ambiguity* may be read as retrieving the voices of Husserl and Hegel and as negotiating the differences between Merleau-Ponty and Sartre.

Redescribing Intentionality

Beauvoir describes intentionality as comprised of two moments: a moment that discloses being, and a moment that identifies the disclosing I with the being it discloses. Beauvoir's account of the first intentional moment echoes Husserl and Merleau-Ponty. In this moment I unveil the

meanings of being, experience myself as the freedom of revelation, and am aware of the intersubjective world as the nexus
of my life. Beauvoir's account of the second intentional
moment echoes Hegel and Sartre. Here I appropriate the disclosed meanings of being by insisting on the my-ness of the
world disclosed by me and/or by identifying myself with the
being I disclose. The moments of revelation and appropriation
contest each other. They are also bound to each other. Their
contested bond is the ground of what Beauvoir calls the ambiguity of the human condition. It is also the source of
Beauvoir's unique philosophical perspective.

In redescribing intentionality, Beauvoir envelops each
intentional moment in a mood. The mood of the first moment
is joyful; that of the second is anxious and assertive. In attending to mood, Beauvoir shows that despite their affinities, the
thought of Hegel and Sartre contest each other. She also shows
that despite their differences, there are parallels between the
Husserl and Merleau-Ponty of the first intentional moment
and the Hegel and Sartre of the second intentionality. We can
better understand what is happening by referring to
Beauvoir's July 1940 letters to Sartre. Reading these letters, we
learn that Beauvoir is reading Hegel three hours a day (using
Wahl to help her decipher him), and that though she finds
Hegel's philosophy analogous to Sartre's, she finds the moods
of their thought quite different. According to Beauvoir, what
Sartre finds gloomy and despairing Hegel turns into joy. She
tells Sartre that she finds both observations to be true and that
she would like to find their point of equilibrium.[2]

The Ethics of Ambiguity may be read as the search for that
point. It cannot, however, be read as finding it. If anything, the
contest between Hegel's joy and Sartre's despair is sharpened.
Once she attends to mood, Beauvoir gives Hegel a place in
both intentional moments: the joy of the first, the assertion of
self of the second. Sartre, however, remains confined to the

---

[2] Letters to Sartre, pp. 312, 314, 326, 336.

second moment of intentionality. Further, Beauvoir upsets the idea of an equilibrium between these intentionalities by privileging the desire of revelation and mood of joy of the first intentionality. Having failed to find a way to align Hegel and Sartre, Beauvoir discovered a link between Hegel and Merleau-Ponty. Merleau-Ponty's marvel and Hegel's joy meet in the first intentional moment, a crucial moment of Beauvoir's thought.

For now, I leave it to others to pursue the historical sources of Beauvoir's account of intentionality. I will follow Beauvoir's analysis of intentionality to discern the ways in which her description of the moods and desires of the two moments of intentionality, and her privileging of the first intentional moment lays the ground for an ethic that affirms the joys of freedom; recognizes the lures of bad faith; identifies generosity as an ethical category; distinguishes the ethical project from the imperialist will; and celebrates the bonds linking us to others and the world.

Keeping the names Hegel and Husserl in mind allows us to see that when Beauvoir moves away from Sartre her moves are not arbitrary. Her influences are his influences. This, in part, accounts for the credibility of her insistence that her voice is his and for our difficulty in seeing their differences. But Beauvoir and Sartre work with their predecessors differently. Understanding this allows us to hear the nuances of her voice and to track their implications.

Central to *The Ethics of Ambiguity*'s project is its account of freedom and it is here, at the crucial point of departure, that Beauvoir distances herself from Sartre. This distancing comes early in the text, in a paragraph that begins by recalling Sartre's description of man as a useless passion. Sartre pursues this description to ensnare consciousness in the bad faith project of the desire to be God. Beauvoir, however, sees things differently. Instead of assigning one desire to consciousness, she will assign two. Pausing to consider the relationship between intentionality and bad faith, Beauvoir fissures the relationship between consciousness and being and establishes consciousness as the site of contested desires: the desire to disclose being and the desire to be. She writes:

> It is not in vain that man nullifies being. Thanks to him being is disclosed and he desires this disclosure. There is an original type of attachment to being which is not the relationship "wanting to be" but rather the relationship "wanting to disclose being." Now there is not failure but success ... I cannot appropriate the snow field where I slide. It remains foreign, forbidden but I take delight in this every effort toward an impossible possession. ... This means that man, in his vain attempt to be God makes himself exist as man ... It is not possible for him to exist without tending toward this being which he will never be. But it is possible for him to want this tension even with the failure it involves.[3]

It is important to stay with this passage for a few moments, for as I read it, it is crucial for understanding the differences between Sartre and Beauvoir; the affinities between Beauvoir and Merleau-Ponty; the argument of *The Ethics of Ambiguity*; and the ethic of *The Second Sex*. In this description of consciousness as disclosure, Beauvoir distinguishes two moods and moments of intentionality: an original mood/moment that delights in disclosure *per se*, and a second mood/moment that wants to be the being originally disclosed. Beauvoir tells us two things about this second mood/moment. First, that its desire is impossible and doomed to failure; second, that it cannot be avoided. She then poses a question: How can this inevitable failure be lived? Her answer: Through the desire of the first moment/mood of intentionality, which delights in the failure of the second intentionality. In this delight, this desire of the original intentionality affirms the desire of the second intentionality in its impossibility.

In this fissured account of intentionality, Beauvoir identifies consciousness as lack without allowing this lack to become a wound. Desire as grounded in the lack is originally and joyfully attracted to being. It is only derivatively and secondarily that the lack triggers the anxiety of the wound articulated in the

---

[3] *Ethics*, pp. 12–13/*Morale*, pp. 16–17.

desire to be of the second moment of intentionality. In this account of intentionality, consciousness is the desire for disclosure that desires to be the objects it discloses. When Beauvoir tells us that "thanks to him being is disclosed and he desires this disclosure," we need to see the desire for disclosure as referring to both the activity of disclosure and the object disclosed. Desiring the object disclosed, consciousness falls into bad faith. Desiring the activity of disclosure, consciousness revels in its spontaneity. Attending to this double desire, we see Beauvoir accepting Sartre's accounts of bad faith but not accepting Sartre's account of intentionality.

Beauvoir's description of the contesting desires of consciousness draws on Husserl's distinction between the noesis and the noema without following it. Her distinction attends to desire rather than to constituting activity *per se*. Like Husserl, however, Beauvoir sees consciousness as a dynamic activity. Describing intentionality as comprised of two moments is her way of noting this dynamic. The original moment of consciousness is drawn to the otherness of Being in a mood of joy and delight. Its desire to disclose Being is met with success. It is not, however, stable. Contested by the desire to be God, the joy and success of this original intentionality gives way to a second mode of intentionality. Driven by the desire to be (an impossible desire) this second moment of consciousness articulates the anxieties of finitude. In privileging the joyful desire of intentionality as original, Beauvoir does not suggest that we can or should condemn the desire to be of the second intentional moment. Instead, Beauvoir asks us to affirm the tensions of these contesting intentionalities and directs us to explore them.

Beauvoir's description of intentionality as a site of contesting desires may be read as a critique of the blind spots in Sartre's and Merleau-Ponty's phenomenologies, for according to Beauvoir, our relationship to the otherness of Being cannot be adequately described as wholly reciprocal or wholly contesting and appropriative. It is both, and it is in being both that the ambiguity of our condition lies.

In directing us to read *The Ethics of Ambiguity* according to the ontology of *Being and Nothingness,* and directing us to read her account of intentionality according to Sartre's account of bad faith, Beauvoir tempts us to either misread this passage or slide over its nuances. We would do well to resist this temptation. Resisting it, we see what Beauvoir does not want us to see. Her philosophy is not Sartre's. Far from reinforcing Sartre's position that bad faith, the desire to be, permeates consciousness, Beauvoir challenges it. There is no desire to be, bad faith, in the first intentional moment.

One of the reasons that Sartre's arguments for the pervasiveness of bad faith are so compelling is that he establishes an essential relationship between the experience of freedom and the experience of anxiety. Though *Being and Nothingness* gives reasons for abandoning bad faith, these reasons are overwhelmed by the desire to elude anxiety and the desire to be. Desire, never being impressed with reasons, prefers the path of repression. Bad faith prevails.

Beauvoir recognizes the relationship between freedom and anxiety. She refers to it as a tension. But she also identifies another relationship between freedom and desire, delight. In identifying the desires of disclosure with joy, delight and success, Beauvoir brings Merleau-Ponty onto the scene. In relegating the anxieties of consciousness to the failures of the desire to be, Beauvoir transforms the issue of bad faith from Sartre's question, Can the powers of anxiety be persuaded by the demands of honesty to forgo the project of alienation?, into a new question, Must the anxieties of freedom that express themselves as the desire to be, prevail over the joys of intentionality that signify themselves by revealing the meanings of Being?

With this new question, the focus of an existentialist ethic shifts. It is now tied to determining the conditions under which the desires of consciousness can be diverted from the desire to be the object/meaning it discloses, to the desire to be itself, the activity of disclosing. Given the ways in which the moments of intentionality intersect, the desire to be cannot be

annulled. It can, however, be lived differently. It can forgo the
bad faith project of collapsing the distance between itself and
the object of its desire by recalling its delight in disclosing the
object of its desire. Contesting the anxieties of the second
intentional moment with the joys of the first intentional
moment, consciousness opens itself to the complexity of its
desire. It embraces the tensions of intentionality bad faith
would escape.

Conceptualizing intentionality as a contest between the
desires of disclosure and the desire to be the disclosed object,
Beauvoir opens new paths. The route to bad faith remains
open and heavily traveled, but other roads beckon. Still working with consciousness conceptualized as freedom, fissured,
and the sole ground of meaning, Beauvoir alters the mood and
meaning of the concepts of freedom and subjectivity.

Bad Faith as History

Bad faith is for Beauvoir what it was for Sartre, a response
to the anxieties of freedom that constitutes a permanent threat
to the possibility of an existential ethic. Unlike Sartre, however,
who links anxiety and freedom immediately and ontologically,
Beauvoir links them derivatively and historically. According
to Sartre, we are inexorably marked by the mood of anxiety
because anxiety is the marker of the nothingness of conscious-
ness/freedom. Beauvoir's account of the nothingness of consciousness is more complex. She sees it marked by two
moments and two moods. Whether consciousness becomes
dominated by one mood or the other is not ontologically
given. It owes at least as much to the contingencies of history
as it does to the demands of ontology.

Beauvoir works out the relationship between social/politi-
cal/personal history and the ontology of freedom in *The
Second Sex*. In *The Ethics of Ambiguity* her scope is more limited.
Though there is mention of the harem and slavery, *The Ethics
of Ambiguity* is fundamentally a-historical. Its account of situated
subjectivity is psychological and she assumes that her psycho-

logical categories are universal. Here Beauvoir examines the relationship between the general features of human development and personal history, and the demands of intentionality. She analyzes the relationship between bad faith and childhood and links the ontology of bad faith with the mood of nostalgia. She develops the idea that the anxieties of freedom are reinforced by our nostalgia for the securities of childhood and that bad faith is the way these anxieties and nostalgias express themselves.

According to Beauvoir, the child lives in the world of the other. Its desire is attuned to its situated existence. Knowing neither the desires nor the joys of disclosure, the child does not contest the givenness of its situation. On the contrary, in experiencing values and meanings as already given, it experiences itself as having a clearly defined place in the world; it experiences itself as the fulfillment of its desire to be. The condition of childhood, Beauvoir says, is "metaphysically privileged."[4]

As we all begin as children, we all begin by experiencing ourselves as dominated by our situation. We experience this domination as natural. We come to know ourselves as free in the existential sense only through the crisis of adolescence. Now we must assume our subjectivity.[5] The joys of childhood give way to the joys of liberation. But these joys are ambiguous. They carry with them the anguish, tension, and confusion of existential freedom. The joy of being liberated from the world of the other, the delight of discovering the power of disclosure, is contested by another mood, nostalgia. Beauvoir writes:

> The misfortune which comes to man as a result of the fact that he was a child is that his freedom was first concealed from him and that all his life he will be nostalgic for the time when he did not know its exigencies[6]

---

[4] *Ibid.*, p. 36/p. 53.
[5] *Ibid.*, p. 39/p. 57.
[6] *Ibid.*, p. 40/p. 58.

The source of bad faith then is not the anxiety of freedom *per se*, but the nostalgia for childhood where the desires to be are unambiguously fulfilled. Ontology and psychology are out of sync. As consciousness, the act of disclosure conditions the act of appropriation. As human, the experience of being predates the experience of openness to Being. As we become aware of the existential requirements of freedom (adolescence) we discover that we must resituate ourselves *vis-à-vis* our original anthropological situation. Some of us never get the chance.

In referring us to childhood and nostalgia, Beauvoir empowers the situation in ways that are foreign to the analyses of *Being and Nothingness*.[7] Not only does she identify the child as innocent, that is, as not being in bad faith, she also identifies others, "the negro slave of the 18th century" and "the Mohammedan woman enclosed in a harem"[8] whose situations bar them from the experience of freedom. In these cases, submission to the authority of the other cannot be counted as an act of bad faith. Those who are ignorant and mystified cannot be accused of evading their freedom. In Beauvoir's words:

> mystification [and] ... ignorance is a situation in which man may be enclosed as narrowly as in a prison ... not everyone has the means of rejecting, even by doubt, the values, taboos and prescriptions by which he is surrounded.[9]

In situations where freedom is foreclosed the category bad faith cannot apply.

The break with *Pyrrhus et Cinéas* could not be more dramatic. There my freedom was secured even from the power of the executioner, here the powers of ignorance and mystification are sufficient to negate freedom. Where *Pyrrhus et Cinéas* insisted on the divide between lived and represented subjec-

---

[7] Jean-Paul Sartre, *Being and Nothingness*, trans. Hazel E. Barnes (New York: Washington Square Press, 1969), pp. 49–85.
[8] *Ethics* p. 38/*Morale*, p. 56.
[9] *Ibid.*, p. 98/p. 141.

tivity, *The Ethics of Ambiguity* negotiates it. My represented subjectivity invades my lived experience. Where *Pyrrhus et Cinéas* privileged lived over represented subjectivity, *The Ethics of Ambiguity* presents the relationship between lived and represented subjectivity as fluid. We cannot know *a priori* how the balance of power will fall. Where the ethics of *Pyrrhus et Cinéas* flowed directly from an ontology of freedom, the ethics of *The Ethics of Ambiguity*, by imbedding consciousness in its situation, calls for a detour through history. We will have to wait for *The Second Sex* for Beauvoir to follow this detour herself.

The Other

In referring us to childhood and nostalgia, Beauvoir's analysis of intentionality alerts us to the significance of the situation. It brings the phenomenological issue of intentionality to the existential issue of freedom within the context of the ethical question of the other.

Consciousness as intentionality-freedom is permeated by desire and imbedded in its situation. It may invoke the desires of disclosure to evade the lures of bad faith; it may succumb to the temptations of bad faith; it may get stuck in its nostalgia or delight in its discovery of freedom; it cannot, however, divorce itself from either its desire or its situation. As situated, consciousness is entangled with the other.

How does it stand with the other? Shall we again take our direction from Beauvoir and read her according to Sartre's paradigm of the look? Shall we say that we each confront each other as the desire to be the one—the only one—whose meaning prevails? Shall we say that the other inevitably robs me of my intentional powers and that I must, in the name of my desire, preemptively strike at the other's freedom?

Reading *The Ethics of Ambiguity*, we discover that the look tells part of the story of our relationship with the other. It tells the story of the serious man, the nihilist, the adventurer, and the passionate man. Though diverse in the assumption of their freedom, these men share the illusion of ethical solipsism.

Reserving the name subject only for themselves, they treat others either as objects to be dominated or as objects of indifference. Beauvoir, appealing to her opening descriptions of consciousness, rejects this individualistic understanding of freedom.

Referring to Hegel's account of the fight to the death rather than to Sartre's account of the look, Beauvoir claims that the desire to negate the other's freedom struggles against itself.[10] This struggle takes two directions. In the first, consciousness recognizes that its disclosures are always grounded in a world that is already there and that the already given meanings it confronts are the signatures of another freedom. In the second, consciousness recognizes that the other, like the first moment of intentionality, challenges its desire to be and is therefore essential to the dynamic of its own subjectivity.

The human past is not a brute fact. It is radically different from the natural past in that it is humanly signified. It is the work of other freedoms. We may rebel against the past, but Beauvoir warns us not to do so lightly. Though hardly an advocate of preserving the past out of a sense of reverence, Beauvoir links the transcendence of freedom and the power of disclosure to an ability to recognize the paths opened up to us by our ancestors.[11]

Rebellion against the freedom of the other is not then the essential mark of transcendence. Transcendence is linked to a relationship to the past and a recognition of the past other. This other may be, as it was for the Renaissance, a source of my contemporary projects; or it may be, as it should for contemporary Germans, the focus of my revolt. Either way, it is a meaning that must be recognized. Were there no already given

---

[10] *Ibid.*, p. 71/p. 102.

[11] *Ibid.*, pp. 92-93/pp. 133–134.
   "I would distrust a humanism which was too indifferent to the efforts of the men of former times ... To assert the reign of man is to acknowledge man in the past ... We must try, through our living projects, to turn to our own account that freedom that was undertaken in the past and to integrate it into the present world."

world of the other, there would be no world for my freedom to engage. No adolescence without childhood.[12]

However it may stand with the tensions between the desire to disclose and the desire to be, without the other to challenge the meanings of my freedom, I risk forgetting the meaning of my subjectivity. I risk mistaking myself for an absolute subject. "Only the freedom of others," Beauvoir writes, "keeps each one of us from hardening into the absurdity of facticity."[13]

Following Husserl's Fifth Cartesian Meditation, Beauvoir's analysis of intentionality links consciousness to the other as firmly as it links it to the world.[14] "The me-others relationship," she writes, "is as indissoluble as the subject-object relationship."[15] Given this equal givenness of the world and the other, Beauvoir will argue that I am as responsible for disclosing the freedom of the other as I am for revealing the meaning of the world.

This responsibility takes two forms. First, it requires that none of my projects assert my freedom without simultaneously affirming the freedom of others. Second, it requires me to liberate those who do not know that they can rebel. The first form of responsibility is grounded in the analysis of intentionality as disclosure. The second is derived from the judgment that submission to authority is not always a sign of bad faith. It may be a sign of mystification. That is, rather than a mark of my refusal to contest the anxieties of freedom, submitting to the authority of the other may signify the other's success in confining me to the conditions of childhood. It is not by accident that slaves are compared to children. According to

---

[12] *Ibid.*, p. 71/p. 102.
   "One can reveal the world only on a basis revealed by other men. No project can be defined except by its interference with other projects. To make being 'be' is to communicate with others by means of being."
[13] *Ibid.*
[14] Edmund Husserl, *Cartesian Meditations*, trans. Dorian Cairns (The Hague: Martinus Nijhoff, 1973).
[15] *Ethics* p. 72/*Morale* p. 123.

Beauvoir, the slave, like the child, is the one who does not know that the world is constituted, not given. For the child this ignorance is a matter of immaturity; for the slave it is a matter of exploitation. The other, according to Beauvoir:

> has succeeded in mystifying [the slave] in such a way that his situation does not seem to him to be imposed by men, but to be immediately given by nature, by gods, by the powers against whom revolt has no meaning; thus he does not accept his condition through a resignation of his freedom since he can not even dream of any other ... [16]

Teaching the slave to dream, freeing the slave from the powers of mystification, showing the slave that revolt is possible, is the responsibility of the one who is not mystified.

In placing the question of bad faith within the context of childhood and the question of nostalgia, and in discerning the ways in which the situation and the other permeate the desires of intentionality, Beauvoir blurs the boundaries between consciousness and its other. The subject, as the source of meaning, is a source of meaning from a particular place in an intersubjective field—a field in which it finds itself already made meaningful by others. These others are my situation as I am theirs. If they are mystified, their mystifications threaten me.

The slave's mystification mirrors the condition of the child and magnifies the power of bad faith. In absolving the slave of bad faith, Beauvoir does not remove bad faith from the condition of slavery. The dynamics of exploitation are the dynamics of bad faith, for it is the bad faith of the oppressor's desire to be the law that accounts for the oppressed's world of the law.[17] Looked at this way, we see that the idea of mystification points to the permeability of subjectivity. To be a situated subject means that as subject I am/can be affected/infected by the other's desire. As the oppressor's world of bad faith cripples

---

[16] *Ibid.*, p. 85/p. 123.
[17] For a discussion of this see Debra Bergoffen, "The Look As Bad Faith," *Philosophy Today*, Vol. 36:3 (Fall 1992), pp. 221–227.

the oppressed's intentional possibilities, the oppressed's mystification fuels the nostalgias of those who are neither tyrants
nor slaves. No one escapes the effects of oppression. No one is
outside the situation. So long as the slave recognizes authority
as absolute, all freedoms are jeopardized. The anxieties of the
desire to be are reinforced against the joys of the desires of disclosure.

In taking up the cause of the other's freedom I am, therefore, taking up my own fight. Beauvoir's remark "to want to
disclose the world and to want men to be free are one and the
same will"[18] is telling. It establishes the crucial link between
the epistemology and the ethics of phenomenology; for
according to Beauvoir, the epistemological desire of disclosure
is also the ethical will of liberation. In linking the epistemology
of intentionality to an ethics of freedom, Beauvoir shows us
that the subjective domain of intentionality is necessarily and
inevitably intersubjective.

None of Beauvoir's talk of commitment to the other is for-
getful of the look. Recognizing the threat we pose to each
other, however, does not lead Beauvoir to reject the idea that
we are fundamentally bound to each other. In a move that is a
mark of her philosophy insofar as it is repeated at crucial junc-
tures, Beauvoir transforms what most of us would see as a
negative limit—failure—into a limiting condition of our
humanity. She then explores this limiting condition for its
meaning for our success as human beings. Here Beauvoir
faces the failures of humanity's history of conflict, oppression,
and exploitation. Instead of appealing to these failures to
support the idea that we are inevitably each other's enemy,
she sees them as evidence of our mutual responsibility for
each other.

The other has the power to recognize or exploit me. The
power of exploitation is derived from the power of recognition. It perverts the meaning of the bond without negating it.
Insisting on this bond is crucial to Beauvoir's ethics.

---

[18] *Ethics*, p. 87 / *Morale*, pp. 124–125.

Confirming what she takes to be Hegel's mood of joy, Beauvoir argues that recognizing the other's freedom belongs to the intentional moment of disclosure and expresses its joy. In her words:

> to will man free ... is to will the disclosure of being in the joy of existence; in order for the idea of liberation to have a concrete meaning, the joy of existence must be asserted ... at every instant; the movement toward freedom assumes its real, flesh and blood figure in the world by thickening into pleasure, into happiness.[19]

The Ethics of the Epoché

So far we have directed our attention to the question: How does Beauvoir's analysis of intentionality become the ground of an ethic? Pursuing this question we have been able to tell a fairly neat story. If we shift the question, however, the story gets tangled. For if we ask: How does Beauvoir's analysis of intentionality alert us to the conflicts of the ethical situation?, we discover that the uneasy relationship between the two moments of intentionality is indicative of a troublesome relationship between the will to let being be (taking delight in disclosure) and the will of the project (marking the world with my meanings). By focusing on the conflict between the moods of the two moments of intentionality rather than on their conflicting desires, Beauvoir aligns the second moment's desire to be the meaning of the world with the first moment's joy through the concept of recognition. Insisting that all of our projects recognize the freedom of the other and that this freedom always refers to a situation, Beauvoir delineates an ethic of the project which eludes the anxieties that fuel the bad faith of the second intentional moment by describing the will of the ethical project as joyfully determining itself as the law which recognizes the other's freedom. Thus the desires of disclosure and Being meet in the phenomenological ethical will.

---

[19] *Ibid.*, p. 135/pp. 195–196.

Aligning the demands of intentionality with the ethical will is not, however, without its problems. Looking closely at Beauvoir's analysis of intentionality, we discover that the language of authorship and the project, though appropriate for the second moment of intentionality, may not speak to the dynamics of the first. For once we see that each moment of consciousness carries its own ethical demands, we not only discover that the language of the project must be very carefully construed if it is to meet the moral requirements of the desire to be, but also see that however carefully it is construed, it may not be possible to reconcile the ethic of the project with the ethical demands of freedom construed as spontaneity/disclosing activity.

The language of the project is the language of teleology and identity. I take up my project as a goal to be achieved; I identify this goal with my present striving and my future self. Bad faith lures me to collapse the distance between my represented-project self and my lived subjectivity. Putting some distance between this represented self and my lived subjectivity, I must remember that I am the *author* of my project. As author I can allow my desires to be to express themselves without constituting myself as an object. As author I establish the project as mine without allowing it to coalesce into me.

So far so good. Taking the idea of the project in this way affirms the failure of the bad faith and tyranny of the desire to be and transforms this failure into an affirmation of freedom. Beauvoir refers to this transformation as a conversion.[20] She asks us to think of it phenomenologically, writing:

> Existentialist conversion should ... be compared to Husserlian reduction: let man put his will to be 'in parentheses' and he will thereby be brought to the consciousness of his true condition.[21]

Clarifying what she means by bracketing the will to be, Beauvoir tells us that it involves:

---

[20] *Ibid.*, p. 13/p. 17.
[21] *Ibid.*, p. 14/p. 18.

refusing to set up as absolutes the ends toward which my transcendence thrusts itself, and by considering them in their connection with the freedom which projects them.[22]

This clarification, however, misses the point of the phenomenological reduction. It is one of those places where Beauvoir, instead of letting her insights cut new paths, directs her thought along traditional existential lines.

Given Beauvoir's analysis of the two moments of intentionality and Husserl's account of bracketing, putting the will to be in parentheses is more than a matter of refusing to set up my ends as absolute. It is a matter of seeing what happens when the will to be, understood as the will of the project (the will of establishing ends whether as absolute or contingent), is put out of play. Husserl discovered that bracketing, far from leaving us empty handed, left us with the riches of the world as phenomena; we discover that putting the will to be, the will of the project, in parentheses, far from depriving phenomenology of an ethics, reveals the ethical fullness of the original intentional moment. With this bracketing, we discover new tensions between the two moments of intentionality, new meanings of our ambiguity. We discover that the will of the first moment of intentionality, the will of disclosure, contests the ethical will of the project. Not grounded in the wound, in no way motivated to elude the anxiety of the void, this will feels no need to impress itself on the world. Its desire lies elsewhere. As a pure willing of relationship, this will expresses itself as an attentiveness to otherness—as the simple desire of revelation. Beyond that it has no aim. Hence its delight.

If we recall that one of the points of Beauvoir's analyses of intentionality is to clarify the sense in which we are and are not a useless passion, this bracketing of the will to be takes us even further. According to Beauvoir, we are a useless passion only if we identify ourselves with the will of the desire to be. If, however, we take the failure of the will to be as a sign of the success of consciousness as disclosure, then, Beauvoir says, we

[22] Ibid.

are ready to assume our role as moral agents. We open ourselves to the joys of existence.

The existential epoché redefines the relationship between the will to be and the project. It links the failure of the one to the other. By directing our ethical attention to the dynamics of disclosure, the existential epoché turns us away from the ethical project of restructuring the failure of the will to be toward the task of delineating the ethical possibilities of the will of disclosure. Looked at in this way, the existential epoché challenges the ethics of the project. By directing our attention to the will of disclosure, this epoché moves the ethical question from the intentionality of the will to be and its failures, to the will which is not a failure—the disclosing will of the first intentional moment.

Given the redirected vision of the epoché, we turn from the task of challenging the imperialist inclinations of the project to other, more radical, issues. We ask: What sort of ethics might appear if we bracketed the will of the project? What sort of ethics would validate the will that delights in letting being show itself—a will with no desire to appropriate the object it reveals? What sort of ethics would emerge if the will of disclosure were not seen as the means to the ends of my will to be, however nuanced that will might be described? What sort of ethics would express consciousness' celebration of its relationship to being?

Pursuing these questions, might we go so far as to say that ethically we are obliged to refuse the will of the project? Might we discover that however careful we are in delineating it, we cannot absolve the project of its participation in the failure of the will to be? Perhaps, but given Beauvoir's attention to ambiguities, and given her description of intentionality, it is more likely that Beauvoir herself would not take this radical route. It is more likely, I think, that if Beauvoir developed her muted voice she would say that an existential ethic must attend to the ambiguity of a will that expresses its gratitude to the being it discloses by refusing to appropriate it for its ends in any way. She would remind us, however, that consciousness cannot let Being be because its being is tied to expressing itself as a project toward a future?[23] She might refer us to Husserl who talks about the inevitability of falling back into the natural attitude. She might remind us that what appears within the context of the epoché as two wills is, in fact, the ambiguity of one will, and, insist that an ethics reflective of the human condition take its cue from the dynamics of the ambiguities of consciousness.

Beauvoir does not systematically pursue this line of thought. She does, however, indicate her concerns regarding the ethic of the project in the various challenges to the project scattered throughout the text. There is, for example, the discussion of the serious man. Here the will to be is construed as an act of submission to the thing which, in turn, is understood as an expression of the desire for mastery.[24] With her portrayal of the serious man, Beauvoir indicates that the will of the project is perverted not only when it posits its ends as absolute but also when it succumbs to the desires of mastery.

The will of the project is not essentially tied to the positing of its ends as absolute. Cognizant of its finitude and contingency and aware of its situated otherness/others, this will can express itself by positing its ends as provisional without negating itself as the will to an end. Unlike the fluidity of the relationship between the desire of the project and the willing of ends as absolute, however, the relationship between the will of the project and the will to mastery may not be negotiable. Here the tie appears to be essential. Can we understand the will of the project as other than the desire to bring some dimension of reality under our power? Can we understand this as other than the will to mastery? However we may wish to construe the difference between mastery and the project, it is difficult to think of a project which does not share with mastery the desire for some sort of control. The very idea of a

---

[23] *Ibid.*, p. 76/p. 110.
[24] "the serious man ... [is] threatened by the whole universe ... since despite all precautions, he will never be the master of this exterior world to which he has consented to submit, he will be constantly upset by the uncontrollable course of events." *Ibid.*, p. 51/p. 74.

project is the idea of directing reality toward certain specified ends. However contingent these ends may be, as ends they are at odds with the attitude of witnessing the emergence of meaning. Merely suggesting that the will to mastery perverts the will of the project does not get to the heart of the issue— that to question the desire of mastery puts the desire of the project on trial.

In bringing up the issue of mastery, Beauvoir alerts us to the fact that between the two moments of intentionality there are two different attitudes toward Being. Though she does not seem to question the compatibility of the project with the requirements of disclosure, once the issue of mastery is raised, the question cannot be avoided.

The project, defined as the positing and pursuit of a goal, contests the attitude of letting be that characterizes the original moment of intentionality. Given Beauvoir's account of the two moments of intentionality, we cannot say that the will of the project is cut off from the will of disclosure. We cannot suggest that the desires of disclosure are insulated from the project's desires of mastery. Presenting one's self as master, as in control of Being, does more than Beauvoir allows, it does more than pervert the will of the project; it infects the desires of revelation. It threatens the attitude of letting be. The joy of these desires is the delight of discovery. Key to this delight is the experience of being in the presence of, but not in control of, the unfolding of Being. To introduce the desire for control undermines this desire's delight. It suggests an attitude of flight and refusal analagous to bad faith.

The discussion of the serious man, with its allusions to mastery, are not the only places where the ethics of the project are problematized. The undertow of Beauvoir's thought sounds again in her discussions of maniacal and generous passion. Again, Beauvoir does not directly challenge the ethic of the project. But as I read her description of generous passion, I cannot help but ask whether it is compatible with the ethics of the project.

Returning to the phenomenology of disclosure, Beauvoir identifies the genuine moment of all passion as the revelation of a thing's worth. This revelation expresses the power of the subject. How, Beauvoir asks, will this power be assumed—generously or maniacally?[25] We are familiar with the maniacal assumption of this power. The other is refused their freedom and treated as a thing. Mastery is another name for this passion. The description of generous passion, however, is striking. It does not go over familiar territory. Beauvoir writes:

> It is only as something strange, forbidden, as something free that the other is revealed as an other. And to love him genuinely is to love him in his otherness and in that freedom by which he escapes. Love is then the renunciation of all possession ...[26]

Beauvoir uses this description of generosity to challenge the assertion of autonomy. As she analyzes it, to generously recognize the other's otherness is to become responsible for protecting the other from being reduced to the object of an alien will. As generous, I acknowledge the bond of the "we" and commit myself to protect it. In this way of thinking, the thought of generosity is subordinated to the idea of the project. It delineates the project's ethical domain.

However, the idea of generous passion may also be seen as contesting the ethic of the project. The generous passion that affirms the other in their strange, transcending freedom, the passion that values the other as the freedom that escapes it, undoes itself as soon as it becomes directive. In its commitment to let the freedom of the other be, generosity renounces the desire of the project—the desire to set goals and to engage the other as the ally. In this renunciation, the desires of generosity are at odds with the desires of the project.

As project, my freedom engages the freedom of the other. It does something to it, for it, or with it. It does not, and cannot, allow the other's freedom to elude it. The passion of the project need not be maniacal, but it cannot curtail its directive energies. It cannot confine itself to an affirmation of otherness.

---

[25] Ibid., p. 64/p. 92.
[26] Ibid., p. 67/p. 96.

Going beyond the simple affirmation of otherness and unable to delight in the elusiveness of the other's freedom, the passion of the project cannot avoid the desire to capture the other's freedom.

We are caught in the requirements of otherness and the forces of the situation. If Beauvoir did not recognize the real power of the situation—if she refused to see the ways in which situations negate the possibilities of freedom, she might have resolved the tensions between the desires of intentionality in favor of the generosity that lets the other be. This generosity, however, requires that both I and the other experience our revelatory powers. When the situation bars the other from this experience, the generosity that lets the other be is empty. Here the situation demands the other form of generosity—the generosity of the we-project. I am, in these circumstances, obligated to work against situations that dehumanize others —to work for liberation. Remembering Beauvoir's attention to the situation, we see that when Beauvoir stops short of challenging the ethics of the project, it is more than a matter of refusing to pursue the implications of the ethical epoché. It is a matter of her Marxist commitment to the material/concrete.

Beauvoir is acutely sensitive to the real conditions of our lives. She is painfully aware of the ways in which we are constrained by reality. Whatever may be true ontologically, we are not, she insists, equally free in the everyday world. Some of us are free. Others are not. Those who are free are responsible for the rest.[27] From this perspective, developing an ethic of generosity that stands outside the demands of the project seems more like a luxury—an aesthetic, abstract exercise—than a credible moral position.

Attending to the relationship between the situation and freedom, it is tempting to propose a two-tier analysis of generosity where the generosity of the we-project sets the stage for the possibility of the generous passion that stands back before the other's transcendence. Given Beauvoir's examples

---

[27] *Ibid.*, p. 74/pp. 107–108.

of situations that call for liberating generosity (the slave, the woman in the harem), it is difficult to quarrel with this resolution of the issue.

There are other examples, however, which show us how difficult it is to distinguish liberating generosity from the horror of the other or the drives of mastery—the missionary working for the salvation of African souls, educators saving Native Americans from their primitive ideas, etc., etc., etc. Without the guidance of historical hindsight, the project that is offended by the freedom of the other is as often as not experienced as a project of liberation. Given these dangers and difficulties, the two-tier solution to the contest between the generosity of the we-project and the generosity of letting be, though logically appealing, is existentially suspect. The contesting ethical demands of these different powers and wills can neither be logically mediated nor dialectically surpassed.

However unresolvable their differences may be, the passions and projects of generosity are crucial to Beauvoir's ethical vision. They are the antidote to the logic of sacrifice. They are central to her rejection of individualism and essential to her affirmation of otherness.

Recognition

Ethical inquiries cannot avoid confronting the question of the relationship between the individual and the community. They usually assume that the interests of the personal and the collective are at odds with each other and look for some way to adjudicate these conflicting interests. Utilitarians privilege the community. Deontologists privilege the individual. Beauvoir rejects this way of formulating the issue. She rejects the utilitarian idea that we can each be measured according to our contribution to the collective.[28] Her affirmation of the individual, however, rejects the deontological idea of subjectivity. She refuses to link individuals to each other by virtue of some

---

[28] *Ibid.*, p. 103/p. 149.

common, universal essence. Rejecting the Hegelian notion of recognition[29] Beauvoir insists that it is through our recognition of the otherness of each subject that we discover our fundamental need of and relatedness to each other. The individual, she writes:

> is a unique and irreducible value ... if individuals recognize themselves in their differences, individual relations are established among them[30]

and

> that is precisely the ambiguity of his condition: in his surpassing toward others, each one exists absolutely as for himself; each is interested in the liberation of all but as a separate existence engaged in his own projects.[31]

Thus we are bound to each other through our differences and separations. The idea of otherness, muted where it might pose obstacles to the ethic of the project, is called upon here to navigate the distance between the individual and the collective. However much our relatedness is affirmed, this affirmation never takes the form of collectivizing the subject. In refusing to establish a universal subject Beauvoir is doing more than following the existential insistence that existence precedes essence. She is introducing the idea of otherness into the concepts of recognition and community.

If the generosity that lets the other be threatens the moral claims of the project, the generosity that affirms the other's otherness is crucial to the morality of the project. The project, as an expression of generosity, affirms a "we" comprised of others different from me. The other of this "we" is not my double. This is the Hegelian error. As other than me, the other is always distinct from me. I cannot call identification with the other recognition—another Hegelian mistake. For Beauvoir,

---

[29] *Ibid.,* p. 104/p. 150.
[30] *Ibid.,* pp. 107–108/pp. 154–155.
[31] *Ibid.,* p. 112/p. 162.

recognition means an acknowledgment of otherness. It is in recognizing our otherness, she argues, that we recognize our need of each other.

Erotic Risks

Once the project of recognition is played out on the theme of otherness, other themes are brought into play—risk and transcendence. For once we discover that recognizing the other entails recognizing the otherness of the other we find that the act of recognition is always and necessarily a risk-taking act. We recall Beauvoir's words,"Only man can be an enemy for man."[32] They speak to the risk we take in acknowledging each other. Why take the risk? Why not refuse recognition? We know the core of the existential answer: we are ethically obliged to take the risk of recognizing the other's freedom. Beauvoir provides a phenomenological ground for this existential imperative. "The individual," she tells us, "is defined *only* by his relationship to the world and other individuals." (emphasis added)[33] Pursuing this phenomenological ground, Beauvoir takes the description of consciousness as intentionality into the domain of love and value. She writes:

> If we do not love life on our own account and through others, it is futile to justify it in any other way.[34]

and

> Let men attach value to words, form, colors, mathematical theorems, physical laws and athletic prowess; let them accord value to one another in love and friendship, and the objects, the events, the men immediately *have* this value; they have it absolutely. It is possible that a man may refuse to love anything on earth; he will prove his refusal and he will carry it out by suicide. If he lives ... there still remains in him some attachment to existence.[35]

---

[32] *Ibid.*, p. 82/ p. 118.
[33] *Ibid.*, p. 156/p. 225.
[34] *Ibid.*, pp. 135–136/p. 196
[35] *Ibid.*, pp. 157–158/p. 228.

These words take us to the unique strain of Beauvoir's
thought. Consciousness brings meaning and value to the
world through love. Distancing herself from Kant and from
Sartre's "Existentialism as a Humanism," Beauvoir links
morality and desire. Our moral obligations are an expression
of our love of the earth and each other. Assuming the risks of
subjectivity is the way we affirm the joy of being. The ethics of
liberation is grounded in the intentionality of disclosure and
its fundamental mood—joy. Thus Beauvoir writes:

> in order for the idea of liberation to have a concrete meaning, the
> joy of existence must be asserted in each one, at every instant.[36]

None of this is sentimental. Beauvoir does not envision a
humanity circled in a mutual embrace. In the concrete world,
love, though an absolute value, is also a precarious one. Risk is
never absent. Violence is ever present. Sometimes, Beauvoir
says, it cannot be avoided. She is under no illusions. There will
always be tyrants—those who use violence to negate the freedom of the other. To liberate the oppressed we may have to
destroy the tyrants. The existential will that Beauvoir invokes
in defiance of this violation is not a self-righteous will but a
passionate one. It is driven by love to undertake the causes of
liberation.[37]

Like the discussions of generosity, these discussions of
love pull in two directions. Both call on different approaches
to the question of recognition. In the approach that dominates
The Ethics of Ambiguity, I express my love of the other and
affirm the joy of existence through acts of recognition that
enact projects of freedom. I accept the risk that the other is to
me. Without negating the power of the other to violate me, I
appeal to the other in the name of our freedom to recognize us
as bound to each other. Here love is lived reflectively.

On the margin of *The Ethics of Ambiguity*, however, a margin
confined to one page, another expression of love and recognition

---

[36] *Ibid.*, p. 135/pp. 195–196.
[37] *Ibid.*, p. 159/pp. 229–230.

is heard. It is introduced with the name Bataille. It is associated with the excesses of the festival. It speaks of the recognition
of the erotic. It refers to another notion of community. It is
essentially unreflective. In this margin, Beauvoir, following
Bataille without objection, speaks of the fundamental link
between existence and destruction and links the expenditures
of existence to recognition and risk. She writes:

> Existence attempts in the festival to confirm itself positively as exis-
> tence ... the ethics of being is the ethics of saving: by storing up
> one aims at the stationary plenitude of the in-itself, existence, on
> the contrary, is consumption; it makes itself only by destroying: ...
> The spending [of the festival] is also a matter of establishing a com-
> munication of the existants, for it is by the movement of recogni-
> tion which goes from one to the other that existence is
> confirmed, in songs, laughter, dances, eroticism and drunkenness
> one seeks both an exaltation of the moment and a complicity with
> other men.[38]

In *The Ethics of Ambiguity* Beauvoir looks to art to fix this
passionate assertion of existence.[39] She brings the unreflective
excess of the festival back to the reflections of the project. She
subordinates the expenditures of erotic, drunken, laughing,
and dancing existential affirmation to the calculations of concern. It is not clear that this solution works. For while the
excesses of eroticism, drunkenness, dancing, and laughter are
identified as forms of recognition that cannot be sustained, the
ethics of the sustainable is said to aim at the *en-soi* of being and
placed at odds with the becoming of the for-itself.

We may linger over the ways this allusion to Bataille,
excess, and the festival unsettles the effect of *The Ethics of
Ambiguity*. Beauvoir did not. Whether she attends to it or not,
however, *The Ethics of Ambiguity* is unsettled; for once we
discover that both festival excess and project transcendence

---

[38] *Ibid.*, p. 126/pp. 181–182.
[39] *Ibid.*, p. 127/p. 183.

distinguish us from the *en-soi*, words intended to describe the project also seem to refer to the festival.

Insisting that we are, as mortal and finite, always at risk and that we must live in recognition of the risk that we are to ourselves and to each other, Beauvoir writes:

> Life is occupied in both perpetuating itself and in surpassing itself; if all it does is maintain itself, then living is only not dying and human existence is indistinguishable from an absurd vegetation.[40]

How are we to understand this surpassing? Is it the aiming toward the goal of the project or the expenditure of dancing, laughing, drunken eroticism? There is, I think, no way to be sure—no way to keep the idea of surpassing within the confines of the project once Bataille is allowed to speak.

The Ethics of Ambiguity speaks in at least two voices. Both are grounded in an analysis of intentionality that describes it as broken into two moments, with each moment characterized by a unique desire and mood. Directed by the thought of ambiguity, Beauvoir never severs these moments of intentionality from each other. Relying on the epoché to attend to the differences between these moments of consciousness, Beauvoir does not confuse the phenomenological view of consciousness with the lived realities of intentionality.

As the project of *The Ethics of Ambiguity* is ethical rather than ontological or epistemological, Beauvoir draws out the moral implications of her descriptions of intentionality by according moral status to the mood and desire of the disclosing moment of consciousness. This leads Beauvoir in two directions. One direction calls on this mood and its desire to contest the bad faith perversions of the project. This direction dominates the analyses of *The Ethics of Ambiguity*. The other direction contests the ethics of the project. Here it is not the bad faith perversions of the project that are called to account, but the desire of the project itself that is called into question. This

---

[40] *Ibid.*, pp. 82-83/p. 120.

direction links the ethical to the joys of the original intentional moment, the generosity of letting be, the risks of the erotic, and the excess of festival disclosures.

Within *The Ethics of Ambiguity*, this challenge to the ethic of the project is muted. We need to put our ear close to the text to catch it. Its unsettling effect, however, cannot be dismissed, especially when we hear the return of its soundings in *The Second Sex*, and "Must We Burn Sade?" where the hope of liberation is linked to the possibilities of the excesses of the erotic and where the powers of patriarchy are linked to its perversion of the meaning of risk, its betrayal of the erotic, and its subversion of women's generosity.

Given the ways in which Beauvoir appears to marginalize this other voice, and given the ways it contests her self-portrait as a disciple of Sartre, we are tempted to ignore and/or minimize its place in Beauvoir's thought. The point I wish to make is that following this temptation is a mistake. However it may unsettle Beauvoir's dominant existential voice, her analyses of the otherness and generosity of letting be and her allusions to excess and the erotic cannot be dismissed. They are grounded in an analysis of intentionality that is crucial to Beauvoir's understanding of the human condition. The emergence of these themes in *The Ethics of Ambiguity* and their persistent return in Beauvoir's other works mark the return of the desires of the original intentional moment.

Toward *The Second Sex*

Though *The Second Sex* acknowledges the influence of other thinkers, it never mentions the influence of *The Ethics of Ambiguity*. More than willing to show us *The Second Sex's* diverse intellectual sources, Beauvoir seems unwilling to show us the ways it is rooted in her own philosophical thought. With or without her guidance, however, the tracks of her debts to herself are visible. The idea of generosity, suggested as an ethical paradigm in *Pyrrhus et Cinéas* and ambiguously aligned with the desires of the project and pure disclosure in *The Ethics*

of Ambiguity, becomes eroticized as the gift in *The Second Sex.*
The situation, dominated by freedom in *Pyrrhus et Cinéas* and
empowered in *The Ethics of Ambiguity,* becomes bodied and
historicized in *The Second Sex.* The phenomenon of failure,
grounds for the affirmation of the human condition in *Pyrrhus
et Cinéas* and *The Ethics of Ambiguity,* becomes grounds for the
project of liberation and the reciprocity of the erotic in *The
Second Sex.*

Like *The Ethics of Ambiguity* which picks up, revises and
rethinks the positions of *Pyrrhus et Cinéas, The Second Sex*
reworks and extends the analyses of *The Ethics of Ambiguity.*
Sometimes this reworking brings a marginal discussion to the
center. Sometimes it retrieves a margin of *The Ethics of
Ambiguity,* not to move it elsewhere, but to pursue, still on the
margin, its radical possibilities. Reading *The Second Sex* as a
continuation of the discussions of *The Ethics of Ambiguity,* we
are alerted to its muted voices and its phenomenological context. Ideas that appear to be ideologically motivated take on
other significations.

For example, what sounds hyperbolic taken on its own,
the claim in *The Second Sex* that the conditions of the woman
and the slave are analogous, warrants our attention once *The
Ethics of Ambiguity*'s analyses of intentionality and mystification
are considered. Without these analyses, the analogy between
women, especially Western middle and upper class women,
and slaves seems tenuous at best, for as long as we focus on
the material conditions of oppression, the hardships of slavery
cannot be compared to the difficulties of women who are not
slaves.[41] Coming from *The Ethics of Ambiguity,* however, we
know that the material conditions of the situation do not
exhaust its reality. We must also consider its structure.

Turning from the materiality to the structure of women's
and slaves' situations we discover the oppressions of mystifi-

---

[41] An analogy that may have seemed far fetched a few years ago has become a fact of
our times. See Amy Fries, "Trafficking in Women and Girls: A Modern Slave
Trade," *Choices* 3:3 (1994), pp. 1–2.

cation. Setting the stage for *The Second Sex*, *The Ethics of Ambiguity* identifies mystification as the source of the slave's, the non-Western woman's. and the Western woman's exploitation. [42] All share the fate of the mystified insofar as they believe that their places in the world are embedded in the order of things. They do not see themselves as unjustifiably positioned because they cannot imagine themselves as other than the inessential other. They cannot see that it is neither nature, nor gods, but human beings who create the conditions of their existence. Oppression goes unnamed and unchallenged. Revolt is silenced before it can even be voiced.[43]

In addition to grounding *The Second Sex's* analogy between woman and slave, *The Ethics of Ambiguity's* idea of mystification is the source of *The Second Sex's* category of the inessential other and of its perhaps most famous line, "One is not born one becomes a woman." Mystification is a unique form of the anti-human. According to the structure of mystification, the mystified human other is by nature incapable of expressing its humanity. It cannot articulate its meaning-giving powers and cannot contest the other's freedom. The mystified subject does not know that it can challenge its subordinate status. It thereby offers its "superior" other risk-free recognition.

Ever the concrete thinker, Beauvoir does not divorce the material conditions of the situation from its power to mystify. Ignorance and economic dependence validate mystifications. Mystifications justify poverty and hardship. Though the slave, the non-Western woman and the Western woman are mystified, given the different concrete conditions of their mystification,

---

[42] "There are beings whose life slips by in an infantile world because, having been kept in a state of servitude and ignorance, they have no means of breaking the ceiling which is stretched over their heads. ... This is the case ... of the slaves who have not raised themselves to the consciousness of their slavery ... This is also the situation of women in many civilizations; they can only submit to the laws, the gods, the customs and the truths created by the males. Even today in western countries, among women who have not had in their work an apprenticeship of freedom, there are still many who take shelter in the shadow of men." *Ethics* p. 37/*Morale* p. 54.

[43] "One of the ruses of oppression is to camouflage itself behind a natural situation since, after all, one cannot revolt against nature." *Ibid.*, p. 83/p. 120.

they each live their mystifications differently. As the material conditions of the situation become more benign, we can speak of the woman or the slave as happy or resigned, and as conditions become compatible with experiences that challenge the myths of mystification, it becomes possible to speak of the oppressed's complicity in their oppression.

Thus while it is important to attend to the analogy between the slave and the woman insofar as it alerts us to the potency of myths and ideologies, it is also important not to carry the analogy too far. The degree to which the material conditions do or do not reinforce the inevitabilities proclaimed by the mystifications must be carefully examined. These differences determine, for example, the sorts of violence that may be necessary to end oppression. They will decide whether the forces of liberation can be cultivated from within or whether they must be imported from without. When writing about a Nazi youth, Beauvoir declares:

> The desirable thing would be to re-educate this misled youth; it would be necessary to expose the mystification and to put the men who are its victims in the presence of their freedom. But the urgency of the struggle forbids this slow labor. We are obliged to destroy not only the oppressor but also those who serve him, whether they do so out of ignorance or out of constraint.[44]

The Second Sex knows no such urgency. It chooses the route of slow labor. Why? Because the oppressor cannot be destroyed? Because women as accomplices would be destroyed? Because, as indicated in the preface to *The Second Sex*, though the oppression of women is structured like other forms of oppression it is also something different?

In historicizing the phenomenology of *The Ethics of Ambiguity*, *The Second Sex* sets itself the complex task of using phenomenology to unmask the mystifications of oppression. Taking up the question of woman, Beauvoir discovers the difference between sex and gender. She also discovers that

---

[44] *Ibid.*, p. 98/pp. 141–142.

patriarchal genders distort the humanity of both women and men. She discovers that at this point in our history, there are men, gendered as patriarchal man, and women, gendered as patriarchal woman, but no humanly gendered subjects.

From the point of view of *The Second Sex* taken by itself, the immorality of patriarchy consists of depriving women as woman of their subjectivity; but if we take *The Second Sex* together with *The Ethics of Ambiguity*, the immorality of patriarchy is more serious and more complex. For, if *The Second Sex* taken by itself suggests that men as man are subjects but that women as woman are not, taken with *The Ethics of Ambiguity*, we discover that neither the man nor the woman of patriarchy are subjects. Both are gendered according to the dictates of the nostalgias for childhood and the anxieties of the second intentional moment. So long as they are captured by the strictures of patriarchal gender, neither men nor women will experience the ambiguity of their condition or the joys of the original intentional moment.

If we carry *The Ethics of Ambiguity*'s analysis of nostalgia to *The Second Sex*, we discover that for women gendered as woman nostalgia is figured as the eternal child, and that for men gendered as man nostalgia is figured as the absolute (impossible) subject. Patriarchy takes up the nostalgias that empower the second moment of intentionality and genders them such that men as man live out their nostalgia according to the desire to be God and women as woman live out their nostalgia according to the desire to be attuned to a world already given to them by the other. A perfect, if immoral, fit. As so gendered, men and women are reified in the failure of the useless, bad faith passion to be.

In moving from *The Ethics of Ambiguity* to *The Second Sex*, Beauvoir draws on both phenomenological and existential categories. The phenomenology of intentionality leads Beauvoir to discover the oppressions of mystification and thereby to identify women as oppressed. It leads her to define subjectivity in terms of the contesting desires of intentionality and thereby to challenge the patriarchal category of the subject. The exis-

tential categories of immanence and transcendence allow
Beauvoir to disengage tyranny from its usual political trappings and to identify women as objects of tyranny. According
to Beauvoir:

> The trick of tyrants is to enclose a man in the immanence of his fac-
> ticity ... The tyrant asserts himself as a transcendence; he considers
> others as pure immanences; he thus arrogates to himself the right
> to treat them like cattle. We see the sophism on which his conduct
> is based: of the ambiguous condition which is that of all men, he
> retains for himself the only aspect of a transcendence which is
> capable of justifying itself; for the others, the contingent and unjus-
> tified aspect of immanence.[45]

The Second Sex discloses how this unique trick of enclosing
man in his facticity works when the "man" in question is a
woman and when the enclosing facticity is our most intimate
facticity—the body. We appreciate the power and perversity of
this patriarchal trick if we recall that for Beauvoir it is as
embodied subjects that we experience the world, and that for
her the body is always intentional. In reducing woman to the
facticity of her body, patriarchy estranges her from the powers, joys, "living warmth" and generosities of her subjectivity.[46]
    The question of woman, the body, and the erotic lie in the
margins of *The Ethics of Ambiguity*. Once Beauvoir moves the
question of woman from margin to center and considers the
meanings of sex and gender, she discovers that the other, identified in *The Ethics of Ambiguity* as a strange freedom that
eludes us, is gendered and that when the other is gendered as
woman, she is marked as inessential. With this discovery,
Beauvoir discovers that the questions of ethics are bodied and
that the erotic is a philosophical-moral category.
    In *The Second Sex* it is more than a matter of rescuing the
original intentional moment from oblivion; it is a matter of
refiguring the meanings of the gendered subject. Further, it is
now a matter of risk; for generosity, the ethical expression of

---

[45] *Ibid.*, p. 102/p. 147.
[46] *Ibid.*, pp. 41-42/pp. 57-58.

the first intentional moment, is now embodied and eroticized and, as Beauvoir makes clear in her essay "Must We Burn Sade?", erotic generosities within the context of patriarchy are more often refused and violated than acknowledged and received.

In *The Second Sex*, *The Ethics of Ambiguity*'s call to generous love becomes fleshed. Here Beauvoir looks to desire's carnal touch to disrupt patriarchy's nostalgic figuring of otherness. Here Beauvoir looks to the fleshed erotic desires of the sexed subject to disrupt the embodied nostalgic desires of the gendered subject. For though patriarchy accommodates and exploits the erotic within its gender codes, the patriarchal erotic, according to Beauvoir, is figured according to the second intentional moment and as such is both perverse and unfulfilling. It misses the joy, the delight and the passion of the openness to otherness; it refuses or exoticizes the risks of strangeness; and it colonizes the mysteries of the forbidden.

The Ethics of Ambiguity's analysis of the generosity of the "we" and the love that animates the project provides the set for *The Second Sex*'s discussions of the bond and risk. Its descriptions of generous love and the festival's celebrations of excess frame *The Second Sex*'s attention to the erotic and the gift. By listening to *The Ethics of Ambiguity*'s muted voices and attending to its nuanced description of intentionality, we are able to distinguish Beauvoir's phenomenological-existential positions from Sartre's and to decipher Beauvoir's philosophical signature. This signature marks *The Second Sex* as it marked *The Ethics of Ambiguity*; for like *The Ethics of Ambiguity*, *The Second Sex* speaks in more than one voice—a voice of the project that appeals to traditional Marxist-existential analyses, and a voice that challenges the ethic of the project by calling on the categories of generosity, the gift, and the erotic to liberate us from the perversions of patriarchal gender.

CHAPTER 4

Perversions:
"Must We Burn Sade?"

Reading *The Ethics of Ambiguity* attentive to the complexities of intentionality, we see that Beauvoir's concept of ambiguity is grounded in a phenomenology that depicts consciousness as the site of contesting desires. This contest is the source of the conflicts of human life: the conflict between the anxieties of the desire to be (bad faith) and the joy of the desires of disclosure; the conflict between the demand to be recognized as the sole author of meaning (the look) and the recognition of my bond with the other and the intersubjective nexus of meaning; and the conflict between the existential ethic of the project, where I call upon the other to become my ally, and the ethic of generosity, where I let the other be in their elusive, uncanny freedom.

The Ethics of Ambiguity explores these conflicts at the theoretical and imaginary levels. For the most part, the text is pure philosophy. It engages the arguments of other philosophers and develops arguments of its own. It creates imaginary persons and situations to provide examples for particular issues. Looking back, Beauvoir expresses extreme dissatisfaction with *The Ethics of Ambiguity*. She writes, "Of all my books, it is the one that irritates me most today."[1] Why? Because it is, she says, too abstract. Though Beauvoir says that she still finds parts of it valid, for example, the polemics and the discussions

---

[1] *Force I*, p. 67.

of asceticism and the artist, her fundamental error, she says, was to try to define a morality independent of a social context.

The Second Sex and "Must We Burn Sade?" correct this error. They show us how Beauvoir does what she would call concrete philosophy. Attending to the concrete for Beauvoir means attending to the body. Not just the phenomenological perceiving body, but what she calls the flesh and blood body —the body of needs and work.[2] Determined to do concrete philosophy, Beauvoir turns to women and the Marquis de Sade. The life of a man, the history and conditions of women, are better sites for ethical digging than the quarry of philosophical arguments.

How shall we approach these writings? So far we have proceeded historically. By reading Pyrrhus et Cinéas and The Ethics of Ambiguity before The Second Sex, we are alerted to the ways in which The Second Sex is an ethic grounded in the notions of failure, spontaneity, and intentionality. We are able to situate its concrete analysis of women within a theoretical frame that goes beyond the set-up of its introduction. We are prepared for the phenomenological-existential complexities of the text.

Here a chronological procedure works to our advantage. Chronology, however, is not always the best director. Sometimes we do better not following it. Flaunting chronology to consider "Must We Burn Sade?" before The Second Sex opens certain possibilities.

As chronology alerts us to the ways in which Beauvoir's unique phenomenological-existential perspective informs The Second Sex, dispensing with chronology to read "Must We Burn Sade?" before The Second Sex allows us to notice things we might have missed. Specifically, it helps us hear the muted voices of the erotic body that speak on the margins of The Second Sex. "Must We Burn Sade?" also establishes Beauvoir as a philosopher of the concrete particular. It shows how Beauvoir moves from the individual case to the general issue

---

[2] Ibid., p. 68.

to establish categories that are concretely universal. Finally, the Sade essay shows us that when Beauvoir refers to the concrete situation, she means to include the body and that the reference to the body is also a reference to the flesh in the phenomenological sense developed by Merleau-Ponty.

An Extreme Case

There is, it would seem, nothing mysterious about Beauvoir's choice of the Marquis. She tells us at the very beginning of her essay that though Sade's writing is often ponderous and his perversions mundane, he has, by virtue of aligning his authorship with his sexuality, assumed "a wide human significance."[3] Sade is, Beauvoir says, an example of a man who justifies his perversions as his own. His self-justification is coupled with an appeal for recognition. As a "pervert," Sade asserts his individuality against the standards of his times. As an author, he inserts himself into the community. As both, he embodies the problem that concerns us all: How can we simultaneously satisfy our desire to be this unique individual and our desire to escape the limits of our finite singularity?[4] Embodying the problem that concerns us all, Sade is unique because he carries his differences with the community "to the point of outrageousness."[5]

Beauvoir tells us that she chose to write about Sade because his is an extreme case of the conflict between the singularity of the subject and the demands of the collective. "His persistent singularity," Beauvoir tells us, "helps us define the human drama in its general aspect."[6] Why this extreme case rather than another? Why choose the case of a man who asserts his individuality through outrageous displays of "perverse" sexuality? Why an author who tries "to communicate

---

[3] Simone de Beauvoir, *"Must We Burn Sade?,"* trans. Annette Michelson in *The Marquis de Sade* (New York: Grove Press, 1966), p. 4/*Faut-il Brûler Sade?* (Paris: Gallimard, 1944), p. 12.

[4] *Ibid.*

[5] *Ibid.*

[6] *Ibid.*, p. 5/p. 13.

an experience whose distinguishing characteristic is, nevertheless a tendency to be incommunicable"?[7] Is Sade the clearest
example of the ethical issue announced by Beauvoir, the question of the relationship between individuality and community,
or is he also and perhaps more fundamentally the clearest
example of another moral issue, the one raised under the
name of Bataille in *The Ethics of Ambiguity*, the issue of excess,
the erotic, transcendence and art?

What was written in the margins of *The Ethics of Ambiguity*
is centered in "Must We Burn Sade?" What is not announced
at the beginning of this text becomes clear by its end—what
makes the Marquis de Sade a perfect study for Beauvoir's
ethics is not so much the fact that he challenged society in fact
and in fiction but rather the fact that his point of opposition
was the point at which we are most vulnerable—the point of
the excessive, erotic body. This is the point at which we are
most readily seduced by the ploys of others. It is also the point
at which we feel ourselves to be most our own. It is here that
the questions of self-affirmation and recognition are raised in
their most intimate, provocative, and dangerous forms.
Theoretical issues assume a dramatic urgency when posed in
moments of passion. The questions: How can I affirm my need
of others without giving myself over to them? How can I insist
on my singularity without risking isolation? take on a unique,
lived meaning when posed at the point of the desiring body
and compressed into the more familiar: Do you love me?

With the Marquis it was never a question of love. And here,
ultimately, is where Beauvoir will find his failure. For however
sharply he presented the ethical question, and however clearly
he saw the point where it was most urgently posed, his obses-
sion with the questions of freedom and recognition never
moved him toward the other generously. Understanding this
we can understand Beauvoir's use of the adjective "perverse"
to characterize Sade's sexuality.

---

[7] *Ibid.*, p. 4/p. 12.

Perversion

To get a handle on what is going on in the Sade essay, we need to pause at Beauvoir's characterization of Sade as perverse. If we gloss over this adjective and assume the obvious, that is, if we assume that in calling Sade perverse Beauvoir is passing judgment on his real and imaginary sexual practices, we will be misled.

Though she may not have agreed with him, Beauvoir knew her Freud. She learned from him what we all learned, our sexuality is originally and naturally polymorphous. Coming after Freud, we know that perversion cannot mean un-natural when applied to the domain of sexuality. There are no un-natural sexual practices. If, coming after Freud, we attach the label perverse to a sexual practice, we know that we are expressing a moral judgment.

By what standards does Beauvoir label Sade's sexuality perverse? Surely not the standards of the aristocratic and post-revolutionary bourgeois societies within which Sade lived. Their moral judgments are not Beauvoir's. Neither is it the more recent Freudian standard of maturity and procreation. There is nothing in Beauvoir's life or writing to suggest that she accepted the Freudian notion of normalcy. Finally, the judgment cannot come from Sade's writings themselves. Though Sade openly affirms the relationship between sexual cruelty and criminality, he clearly does not accept the usual association of criminal and perverse. Though Sade acknowledges that the sexual criminal perverts social morality, he never grants moral authority to society. Unlike Freud, who couldn't utter the word polymorphous without linking it to the word perverse, for Sade the polymorphous accurately describes mature sexuality. There are no perversions. There are, to be sure, idiosyncracies, but as there are neither norms nor generalities of desire, there are no standards by which we might measure deviations and no criteria by which we could establish perversions.[8]

---

[8] Annie Le Brun, *Sade, A Sudden Abyss*, trans. Camille Naish, (San Francisco: City Light Books, 1990), pp. 94–95.

The standards by which Beauvoir judges Sade to be perverse are laid out in *The Ethics of Ambiguity* and reflect the
diverse voices of that text. Determining that Sade's sexuality
violates the reciprocity of the we-project and the generosity of
the gift, Beauvoir condemns Sade's sexuality as a maniacal
passion that refuses to recognize the other. The Sade essay is
an extended reflection on the perversion of this maniacal passion and the other perversions it draws to it—the perversions
that prefer the imaginary to the real; the perversions of pleasure and resentment; the perversion of refusing to relinquish
one's status as the absolute subject.

Following Beauvoir's critique of Sade is tricky. It is almost
as if Beauvoir uses one set of criticisms to camouflage another.
On the one hand Sade is important, Beauvoir tells us, because
he made eroticism the meaning and expression of his whole
existence.[9] On the other hand, Beauvoir condemns Sade for
choosing the erotic rather than the project to fulfill his existence.[10] According to Beauvoir, Sade's eroticism only seems to
be an act of rebellion. Though he flouts the authorities, nothing he does challenges authority. His actions are imaginary
escapes into an already bypassed world of feudal authority.
They express a nostalgia for a dissipated world and are
grounded in an illusionary notion of power. Rather than confront reality, Sade, Beauvoir says, retreated to the bedroom to
re-enact the role of the despot.

Beauvoir's charge that Sade abdicated action in the real
world for reveries in a fictional one is curious. The Keller inci-
dent, as Beauvoir herself notes, is a serious provocation of the
authorities. To beat and torture a destitute woman is one
thing; to beat and torture her on Easter Sunday is quite another.
Further, that he spent the better part of his life in jail would
seem to indicate that he was perceived as a threat by the
regimes under which he lived. Finally, the fact that Sade began
to write after he was imprisoned, that is after action in the

---

[9] "Must We Burn Sade?" p. 19/pp. 29–30.
[10] *Ibid.*, p. 9/p. 18.

social world was no longer possible, would seem to undermine the claim that Sade used the imaginary to escape the
demands of reality. With Sade, the imaginary was a provocation. Here he is more an ally than Beauvoir allows. For though
his understanding of the revolutionary project is at odds with
Beauvoir's, like Beauvoir, Sade understands the powers of
mystification and like Beauvoir, he writes to unmask the fic-
tions of patriarchy's gender constructs. If Sade works in the
imaginary it is not to escape reality but to engage it. He claims
that his imaginary mirrors the real. When he writes:

> What does one want when one is engaged in the sexual act? That
> everyone around you give you its utter attention, think only of
> you, care only for you ... every man wants to be a tyrant when he
> fornicates.[11]

he puts himself before us as someone exposing the reality of
men's desire.

Is Sade right about what every man wants? Perhaps.
Given the categories of *The Second Sex*, Sade's description of
fornication cannot be dismissed. It seems to get at the heart of
patriarchal sexuality. His so-called perversion may reveal the
secret of patriarchal desire and it is in this possibility that his
importance for Beauvoir and for us lies. Far more than object-
ing to the fact that Sade preferred an imaginary eroticism to
real acts of rebellion, Beauvoir objects to the meaning that
Sade gives to the erotic. What first sounds like a condemnation of the erotic, the charge that it represents a flight from
reality, turns out to be a charge against Sade's perversion of
the erotic; for once we attend to the standard by which
Beauvoir judges Sade's sexuality, we discover that it is perverse insofar as it misses the fundamental way in which the
erotic expresses the ambiguity of our condition as consciousness, as flesh, as subject, and as other.

If Sade is right in claiming that his desire expresses the
truth of men's desire, and if Beauvoir is correct in attributing

---

[11] *Ibid.*, p. 8/p. 17.

men's desire to the socialization processes of patriarchy, then understanding Sade is essential to understanding patriarchy. Condemning his perversion of the erotic entails a condemnation of the patriarchal erotic. As *The Second Sex* depicts the perverse subjectivity of women who become woman, "Must We Burn Sade?" depicts the perverse subjectivity of men who become man. In giving us these two pieces, Beauvoir gives us a portrait of the patriarchal couple.

According to Beauvoir, it is as erotic that I recognize my passivity in the passivity of the other and it is as erotic that I recognize my freedom in the freedom and consciousness of the other. The erotic is the moment in which I recognize myself in the other without reducing the other to my double or dissolving myself in their otherness. The intoxication of the erotic is an intoxication of ambiguity not identity. In Beauvoir's words:

> The state of emotional intoxication allows one to grasp existence in one's self and in the other as both subjectivity and passivity. The two partners merge in this ambiguous unity; each one is freed of his own presence and achieves immediate communication with the other.[12]

Beauvoir's quarrel with Sade is not then that he chooses to fulfill his existence in the domain of the imaginary erotic but that he alienates the meaning of eroticism. It is not a matter of escaping into the imaginary from the real but a matter of dismissing the ethical intentionality of generosity for the unethical project of tyranny.

The possibilities of the erotic mirror the contesting desires of intentionality. Like the phenomenological epoché which upsets the common sense and traditional Western philosophical distinctions between subject and object, the intimacies of the erotic disturb the boundaries that mark consciousness off from the body and separate self and other. The erotic, like intentionality, is grounded in an original openness to otherness that is

---

[12] *Ibid.*, pp. 21–22/p. 33.

challenged by the desire to be. In its originality, the erotic gives us to each other as fleshed.[13] Here we seem to reach the other in their otherness. In its second moment, the erotic becomes the project of possession. Here the desires of the same prevail. Sade seems to understand the revolutionary possibilities of the erotic. He seems to understand that in its original disclosing moment the erotic challenges the tyranny of the social order. He seems to offer himself to Beauvoir as an ally in her turn to the ethic of the erotic. The appearance is deceptive. Betraying both Beauvoir and the erotic, Sade refuses the risks of intimacy to pursue the pleasures of the libertine.

The Cartesian Despot

According to Beauvoir, the radical communicative possi- bilities of the erotic lie in its power to disturb the conscious- ness-body divide. Here is the irony of Sade. Committed to writing about what barely lets itself be communicated, the erotic, Sade, refusing the disturbances that are unique to the erotic, was least able to understand the meaning of eroticism. Never succumbing to emotional intoxication, Sade surfaces as the Descartes of the bedroom.

> Never in his stories does sensual pleasure appear as self-forgetful- ness, swooning or abandon ... The male aggression of the Sadean hero is never softened by the usual transformation of the body into flesh. He never for an instant loses himself in his animal nature; he remains so lucid ... that ... philosophical discourse ... acts as an aphrodisiac ... desire and pleasure explode into furious crisis in this cold, tense body impregnable to all enchantment. They do not constitute a living experience within the framework of the subject's psycho-physiological unity. Instead, they blast him, like some kind of bodily accident.[14]

Pursuing the aims of the erotic, the discovery of the other, but dedicated to lucidity and enamored of his own subjectivity,

---

[13] *Ibid.*, p. 22/p. 33.
[14] *Ibid.*, p. 21/p. 32.

Sade discovers cruelty. Having no recourse to God to save him from his isolation, this confirmed atheist finds the route to the other through torture. She screams therefore we exist.

Sade as one of the consequences of Descartes? Isn't this too problematic? Perhaps, but less and less so as we stay with Beauvoir's text. And more and more so if we go to the French. For there we discover that what is rendered emotional intoxication in the English is the French *le trouble;* and though *le trouble* may, given the context and translator's poetic license, be rendered emotional intoxication, it is more literally understood to mean a disturbance, a confusion, or an agitation relating to sexual desire. Thus, what Sade refuses, according to Beauvoir, are the confusions of the erotic. He will not sacrifice his lucidity to the erotic's power to disturb the clear and distinct differences between self and other. Beyond the implications of this word *le trouble,* we find Descartes' issues running through Sade's orgies: the status of the subject, the question of the other, the relationship between body/flesh, and soul/consciousness.

It is because he insists on his status as subject that Sade refuses the reciprocities of the erotic and pursues the pleasures of sadism. It is because he insists on the absolute sovereignty of the subject that Sade distances himself from the erotic other; and it is because he equates subjectivity with the lucidity of consciousness that he defends the body against the flesh and figures it as the mechanized site of cruelty and degradation.

Sade's commitment to the Cartesian ideal of consciousness marks the uniqueness of his project. He embodies, Beauvoir says, "the tension of a will bent on fulfilling the flesh without losing himself in it."[15] To fulfill himself as flesh Sade had himself beaten. To maintain himself as consciousness he dashed to the mantel every few minutes to notch the number of lashes he had endured.[16] Wherever we look we discover the same

---

[15] *Ibid.,* p. 27/p. 39.
[16] *Ibid.*

thread. What distinguishes Sade is the way he combines "passionate sexual appetites with a basic emotional apartness."[17]

Spontaneity has no place in Sade's rationally ordered universe. Desire, orgasm, and cruelty are premeditated and programmed for their maximum effect of heightening the torturer's experience of pleasured subjectivity. Everything must be ordered to establish the body as the ally of consciousness. Without such ordering, the body threatens to become for Sade what it was for Descartes—a threat to one's identity.

Where Descartes combatted the powers of the body by turning to the soul, Sade remained fascinated with the conflict between consciousness and the flesh.[18] Lured by the pleasures of the flesh but repelled by its threat to his sovereignty, Sade links the flesh with vileness, old age, filth, and bad odors. He recoils before its call to intimacy.[19] He cannot figure the erotic disturbance of autonomy as other than loss. For him the flesh is the site of the humiliated/annihilated subject. As desiring flesh, Sade pursues the humiliations. As the insistent subject, he pulls back before being consumed. As sadist, he cannot negotiate the distance between himself and the other. It is either sovereignty or humiliation.

This then is the meaning of Sade's perversion: the either/or of the lucid consciousness that refuses the opacity of the flesh and the ambiguity of subjectivity. Sade's perversion is the perversion of the imaginary not because he wrote to escape reality, and not because he acted in the bedroom rather than in the world, but because he chose to live his subjectivity in the register of the imaginary ego-imago.

According to Beauvoir, the Sadean subject "possesses himself only as an imago."[20] Drawing on Sartre's analysis of the imaginary, Beauvoir characterizes this imaginary existence as one of absence. Drawing on one of the crucial themes of her own thought, she characterizes the imaginary as the realm of

---

[17] *Ibid.*, p. 21/p. 32.
[18] *Ibid.*, p. 29/p. 41.
[19] *Ibid.*, p. 26/p. 38.
[20] *Ibid.*, p. 32/p. 45.

certainty. There is no risk in the imaginary. The dominated other poses no threat. Drawing on this idea of the imaginary as a retreat from the threat of the real, Beauvoir strips Sade of his claim to be an artist.[21]

Sade's flight to the imaginary is quite different from the liberating imagination of *The Ethics of Ambiguity*. In *The Ethics of Ambiguity*, Beauvoir sees the imagination as an ally of freedom. There, she envisions the relationship between the author and the erotic quite differently from the one she sees in the work of Sade. In *The Ethics of Ambiguity*, the author is described as being grounded in the risks of reality and as revealing us to ourselves as ambiguously situated amidst the resistances of the world.

Sade, Beauvoir says, is grounded elsewhere. Refusing to confront the real other before whom we must risk our subjectivity, Sade insisted on occupying the place of the despotic subject. He secured his subject status by creating images which were "perfectly submissive and pliant."[22] In Sade:

> The victim is never more than a symbol; the subject possesses himself only as an imago, and their relationship is merely the parody of the drama which would really set them at grips with their incommunicable intimacy.[23]

Though she does not mention him, it is difficult to read these indictments of Sade's ego-imago, imaginary commitments without recalling Lacan's accounts of the mirror stage and the imaginary. Beauvoir's account of the ways in which Sade's immersion in the imaginary perverts the desires of the erotic by rigidly asserting the subject's authority, parallels Lacan's critique of the fortress ego-imago which models itself on an imaginary *méconnaissance* in order to assure itself that it is the (m)other's desire absolutely. But where for Lacan the ego-imago, however it may misrepresent the subject, speaks

---

[21] *Ibid.*, p. 37/p. 50.
[22] *Ibid.*, p. 37/p. 51.
[23] *Ibid.*, p. 32/p. 45.

for/to the infant's future, for Beauvoir, there is no future either for or in Sade's world. Here the perversion closes in on itself.

What Lacan identifies as stages in infant development, the *méconnaissance* of the mirror and the doubling aggressivity of the eighteen month old, Beauvoir identifies as a stable feature of Sade's psyche. Aggressive doubling was his preferred way of being in the world. His favorite fantasy, one which he often acted out, Beauvoir tells us, was "to be penetrated and beaten while he himself was penetrating and beating a submissive victim."[24]

Though we may be tempted to pursue this Lacanian thread by asking whether the paternal metaphor ever got hold of Sade, we would be wrong to suggest that he was stuck in the imaginary. As author, torturer, and criminal, Sade takes his place in the symbolic order. What he does not do is accept the usual symbolic anchors. Gender identities, metaphysical systems, temporal flows, and spatial markers are deliberately confounded. The phallus as the master signifier anchoring the symbolic chain is unmoored, giving us a symbolic without boundaries. With Sade the phallus is an instrument of destabilization.

In his disturbance of the place of the phallus, Sade may be more radical and more insightful than Beauvoir. Whether or not it is her intention, Beauvoir's analyses of patriarchy stabilize the power of the phallus. Identifying woman as the inessential other and identifying the position of the subject as culturally not biologically given, Beauvoir, refusing as always to establish dichotomies, notes that nature (biology) and culture are ambiguously related. The subject is the human embodiment of transcendence. In *The Ethics of Ambiguity*, Beauvoir linked the experience of transcendence to the crisis of adolescence. In *The Second Sex*, she remembers that adolescents are bodied, sexed, and gendered long before they become teenagers. She tells us that bodily differences invite boys and girls to experience their subjectivity differently and

[24] *Ibid.*, p. 27/p. 39.

that this difference makes a difference in the way the crisis of adolescence is experienced.

Without claiming that men's subject and women's inessential other positions are naturally grounded, Beauvoir does say that the boy's penised body and the young man's stronger body produce spontaneous experiences of transcendence which culture then reinforces. The girl's and young woman's body, according to Beauvoir, makes no such offering. Its spontaneities speak of immanence. In linking the spontaneous experience of transcendence/subjectivity to the penis, Beauvoir points to the structural confusion between the penis and the phallus. For her, as for Lacan, the question is whether this confusion is contingent or essential, and she, like Lacan, insists that the confusion is contingent. Biology is not destiny.

Beauvoir's point in revealing the confusion of penis and phallus is not to challenge the relationship between subjectivity and the phallus but to challenge the relationship between subjectivity and the penis. Her solution to the immoralities of patriarchy requires a redistribution of phallic power such that experiences of subjectivity are not foreclosed from bodies without the penis. Beauvoir's solution, however, requires a clarity regarding the difference between the imaginary and the symbolic phallus that her empirical and theoretical observations suggest may not be possible. Further, if we pursue her theories of ambiguity and intentionality, we discover that defining the subject in terms of the experience of transcendence may not capture the nuances of human subjectivity and may not be adequate to the task of dismantling the patriarchal subject.

Sade sees things differently. For him it is neither the penis nor the phallus that grounds the patriarchal subject but the regulated woman's body; and for him the woman's body is regulated not because it carries the threat of castration (loss of identity) but because it speaks of the excess that explodes the category of the subject. Sade is forever showing us how women's polymorphous bodies threaten the phallic symbolic order. He never tires of telling us that women's bodies are artificially regulated to meet the demands of procreation and repeatedly insists that women's bodies are not naturally heterosexual. The woman's body is the perfect libertine site because it is fluid. Sodomy is the ultimate libertine act because it unhinges the so-called fixities of biology, identity, and sexual desire that are called upon to justify patriarchy.

The destabilizing effects of libertine license, however, are limited. They do not extend to the libertine subject. Like Beauvoir, Sade identifies the subject with the power to give meaning. Beauvoir links the subject as meaning-giver to the project of liberation—the creation of a non-exploitive order. Sade links the subject as meaning-giver to the project of destabilization—hence the powerful effects of blasphemy and its central place in the libertine economy. Rejecting a system that stabilizes the subject in order to regulate desire, Sade will not, however, go so far as to threaten the libertine subject with destabilization. Throwing everything else into confusion for his/her own pleasure, the libertine returns to himself/herself after the orgy. Though the origin and end of Sade's critique of patriarchy differ's from Beauvoir's, it is grounded in the same place and faces the same problems. A critique of patriarchy that leaves the concept of the subject intact touches the trappings but not the groundings of patriarchy.

Reading Sade we cannot conclude that man's desire for woman is a heterosexual matter. The libertine's sexual preferences are anal. Anal sexuality does not require woman. Indeed Justine's Clement calls vaginal intercourse "woman worship" and rejects it as a preferred or exclusive source of erotic pleasure.[25] Why then are Sade's novels strewn with harems filled with girls and women rather than with boys and men? Why is it that even when women are used as men it is as women that they are beaten, tortured, and abused? Why is it that in Justine Clement insists that "women ... are nothing but machines designed for voluptuousness ... nothing but targets

---

[25] Marquis de Sade, Justine, Philosophy in the Bedroom and Other Essays, trans. Richard Seaver and Austryn Wainhouse (New York: Grove Press, 1965), p. 602.

of lust ... "[26] when the site of rapture is the ass, not the cunt? It may be, as Sade says, that woman's weakness makes her vulnerable to man's domination, but it is not her weakness that makes her the target of lust. It is woman's body as sexed, not as weak, that makes it voluptuous; and given Sade's account of pleasure, it is not as *the* sex that she is desired, but as the body that invites transgression that woman inflames man's desire. Barthes shows us what is at stake when he writes:

> Libertine morality consists not in destroying but diverting; it diverts the object, the work, the organ from its endoxal usage; however for this theft to occur ... the meaning must persist. Woman must contrive to represent a paradigmatic area with two sites, one of which the libertine, a linguist respectful of the sign will mark, and the other which he will neutralize. Of course by concealing the female's sexual organs, by baring her buttocks, the libertine seems to be making her into a boy and seeking in Woman what is not Woman, however the scrupulous abolition of difference is a trick, for this asexual Woman is still not the other of Woman (the boy): among the subjects of debauchery, Woman remains pre-eminent ... the paradigm must function; only Woman offers the choice of two sites of intromission; in choosing the one over the other *in the area of the same body*, the libertine produces and assumes a meaning, that of transgression. The boy because his body provides the libertine with no opportunity for stating the paradigm of sites (he offers but one) is less *forbidden* than Woman: Thus systematically he is less interesting.[27]

Barthes' observations are echoed in the psychoanalytic theory of the part object; for we may infer from the theory of the part object that it is not as the object of heterosexual desire that the woman's body interests us, but as the body with the most part objects that it elicits and sustains our desire. Distinguishing normal from abnormal development, psychoanalysis portrays this attention to the part object *per se* as

---

[26] *Ibid.*, p. 605.
[27] Roland Barthes, *Sade, Fourier, Loyola*, trans. Richard Miller (New York: Hill and Wang, 1976), p. 124.

temporary. Ultimately we want to integrate the part object into the valorized whole object of our love. Lacan, noting the rule of reciprocity that governs *Juliette:* "Lend me the part of your body that will give me a moment of satisfaction and, if you care to, use for your pleasure that part of my body that appeals to you."[28], pauses to consider what he takes to be Sade's suggestion: the part object has a pull on us that is independent of its relationship to either love or the whole object. What for Lacan is a psychoanalytic issue, just how connected (or estranged) is the part object from the full loved object, is for Sade and Beauvoir a philosophical-political issue.

Sade claims that his part object economy liberates us from the alienating whole object economy of patriarchy. Beauvoir agrees with Sade regarding the alienating effects of the whole object economy of patriarchy. The problem as she sees it, however, is not that patriarchal sexuality transforms our part object bodies into regulated heterosexual whole objects but that the whole body object of patriarchy is modeled after the part object. That is, as gendered, the person only appears to be a whole object. Men gendered as man and women gendered as woman function like the part objects of Sade's libertine world. As part objects, they fulfill each other's nostalgic desires.

From Beauvoir's perspective, Sade's part object eroticism destabilizes the heterosexual structures of patriarchy while repeating its nostalgic codes. Sade's world, like the patriarchal world it claims to repudiate, refuses the risks of intimacy to follow the laws of exploitation. In both worlds, the affirmation of subjectivity is linked to the exercise of violence. Beauvoir exposes the fallacy of this link. Subjectivity, according to Beauvoir, cannot be divorced from the realities of risk, but risk, she insists, cannot be reduced to violence.

In distinguishing risk from violence and in accusing patriarchy of perverting the meaning of risk, Beauvoir distinguishes the body which constitutes itself/is constituted as a

---

[28] Jacques Lacan, *The Seminar of Jacques Lacan: Book VII The Ethics of Psychoanalysis, 1959–1960,* trans. Dennis Porter (New York: W. W. Norton, 1986), p. 202.

part object from the body which constitutes itself/is constituted as a whole object. The part object body is patriarchal. It remains committed to the desires of possession and is contaminated by the project of domination. It alienates us from the intimate possibilities of the erotic. The whole object body escapes patriarchy's perversions. It takes up the risks of recognition and opens us to the possibilities of love.

Sade is a troubling figure for Beauvoir. She validates his decision to become an author and then denies him his authorial place. She affirms the way he assumed his sexuality but discredits it as perverse. Insisting that the erotic is a unique human experience which reveals us to each other as freedom and flesh, Beauvoir accuses Sade of repeating the errors of Cartesian dualism. He severs the domains of body and spirit and reduces the erotic flesh to a mechanical body whose spatial extensions are manipulated according to the geometries of the orgy.[29]

Though Beauvoir accuses Sade of injecting the Cartesian subject into the erotic relationship, she also sees Sade as engaging the ambiguity of the flesh. In engaging this ambiguity Sade becomes an inconsistent Cartesian, for though the libertine orgies figure the body as an object, libertine pleasures require that the body be consciously fleshed. The sadist, Beauvoir argues, is distinct from the tyrant. Sade, Beauvoir says, understands this distinction.

Refusing the Risks of the Real

According to Beauvoir, Sade's refusal to impose the death penalty indicates that he distinguished sadism from tyranny. The project of tyranny is the project of the look: to assert one's autonomy by transforming the fleshed other first into a bodied subject and then into an objectified quasi-thing available for domination. The project of sadism is the project of cruelty. Here the other must remain fleshed and other. Its conscious-

---

[29] "Must We Burn Sade?," pp. 37–38/pp. 50–51.

ness must remain in play, for the pleasures of cruelty depend on a simultaneous valorization and degradation of the particular individual in its fleshed humanity. These pleasures depend on revealing the unique ambiguity of the subject and on exploiting the unique vulnerability of the other. Reduce the fleshed other to a quasi-body-thing and the pleasures of sadism disappear.[30] Tyranny is a version of the bad faith of the second moment of intentionality. Sadism is a perversion of the original disclosing moment of intentionality. It refuses the joy of affirming the elusive otherness that it discloses. In refusing to execute political prisoners, Sade rejects the project of tyranny. In affirming the pleasures of torture, Sade embraces the project of sadism.

It is not the case, however, that the sadist and tyrant have nothing in common. Like the two moments of intentionality whose contesting desires are bound to each other, these betrayals of the other and the "we" are linked. Both refuse to renounce the useless passion of the autonomous subject. The tyrant's refusal may be traced to his project of objectification. Sade's is traced to his distortion of the erotic. For though Sade may be said to have succeeded in disclosing the ambiguity of our fleshed subjectivity, he failed to disclose the ways in which this ambiguity opens us to each other.

The subject who recognizes itself as ambiguously fleshed and open to other recognizes that this openness is dangerous. The tyrant who recognizes no other subjects and the sadist who recognizes the other only as the subject of cruelty deny the risks of reciprocity. In this denial they flee their vulnerability, their flesh, their embodied subjectivity.[31] The tyrant and the sadist are cowards.

Given that Sade risked his freedom to oppose tyranny but that he was blind to the tyrannies of sadism, we need to look more carefully at Beauvoir's charge that Sade's eroticism, as grounded in the imaginary, misfires as a political protest. To do this we need to return to the question of Sade's sexuality

---

[30] *Ibid.*, pp. 15–16/pp. 25–26.
[31] *Ibid.*, p. 59/pp. 76–77.

and ask: What are the philosophical/political implications of adopting Sade's attitude toward sexuality? Posing this question we discover, surprisingly, that Beauvoir does not dwell on Sade's essentialism or metaphysics of evil. Her focus is on Sade's association of cruelty and sexuality and on the meaning of this association for the question of the other and the problem of recognition.

The political is the domain of the project. For a protest to have political implications it must do more than assert the integrity of the individual. It must call upon the "we"—an intersubjectivity of allies where each one validates the other as its equal. Projects of liberation reject the politics of the scapegoat and sacrifice. This, it seems to me, is Beauvoir's basic philosophical/political intuition.

Given this intuition, Beauvoir finds the project of sadism unacceptable on two counts. First, it accepts the principle of sacrifice. Second, the basis of the social bond is the recognition of inequality. As Beauvoir describes it:

> What the torturer demands is that, alternating between refusal and submission, whether rebelling or consenting, the victim recognize, in any case, that his destiny is the freedom of the tyrant. He is then united to his tyrant by the closest of bonds. They form a genuine couple.[32]

Sade, as the criminal, begins correctly enough. Beauvoir accepts the maxim of Sade's ethic—that one must be a criminal in a criminal society. Further she agrees with Sade when he asserts the rights of the individual against the demands of the collective. Sade's fault, according to Beauvoir, lies in stopping at the individual and in ignoring the concrete other. Applying the existential categories of immanence and transcendence, Beauvoir finds the sadist guilty of enclosing the subject in its immanence and autonomy. On the one hand the torturer and victim form a genuine couple. On the other hand this couple does not constitute a "we," for according to Beauvoir:

---

[32] *Ibid.*, p. 60/p. 77.

the only sure bonds among men are those they create in transcending themselves into another world by means of common projects.
The only project that the hedonistic sensualism of the eighteenth
century has to offer the individual is to 'procure pleasant sensa-
tions and feelings.' It fixes him in his lonely immanence.[33]

In distinguishing the hedonist couple from the "we" of the
project, Beauvoir accuses Sade of refusing the risks of the real;
for the real, according to Beauvoir, is the realm of resistance.
To recognize the other as really free is to understand the other
as a point of resistance to me. It means accepting the dangers
of the other. Sade never positions the sadistic subject as vulnerable to this danger. The Sadean libertine demands the
recognition that Hegel identifies as crucial to subjectivity, but
refuses to accept the risks of the Hegelian dialectic.[34]

The criteria of the we-project are not the only criteria at
work in Beauvoir's judgments. There are also the criteria of
the disclosing moment of intentionality. These criteria are no
more benign to Sade than those of the project. Here, however,
the issue concerns *jouissance* and pleasure rather than cruelty
and crime.

Compare Beauvoir's description of the meaning of the
erotic with her description of Sadean *jouissance*. For Beauvoir,
the erotic is a unique expression of reciprocity and generosity.
It opens the boundaries between consciousness, flesh, self, and
other. For Sade, the erotic is the site of pleasure. And pleasure,
Beauvoir tells us, has nothing in common with generosity. It is
a "tyranny ... of avarice which chooses to destroy what it cannot assimilate."[35] Pleasure overrides the joys of disclosure with
its demands of possession. Sade's pleasure is the failed, useless passion of *The Ethics of Ambiguity*. There is no joy in this
jouissance.[36]

Sade, as portrayed by Beauvoir, is driven by a maniacal,
single-minded pursuit of pleasure which knows no joy, evades

---

[33] *Ibid.*, p. 58/pp. 75–76.
[34] *Ibid.*, p. 59/p. 77.
[35] *Ibid.*, p. 26/p. 38.
[36] *Ibid.*, pp. 53–54/p. 79.

the real, and fails to touch the other. He is the absolute subject as coward, preferring the bad faith of despotic power to the dangers of an eroticism willing to expose itself to the uncanny otherness of another's freedom.

The Worthy Enemy

Powerful as her indictments may be, Beauvoir remains drawn to Sade. Though she insists that he failed to articulate the truths of the erotic, she credits him with giving us "insights of surprising depth into the relation of sexuality to existence."[37] Ultimately she believes that his work deserves our attention.[38] In explaining the attention she gives to Sade, Beauvoir tells us that "circumstances and my own pleasure led me to write about Sade."[39] The circumstances were that she was asked to write a preface for *Justine*. The pleasure was discovering that:

> Justine's epic extravagance was a revelation. Sade posed the problem of the *Other* in its extremist terms; in his excesses, man-as-transcendence and man-as-object achieve a dramatic confrontation.[40]

In titling her reflections on Sade "Must We Burn Sade?" Beauvoir alerts us to her ambiguous relationship to him. Picking up the piece cold, we are struck by the title's originality. Reading Beauvoir's memoirs, however, we learn that the title has a tradition. It repeats the title of a 1946 symposium in *Action* concerned with *literature noire* titled, "Must We Burn Kafka?" and revives the title of an article in *Combat* which responded to attacks on Sartre titled, "Should We Burn Sartre?"[41] Whether Beauvoir would place Sade alongside Kafka and Sartre is unclear. What seems clear, however, is that for all her attacks on Sade's perversions, Beauvoir is not willing to dismiss him.

[37] *Ibid.*, p. 38/p. 70.
[38] *Ibid.*, p. 20/p. 30.
[39] *Force I*, p. 243.
[40] *Ibid.*
[41] *Ibid.*, pp. 44, 230.

Sade is Beauvoir's Nietzschean worthy enemy. He is her adversary and ally. As ally he sees what she sees: that the erotic is neither an innocent nor a private sphere, that sex and gender are divisible, that feminine virtues are ideologically grounded. As adversary he challenges her visions of mutuality, freedom, reciprocity, otherness, generosity, and joy.

Beauvoir says that she sees Sade in his character Juliette, but that she finds him most insightful in his book *Justine*. The sisters Justine and Juliette might not seem to be the best introduction to *The Second Sex*, but appearances might be deceptive. The ideas of mystification, myths, and ideology are crucial to *The Second Sex*. They also go to the heart of Justine and Juliette. Justine epitomizes feminine virtue. She is what all women are taught to be, passive, submissive, attentive to the dictates of femininity. Her reward is abuse and suffering. Her virtues benefit neither herself nor anyone else. In Angela Carter's words:

> Justine is a good woman in a man's world. She is a good woman according to the rules for women laid down by men and her reward is rape, humiliation and incessant beatings. Her life is that of a woman martyrised by the circumstances of her life as a woman.[42]

Anne Le Brun, taking up a similar theme, describes Justine as a body mutilated by ideology.[43] Could Beauvoir ask for a more concrete portrait of the exploitive meaning of femininity?

If Justine embodies the mystified woman, Juliette is her explosion. Angela Carter calls Juliette a sexual terrorist who, in her preference for anal sex and choice of infertility, demystifies the association of woman and womb and demythologizes the womb's sacred meaning. Juliette's womb is an organ like any other. If she wishes to have children it is useful; if not it is an appendage without value.[44] Generalizing from Juliette,

---

[42] Angela Carter, *The Sadeian Woman, and the Ideology of Pornography* (New York: Pantheon Books, 1978), p. 38.

[43] Le Brun, p. 145.

[44] Carter, p. 109.

Joseph McMahon notes that though Sade portrays women as heros (not heroines), he allows them to escape their subordinate position only if they renounce their femininity and woman's body for male homosexual practices where the anus and clitoris prevail.[45] Though Beauvoir fails to validate Juliette's sexual terrorism, she does not challenge Juliette's decision to sever her sexuality from her maternal desire.

If Sade is Beauvoir's ally when it comes to exposing the arbitrary relationship between sex and gender and when it comes to revealing the exploitive powers of gender roles, he is not her unconditional ally. For though he creates worlds where, "male means tyrannous and female means martyrised no matter what the official genders of the male and female being are,"[46] in his worlds, sexual gratification is linked with pain and sexual relations are expressions of tyranny. No vision of liberation accompanies his revelations.

Both Sade and Beauvoir betray their Cartesian lineage in the way they pose the question of the erotic. Both begin with the concrete existing subject and ask how it stands with/to the other. Both ask whether the boundaries of the self can be broken. For Sade these boundaries can be forcefully and momentarily violated; ultimately, however, they are not permeable. Pleasure is always self-contained and solitary.[47]

Beauvoir works with her Cartesian heritage differently. She proposes that the boundaries of the subject can be transgressed without violating subjectivity. Though she recognizes the place of violence in human desire, Beauvoir challenges the victory Sade gives to erotic cruelty. Sade is correct, the erotic is disruptive and threatening. But he is also wrong. In its disruptions of the alienations of patriarchy, the erotic disrupts the boundaries of the self that foster the illusions of the sovereign subject—illusions that Sade and patriarchy insist on maintaining. Against Sade's valorization of a subject centered sexual tyranny,

[45] Joseph McMahon, "Where Does Real Life Begin?," *Yale French Studies*, no. 35 (1965), p. 107.
[46] Carter, p. 24.
[47] Le Brun, pp. 61, 72.

Beauvoir validates the generosity and gifting that mark the lived meaning of the ambiguously fleshed erotic subject. Beauvoir's critique of Sade follows the two lines of her thinking. In chastising Sade for refusing the demands of reciprocity, Beauvoir criticizes him from the perspective of the ethic of the we-project. In chastising Sade for refusing the ambiguities of the erotic, Beauvoir criticizes him for injecting the Cartesian subject into the erotic relationship.

What is especially interesting about the Sade essay is the way it weights what is muted in Beauvoir's other texts. Where Beauvoir's other works focus on the requirements of the project, "Must We Burn Sade?" focuses on the requirements of the erotic. As I read the Sade essay I cannot avoid feeling that more than being displeased with Sade for not engaging in projects of liberation, Beauvoir is distressed by Sade's perversion of the erotic.

Sade and *The Second Sex*

Reading "Must We Burn Sade?" within the context of *The Ethics of Ambiguity* brings the concrete realities of desire and sexuality to the discussions of subjectivity, intentionality, the project, and freedom. Reading "Must We Burn Sade?" as part of the horizon of *The Second Sex* gets us to pause where we might have hurried on. For though sex, sexuality, and gender are central issues in *The Second Sex*, the question of the erotic seems to be peripheral. "Must We Burn Sade?" suggests that this appearance may be deceptive. It alerts us to the relationship between the erotic and the meanings of femininity, subjectivity, and intersubjectivity. It shows us that the political project of liberation and the philosophical project of re-envisioning the subject are essential to each other.

As I listen to Beauvoir reading Sade, I hear her criticizing him for not understanding the limits of autonomy. His political refusal to submit to the demands of the collective is grounded in his affirmation of his individuality. As a consciousness/subject he will define himself, assume responsibility for this definition, and live out this meaning of his existence. So far, so good. But how will he live among others? Only at a distance and in defiance? For Beauvoir this is not adequate. A morality that limits itself to affirming the individual misses the full meanings of freedom. My freedom is engaged with the freedom of the other. Sade revealed the point of this engagement, the erotic; but by figuring the erotic according to the dictates of autonomy, the look, and pleasure, he misses the engagement itself.

Beauvoir's *The Second Sex* shows us how to engage the erotic and escape the tyranny of pleasure. It situates Sade's ethic of the erotic against another erotic ethic, a feminist one. This ethic is grounded in the courage to accept the risks of fleshed subjectivity. This ethic affirms the erotic intoxications that disrupt the tyrannies of pleasure. It forgoes the securities of possession for the generosities of gifting.

CHAPTER 5

Risking: An Ethic of the Erotic:
The Second Sex

Consistent with her decision to present herself as philosophically barren, Beauvoir identifies *The Second Sex* as "an almost chance conception" induced by Sartre.[1] It was Sartre, she says, who questioned her assumption that being a woman was a peripheral fact of her life. It was only in response to his question, she says that she discovered:

> this world was a masculine world, my childhood had been nourished by myths forged by men, and I hadn't reacted to them in at all the same way I should have done if I had been a boy. I was so interested in this discovery that I abandoned my project for a personal confession in order to give all my attention to finding out about the condition of woman in its broadest terms.[2]

Without disputing Beauvoir's claim that it was Sartre who provoked her to take up the question of woman, we would do well not to take Sartre's paternal role in the birth of *The Second Sex* too seriously.[3] If, rather than following Beauvoir's direction to look to Sartre, we attend instead to the direction of Beauvoir's philosophical writings we see that more than Sartre's questioning is involved in Beauvoir's decision to investigate the meanings of the sexed and gendered embodied subject.

---

[1] *Force I*, p. 185.
[2] *Ibid.*, pp. 94–95.
[3] As Elaine Hoffman Baruch does in saying that *The Second Sex* "was in a sense Jean-Paul Sartre's baby" in her essay "The Female Body and the Male Mind," *Dissent*, no. 34 (Summer 1987), p. 351.

Given our reading of *Pyrrhus et Cinéas, The Ethics of Ambiguity*, and "Must We Burn Sade?" we know that Beauvoir was, from the very beginning, sensitive to the ways in which women were assigned inferior roles and relegated to passive positions. In the more abstract works, *Pyrrhus et Cinéas* and *The Ethics of Ambiguity*, this shows up in her examples; in the concrete "Must We Burn Sade?" it becomes a central issue. Taking a developmental view of Beauvoir's work, we might say that as *The Ethics of Ambiguity* abandons the *Pyrrhus et Cinéas* position of absolute freedom for the concept of situated freedom, *The Second Sex* concretely develops *The Ethics of Ambiguity*'s thesis that one's freedom is historically conditioned rather than ontologically guaranteed.

Reading Beauvoir's memoirs and letters we see her successfully rebelling against her feminine bourgeois destiny. We also see (and we know Beauvoir understood) that her father's economic circumstances made her escape possible. She could have been Zaza. The Beauvoir who was neither seduced by the norms of heterosexual desire nor determined by her culture's categories of traditional female roles, the Beauvoir who saw herself as an equal among men and who lived and moved as freely as any man, was not, however, immune from the myth of femininity. One day, after a poor day of skiing she writes:

> I came down pretty poorly—lacking the Christie and courage. It should also be said I was in a state of feminine inferiority; I'm feeling so well it's barely noticeable, but it does weaken you all the same.[4]

We hear nothing more about these bouts of feminine inferiority, but this paragraph tells us that in becoming an independent woman and in sustaining her status as an equal among men, Beauvoir was haunted by the myth of femininity.

---

[4] *Letters To Sartre*, p. 232.

Myths and Mystifications

Reading *The Second Sex* within the context of Beauvoir's experience of being a woman and against the horizon of her philosophical categories of ambiguity, intentionality, embodiment, generosity, and situated freedom, I find the concepts of myth and mystification central to its investigation of woman's inessential otherness. More than providing Beauvoir with a lens through which the phenomenon of woman is clarified, these concepts allow Beauvoir to critique patriarchy from the dual ethical perspectives of the we-project and erotic generosity.

In accusing patriarchy of mystifying women, Beauvoir condemns it for validating particular myths and for endorsing a way of engaging the world that is fundamentally alienating. As a mythical system, patriarchy is anti-human. It engulfs us in an imaginary, a-historical reality which ignores Husserl's discovery of intentionality and rejects Hegel's discovery of historicity. Alert to the phenomenological insights of Husserl and Hegel, Beauvoir will use the principles of their phenomenologies to demystify the "truths" of patriarchy. Drawing on Husserl and Hegel, Beauvoir situates her critique at both the individual and political levels. Though Beauvoir argues that we are ensnared by myths as individuals, she also insists that individual mythical thinking is called into play and sustained by social and political institutions and structures. Not accepting Hegel's dialectic of the Absolute Spirit but relying on his account of the ways in which cultures mistake their constituted and relative values for absolute and universal standards, Beauvoir's *The Ethics of Ambiguity* identifies this mistake as a willed refusal to recognize the constituting powers of consciousness and engage the contesting desires of intentionality. In sexing these insights, *The Second Sex* exposes the ways in which patriarchy obfuscates the liberating powers of consciousness when consciousness is embodied as woman and when woman is the fantasy of the feminine.

Patriarchy appears to endorse multiple visions of women. Beauvoir discovers that this appearance is deceptive. There is, she discovers, a single patriarchal myth regarding women—the myth of the eternal feminine. Whether she is figured as the erotic, birthing, or nurturing body, woman is imaged as the sex and wrapped in a mythical body. Embodied as the eternal feminine, woman is barred from the domain of the subject.

Orienting ourselves to *The Second Sex* through the concepts of myth and mystification, we see that the most famous line of this text, "One is not born, but rather becomes a woman"[5] is not, as a philosophical insight, original to *The Second Sex*. It is a specification of *The Ethics of Ambiguity*'s account of the crisis of adolescence. In *The Ethics of Ambiguity*, all adolescents are said to be capable of transcending the innocence of childhood and competent to challenge the myths that place them in a predetermined world. They are expected to rebel—to insist on their position as meaning giving subjects. In citing the extreme cases of the harem and the slave, however, *The Ethics of Ambiguity* recognizes that myths are not always sustained by innocence and that adolescence (understood as the assumption of subjectivity) is not a universal possibility. In the cases of the harem and the slave, the possibilities of adolescence are foreclosed. Exploited by myths that encase them in a perpetual childhood, the slave and the harem woman are duped into believing that their condition is given and immutable. In *The Second Sex* Beauvoir discovers that victimizing myths are more pervasive than she originally suspected. For in discovering the myth of femininity, Beauvoir discovers that so-called enlightened social orders hide a system of exploitation so pervasive and invisible that no social critique has targeted it and no liberation movement has taken up its cause.

The statement "One is not born but rather becomes a woman" concerns the ways in which girl children are barred from the possibilities of adolescent revolt. As a statement of fact it is grounded in a question: How is it that girls are not transformed by adolescence into subjects, but rather become

---

[5] *The Second Sex*, p. 301./ *Le Deuxième Sexe*, vol. I, p. 285.

woman, the inessential other, who like the child is mystified and who as mystified remains a child?

Beginning from her insight that boy and girl children are nourished by the same man-made myths and that boys and girls respond to these myths differently, Beauvoir discovers the patriarchal lie of the neutral subject. The myths that situate/prepare us for subjectivity are made by men; whether one is a boy or a girl matters in how these myths are appropriated. The child who approaches adolescence is already sexed and gendered. Adolescence (within patriarchy) does nothing to subvert these genderings. In challenging the myth of an immutably given universe and in calling all children to assume their subjectivity, patriarchal adolescence embraces the image of the subject empowered to give the world meaning without overtly identifing it as masculine. It holds up the ideal of the neutral subject as it characterizes it according to man-made myths. Within patriarchy the promise of adolescence is undermined by the man made myth of femininity. The ideal of the neutral subject is simultaneously affirmed and betrayed. Beauvoir calls this betrayal immoral. She sees this collusion between the promise of a subjectivity available to all and the myth of femininity which bars women from their subjectivity as crucial to the power of patriarchy and sets herself the task of exposing the lie of the neutral subject.

According to the promise of adolescence, the subject is neutral and all children have an equal opportunity to become subjects. According to the myth of femininity, the position of the subject belongs to man, for the characteristics of subjectivity are decidedly masculine. The subject is the one who imposes his will on the world; the subject is the one who challenges the status quo; the subject is the one who fights for his rights. Given these images of subjectivity—imposing, willing, challenging—a woman would have to give up her feminine identity to assert her identity as a subject.

Beauvoir insists that the promise of adolescence ought to be universal and that the criteria of subjectivity ought to be phenomenologically neutral. As we examine Beauvoir's defense of the neutral subject, however, we discover the two voices of *The Second Sex*. Both voices appeal to the phenomenological-existential categories of transcendence and immanence to critique the patriarchal lie of the neutral subject. One voice accepts the patriarchal intuition that associates subjectivity with violence but objects to the exploitive way in which patriarchy structures the relationship between subjectivity and violence. The other voice challenges the intuition itself. The first voice identifies transcendence as the mark of subjectivity and sees immanence as a threat to the subject. The second voice identifies subjectivity with the ambiguities of transcendence and immanence. This second voice takes up the muted voices of Beauvoir's other texts. It lies in the margins of *The Second Sex*.

Defining the Neutral Subject: Transcendence

A: The Penis

Speaking in her dominant voice, Beauvoir defines subjectivity as transcendence. She writes:

> Every subject plays his part as such specifically through exploits or projects that serve as a mode of transcendence; he achieves liberty only through a continual reaching out toward other liberties. There is no justification for present existence other than its expansion into an indefinitely open future.[6]

With these words, Beauvoir characterizes transcendence as: (1) an attitude toward time; (2) a mode of activity; and (3) an affirmation of freedom. To be a subject is to challenge the powers of immanence, powers that would freeze me within prescribed categories and/or convince me that I can do no more than submit to forces that determine my destiny.

As a human subject my affirmation of transcendence and struggle against immanence must engage the body. Disputing

---

[6] *Ibid.*, p. xxxiii/I, p. 34.

Descartes and aligning herself with Merleau-Ponty and Sartre, Beauvoir argues that the body is not the alienating other of the subject, but the ambiguity of subjectivity. It is the site of the subject's possibilities of transcendence and the place where the subject can be reduced to immanence. As a material thing in the world, the body comes under the gaze of the other and can be reduced to an object. As the instrument of my grasp on the world, the body is the way the subject enacts itself as a constituting activity.[7]

The objectivity of the body cuts two ways. When I affirm my transcendence through it, it is the objective expression of my subjectivity.[8] When it is fixed by the other's look it is the object that alienates me from myself.[9] The fundamental ambiguity of the body is that though it is me and mine, it exists for others and can become, in its existence for others, the anti-subject (the subject made object) that alienates me from myself. As my otherness, however, my body is not an other. Though I may wish to deny it, the fleshed body is me.[10]

Grounded in this understanding of the alienating possibilities of the ambiguous body, *The Second Sex* observes the ways in which these possibilities are complicated by the phenomenon of sex. It describes the ways in which the female body has been reduced to an alienating immanence and depicts the means by which the male body has come to signify transcendence. In tracing the ways in which activities identified with transcendence were made available to and demanded of men but rendered taboo for women, and in examining the ways in which activities associated with immanence were identified with women, *The Second Sex* describes the ways in which the single phenomenologically ambiguous body was rendered unambiguously male or female.

To adequately track the complex argument of *The Second Sex*, we need to attend to Beauvoir's concept of the ambiguous

---

[7] *Ibid.*, pp. 36, 301/I, pp. 51, 285.
[8] *Ibid.*, p. 372/p. 377.
[9] *Ibid.*, pp. 303, 393/pp. 287, 404.
[10] *Ibid.*, p. 424/I, p. 446.

body and to her complex definition of transcendence. Beauvoir uses the concept of the ambiguous body to challenge patriarchy's image of the sexed either/or body. Defining transcendence as a way of being in the world that confronts the anxieties and affirms the spontaneities of freedom/intentionality, Beauvoir challenges patriarchy's equation of transcendence, subjectivity, and violence.

Directed by the concept of ambiguity, Beauvoir refuses to identify the body as either a blank slate waiting to be coded or as already given and "naturally" meaningful. Unwilling to allow biology to become destiny, Beauvoir is also unwilling to declare biology irrelevant. Instead she notes the ways in which our diversely sexed bodies invite us to experience our subjectivity differently and distinguishes the natural invitations of the body from the categorical demands of patriarchy. In tracing the ways in which biological suggestions became cultural mandates, Beauvoir demonstrates that in identifying men with transcendence and women with immanence patriarchy picks up invitations to transcendence and immanence carried in men's and women's bodies and transforms them into immoral social, cultural, and political necessities.

Though Beauvoir will ultimately argue that it is the economies and myths of patriarchy that establish the male body as privileged, her analysis of embodiment suggests that the body with the penis has certain advantages.[11] According to Beauvoir, children first experience their bodies as a mystery and a threat, an otherness.[12] With the girl this original experience becomes the fundamental experience. In menstruation, pregnancy, and lactation she experiences herself at the whim of alien and alienating bodily processes. Only menopause promises relief.[13] The pre-menopausal embodied woman, according to Beauvoir, experiences herself in service to the

---

[11] For more on this issue see Toril Moi, "Ambiguity and Alienation in *The Second Sex*," *Boundary* 2 19:2 (1992), pp. 96–112.
[12] *The Second Sex*, p. 313/*Le Deuxième Sexe* I, p. 300.
[13] *Ibid.*, p. 34/I, pp. 48–49.

species and at the mercy of obscure powers. She does not and cannot, given the myth of femininity, see herself as the initiator of projects through which she transcends her natural condition.[14]

With the boy, things are different. His experience of his body as mysterious and alien is overridden by the presence of the penis; for the penis shows him how to transform the body from a site of alienation to an affirmation of subjectivity. In experiencing himself as a sexed body, the boy experiences his penis as his double and in this doubling begins to experiment with/experience his transcendence. He can, as in urinating games for example, use his penis to transform a natural process into a subjective project.[15] In Beauvoir's words:

> The individual's specific transcendence takes concrete form in the penis and it is a source of pride. Because the phallus is thus set apart, man can bring into integration with his subjective individuality the life that overflows from it.[16]

Lacking a penis, the girl cannot see her embodiment marked by transcendence. She remains opaque to herself, immersed in the mystery of life.[17] She is given a phallic substitute—a doll, and is encouraged to identify with this embodied other, but the doll is not a part of herself; it does not exhibit the dynamic of passivity and action which characterizes the ambiguity of the body-subject.

In identifying with the phallus, the boy identifies with the erection that transforms the inert flesh into an expression of power. He identifies this erection with a transcendence that is already his. In identifying with the doll, the girl identifies with an objectified, passive body. If it represents transcendence at all, it can only be the transcendence of a promise. This will be

---

[14] *Ibid.*, pp. 33, 354/I, pp. 46–47, 344–345.
[15] *Ibid.*, p. 308/I, pp. 292–293.
[16] *Ibid.*, p. 53/I, p. 64.
[17] *Ibid.*, pp. 313–314/I, pp. 300–301.

yours someday if ... The girl might invent more suitable doubles for herself, and Beauvoir believes that she will when she establishes herself as a subject. But the point not to be missed is this: what she will have to invent, he is given.[18]

To adequately understand the importance Beauvoir assigns to the penis, we need to see that, according to Beauvoir, the task of becoming a subject engages the processes of self-objectification and alienation.[19] In reflections that bear the marks of Hegel and Marx and allude to Lacan's account of the mirror stage, Beauvoir tells us that though it is true that in objectifying myself I alienate myself, it is also true that this alienation is a mode of transcendence which is crucial to the formation of the subject. In finding myself objectified in the world, I discover that I can be/become what I am not. Alienation and subjectivity are not simple opposites. They are dialectically related in a dynamic of desire that engages the sexed body.

We are each faced with the same task—the task of becoming a subject. We are not, however, given the same tools. The boy's body gives him a ready double. He can alienate himself in his penis, see himself as other, appropriate this otherness to himself—playing with it, controlling it, determining its meanings. The girl's body makes no such offering. Unable to alienate herself in a part of herself, her whole body must become the site of her self-alienation and retrieval. Given a more complex and dangerous task, patriarchal structures will compound the girl's difficulties. More than not having a penis to sign her transcendence, patriarchy will code her ovaries and uterus as signs of immanence. Following the invitation of the penis, patriarchy will identify the male body with the alienations of

---

[18] For an alternative understanding of the girl and the doll see Luce Irigaray, *Sexes and Genealogies*, trans. Gillian C. Gill (Columbia University Press: New York, 1993), p.97. Irigaray writes:" ... playing with dolls is not simply a game girls are forced to play, it also signifies a difference in subjective status in the separation from the mother. For mother and daughter, the mother is a subject that cannot easily be reduced to an object, and a doll is not an object in the way that a reel ... etc. are objects and tools used for symbolization."

[19] *The Second Sex*, p. 63/*Le Deuxième Sexe*, p. 73.

subjectivity and claim that the girl's body, as lacking the penis, is cut off from the transcendent possibilities of the subject.

Beauvoir's discussion of the body shows certain signs of being taken in by the myths of femininity. Though she is not taken in by the idea that the penised body is the transcendent (subject) body or by the idea that bodies without penises lack the prerequisites of subjectivity, she seems to accept the idea that ovaries and uteri are marks of immanence. In moving against the patriarchal idea that motherhood is woman's destiny, Beauvoir seems to have uncritically accepted the idea that the body marked as mother is subjectively disadvantaged.

Most of the time Beauvoir is not duped by the myth. Most of the time she uses it to her critical advantage. Without her attention to the myth of femininity Beauvoir would not have seen the distinction between the phenomenological and the patriarchal body and would not have developed the concept of gender. Without her schooling in phenomenology she might have seen the body as a thing and misunderstood the function of the myth. The concept of gender would have eluded her. Schooled in phenomenology, Beauvoir knows that it is through the body that we are imbedded in the world and that the body is the instrument of our grasp on the world. Knowing that "the world is bound to seem a very different thing when apprehended in one manner or another,"[20] Beauvoir sees that the point of the myth of femininity is to give men and women two different worlds and that the way to do this is to give them different bodies.

Enter the concept of gender. According to the concept of gender, it is not the biological body but the mythical body that encloses women in a world of immanence; and according to the concept of gender the credibility of the myth derives from its reference to the biological body. As a phenomenological category intended to critique patriarchy, the concept of gender, straddles the divide between a naturalist essentialism that would justify women's position as woman, and an idealist

---

[20] *Ibid.*, p. 36/I p. 51.

constructivism that would fail to see the materialist groundings of the myth of the feminine. Straddling this divide, the concept of gender shows us how the myth of femininity renders the capacities of the phenomenological body inoperative for women.

Iris Young helps clarify this relationship between phenomenology and feminist critique. Sensitive to the connection between Merleau-Ponty and Beauvoir, she draws on the phenomenological distinction between transcendence and immanence to show how the feminine body is "overlaid with immanence."[21] Developing this idea, Young suggests that we compare women who are woman to those who are physically handicapped. She writes:

> Insofar as we learn to live out our existence in accordance with the definition that patriarchal culture assigns us we are physically inhibited, confined, positioned and objectified. As lived bodies we are not open and unambiguous transcendences that move out to master a world that belongs to us ... [22]

Elaine Scarry pushes Beauvoir's and Young's phenomenological analyses of gender and gendering to its dramatic limit when she observes, "men have no bodies, women have emphatic bodies."[23] Seeing the issue of femininity formulated in this way, we see that it is not the transformation of women into woman as the sex, but the transformation of women into woman as the immanent rather than the phenomenological body which is crucial to the power of patriarchy. Further, seeing the issue of gender as a matter of the body rather than as a matter of sex allows us to see that women as woman are, like other exploited groups, rendered powerless by being reduced to their bodies. Elaine Scarry puts it this way:

---

[21] Iris Marion Young, *Throwing Like a Girl and Other Essays in Feminist Philosophy and Social Theory* (Bloomington: University of Indiana Press, 1990), p. 148.

[22] *Ibid.*, p. 153.

[23] Elaine Scarry, *The Body in Pain* (Oxford: Oxford University Press, 1985), pp. 359–360, footnote # 20.

... to have no body is to have no limits on one's extension out into the world; conversely, to have a body, a body made emphatic by being continually altered through various form of creation, instruction ... is to have one's sphere of extension contracted down to the small circle of one's immediate physical presence. Consequently to be intensely embodied is the equivalent of being unrepresented and ... is almost always the condition of those without power.[24]

Attentive to the phenomenology of the body, Beauvoir discovers that though the myth of femininity would have us see woman as the sex, we are taken in by the myth if we attack it at this point. For it is not simply as the sex that woman's body is gendered. One becomes a woman by following a precise course in femininity; by learning how to sit, walk, carry books and packages. Pierre Bourdieu, describing the general practices of acculturation rather than the specific practices of gendering, corroborates Beauvoir's insights regarding the myth of femininity and the strategies of gendering. He shows us that in attending to questions of fashion and custom Beauvoir is getting at essential feminist issues; for Bourdieu's studies lead him to conclude that:

The seemingly most insignificant details of *dress, bearing,* physical and verbal *manners* ... form the fundamental principles of the arbitrary content of the culture. The principles embodied in this way are placed beyond the grasp of consciousness ... nothing seems more ineffable, more incommunicable, more inimitable and therefore more precious than the values given body, *made* body by the transubstantiation achieved by the hidden pedagogy, capable of instilling a whole cosmology, an ethic, a metaphysics, a political philosophy through injunctions as insignificant as stand up straight and don't hold your knife in your left hand.[25]

All of this happens invisibly. We get a sense of how and why it happens if we compare the practices which transform girls into woman to the practices that transform civilians into

---

[24] *Ibid.,* p. 207.
[25] Pierre Bourdieu, *Outline of a Theory of Practice,* trans. Richard Nice (Cambridge: Cambridge University Press, 1977), pp. 94-95.

soldiers. Making this comparison we see that the point of boot camp, like the point of the myth of femininity, is to establish a uniform and manageable body. The military, working with adults whose bodies are already culturally and regionally marked and having determined that these marks of diversity are militarily divisive, relies on drills and dress codes to erase these signs of difference. What looks petty from a civilian point of view, the exact shine of a shoe for example, is from a military point of view crucial to the project of emptying the body of its civilian content.[26] If we think of gendering as a boot camp for children, we discover that gender is mistaken for sex not because it is grounded in sex but because the myth of femininity silently erases the phenomenological markings of sex and substitutes for them the mythical markings of gender.

Seeing the phenomenological ground of Beauvoir's discovery of gender, we see that Beauvoir can neither reduce sex to gender nor ignore the givenness of the sexed (as distinct from the neutral) body. In basing her argument for the neutral subject on the givenness of the ambiguous, sexed body, Beauvoir indicates that differently sexed bodies carry the meaning of transcendence differently but that all human bodies are phenomenologically transcending.

Taken outside of its phenomenological context, Beauvoir's claim that differently sexed bodies invite us to experience ourselves as either transcendent or immanent seems to anchor patriarchal categories in the givens of biology. Taken within its phenomenological context, the point of the analysis is understood quite differently. As anchored in the givens of the ambiguous body Beauvoir's analysis is intended to teach us the difference between an invitation to and a codification of certain expressions of subjectivity. Beauvoir, noting that the penis invites the boy to experience the transcendent possibilities of embodiment, distinguishes the invitation of the real penis from the myth of the patriarchal penis. Where patriarchy identifies the penis with transcendence, the real penis is

---

[26] Scarry, p. 118.

ambiguous. It, like the woman's body, is also experienced "as merely passive flesh through which [man] is the plaything of the dark forces of Life."[27] Patriarchy forgets the flaccid penis and the penis of the involuntary wet dream. Its categories appeal to mythical biologies which image the penis as the unambiguous sign of transcendence and ignore (or misrepresent) the signs of transcendence given in the woman's body. Instead of inviting us to explore the ambiguities of the lived body, these biologies bifurcate the ambiguous body according to sex. They ground and validate patriarchy's categories of sexed subjectivity.

B: Violence

This relationship between imaginary biologies and the patriarchal definition of subjectivity becomes clearer as Beauvoir moves from the issues of subjectivity, transcendence, and the sexed body to the issues of subjectivity, the sexed body, risk, and violence. In coming to these issues, we come to some of the most controversial sections of *The Second Sex*. Like the discussions of the invitations of biology, which seem to justify the idea that patriarchal distinctions reflect natural differences, these discussions seem to equate transcendence with violence and seem to endorse arguments that justify women's inferior status.

Reading Beauvoir's discussions of violence, transcendence, and subjectivity, we see that so long as she defines subjectivity as transcendence, Beauvoir will affirm the relationship between transcendence, subjectivity, and violence. Her critique of patriarchy will not be that its validation of violence is illegitimate but that in excluding women from the subjectivizing powers of violence and in reducing the meaning of transcendence to violence, patriarchy illegitimately reserves the domain of violence for men and forgets that transcendence is realized in risking and that violence is only one expression of risk. So long as Beauvoir defines subjectivity as transcendence,

---

[27] *The Second Sex*, p. 184 / *Le Deuxième Sexe* I, p. 224.

her prescription for the exploitations of patriarchy will be limited to demanding that society open the domain of violence to women and validate the subjectivizing powers of non-violent transcendent/risk-taking actions.

As Beauvoir does not always identify subjectivity with transcendence, however, she does not always legitimate patriarchy's validation of violence. Again it is a matter of listening for Beauvoir's other voice; for when Beauvoir's muted voice identifies subjectivity, rather than just the body, with ambiguity it is the risks of the erotic, not the risks of violence which are identified as situating us within the domain of the subject. Though we never hear Beauvoir accepting the specifics of patriarchy's culture of violence, in listening to Beauvoir's dominant voice, we hear her supporting patriarchy's alignment of violence and subjectivity. Nowhere is this clearer than in that (in?)famous passage of *The Second Sex*:

> The worst curse that was laid upon woman was that she should be excluded from these warlike forays. For it is not in giving life but in risking life that man is raised above the animal; that is why superiority has been accorded in humanity not to the sex that brings forth life but to that which kills.[28]

With these words Beauvoir, echoes Hegel. She declares that the task of becoming a subject requires that the value of life be subordinated to the value of death and that it is by risking death that we affirm ourselves. This categorical alignment of violence and subjectivity is not supported by Beauvoir's comparisons between pre-patriarchal and patriarchal societies. For though she shows that women are excluded from violence in both societies, the meaning and effect of this exclusion is not the same. According to Beauvoir, when pre-patriarchal societies segregate the ambiguous body into the female immanent and the male transcendent body, they identify woman as other without reducing her to the inessential other. Suggesting that

---

[28] *Ibid.*, p. 72/I, p. 84.

the pre-patriarchal exclusion of women from the realm of violence reflects an ecology of survival, Beauvoir also suggests
that though pre-patriarchal women may have been regarded
as inferior and/or different, they were not designated as non-
subjects. Insisting on the radical difference between being the
inferior and/or different other and the inessential other,
Beauvoir accuses patriarchal, but not pre-patriarchal society of
exploitation. In patriarchal societies it is neither the vicissi-
tudes of survival nor the biology of the weaker body that bar
women from the domain of violence. Here it is the mythical
biology of immanence and the image of the feminine body
that keeps women from developing their bodily strength,
learning to fight, and experiencing the transcending lessons of
violence.[29] In patriarchy, barring women from the realm of
violence serves the purposes of domination, not survival.
Without recourse to violence in a culture that equates
expressions of violence with affirmations of subjectivity and
submission to violence as a loss of sovereignty, women find
themselves reduced to the position of the inessential other.
The patriarchal image of femininity transforms women's rela-
tively weaker bodies into the absolutely weak body which is
permanently barred from the domain of the subject.

In attacking the myth of femininity for imaging women's
bodies as powerless and absolutely weak, and in urging
women to enter the domain of violence, Beauvoir does not
argue that violence is the only way to become a subject and is
not proposing that women become more like men. Refusing to
reject the relationship between violence and transcendence,
and refusing to claim that the weaker woman's body can
effectively express its transcendence through violence,
Beauvoir does not accept the apparent conclusion of her argument: that without recourse to violence women cannot
embody their subjectivity. Instead she returns to the original
meanings of transcendence, challenge, risk, domination, and

---

[29] *Ibid.*, p. 317/I, p. 305.

violence to argue: (1) that in equating transcendent activity with violence, patriarchy has lost sight of the full meaning of transcendence; (2) that this forgetfulness is a forgetfulness of the ambiguity of the body; and (3) that this privileging of violence is immoral.

In essence, Beauvoir accuses patriarchy of misreading the meaning of transcendence and of inscribing its misreading on the sexed body. As misread, transcendence is read as violence instead of risk. As inscribed on the body, transcendence as violence marks the male body as powerful. Lacking this mark of transcendence, woman's body is inscribed as immanence. Thus woman is transformed from the other to the inessential other through the *méconnaissance* of violence. Undoing patriarchy requires an understanding of this *méconnaissance* and a refusal to succumb to its alienations. The meaning of violence must be demystified.

The *méconnaissance* of the body comes from several directions: its being experienced as flesh; its vulnerability to the forces of nature; its objectification under the gaze of the other. The embodied subject must transcend these alienations. As woman or man it must affirm its desire to transcend the givenness of the world and resist the domination of the look. Women and men confront the same task. They must affirm the subjectivity of their bodies by challenging its appearance as an object in the world. They must act in ways which demonstrate that the lived body is not a reactive mechanism, i.e., that it is not, for example, determined by the laws of pleasure and pain or by the demands of survival.

The structure of such action is the structure of the body at risk. Beauvoir makes it clear that there are many ways to articulate the structure of the body at risk. She also makes it clear that within patriarchy the way of violence is privileged. It is identified as the only way the body expresses its subjectivity. Noting this patriarchal prejudice, Beauvoir insists that girls be given access to the ways of violence; for, so long as the prejudice of patriarchy prevails, girls must be allowed to fight their

way out of their condition of inessential otherness.[30] Neither
the structures of patriarchy, however, nor the way of violence
is sacrosanct. There are other ways of transcending the alienations of subjectivity.

If we are duped by patriarchy and equate subjectivity with
transcendence, transcendence with risk, and risk with violence,
we will forget that risk is crucial to subjectivity because it
affirms the spontaneities and anxieties of intentionality/free-
dom, and forget that those spontaneities and anxieties can be
lived in more than one way. They can be lived through the
violence that destroys the given or the challenge that transforms it. They can be lived in the act that marks the world
with my meaning or by the gift that lets reality be. Nothing in
the meaning of risk justifies establishing violence as the only
route to subjectivity. Sports, adventures, erotic love are also
routes to subjectivity. Like violence they humanize the body.
Unlike violence they do not privilege the stronger body and
do not validate the objectification or subjugation of the other.

In appealing to Hegel's dialectic of violence but in situating
this dialectic in the material conditions of scarcity and the pre-
patriarchal hunt and "warlike forays" rather than war *per se*,
Beauvoir decouples the subject's assumption of the risks of
death from the subject's desire to dominate the other. Risking
death for Beauvoir distinguishes the embodied subject from
the thing. It does not entitle one to assume the position of master.
Where Hegel's dialectic establishes the necessity and intelligi-
bility of domination, Beauvoir's does not. On her account of
the values of violence and death, we cannot attribute woman's

---

[30] Eva Lundgren-Gothlin, "Simone de Beauvoir and Ethics," *History of European
Ideas* vol. 19, Nos. 4–6, (1944), pp. 899–903, makes the point that so long as women
accept their status as the inessential other the battle of the sexes is muted in that as
the inessential other women are outside the master-slave dialectic. In demanding
their freedom, women enter the dialectic and the battle of the sexes intensifies.
Lundgren-Gothlin argues that for Beauvoir and Hegel, entering the master slave
dialectic is the condition of authentic human relationships and that women therefore must enter it. I agree that this is true for Hegel but suggest that this is where
Beauvoir departs from a strict Hegelian account of subjectivity and recognition.

subordination to man to her retreat from the risk of death. Ultimately women's position and exploitation are historical contingencies that lack all marks of justification. The conversion of women to woman can be witnessed and described. It cannot be explained.

Defining the Neutral Subject: Ambiguity and the Erotic

The difficulties with Beauvoir's discussions of violence, transcendence and subjectivity parallel some of the difficulties of her discussions of the we-project. Though Beauvoir never intends to validate the dominations associated with violence or projects of liberation, she cannot erase them. So long as she is committed to the ethics of the we-project and the definition of subjectivity as transcendence, Beauvoir will find it impossible to affirm freedom and subjectivity without running the risk of violating the other. When she turns to the ethic of generosity and defines the subject as the ambiguity of immanence and transcendence, these risks disappear. As the ethic of generosity recognizes the otherness of the other for itself, defining the subject as ambiguous deprives violence of its subjectivizing possibilities. Once the definition of the subject as ambiguous is put into play, it is the erotic, ambiguous body, not the violent, transcending one that becomes the privileged site of subjectivity.

Beauvoir's muted voice challenges the equation subjectivity equals transcendence. It proposes an alternative formula for subjectivity: subjectivity equals the ambiguity of the body. In this equation, transcendence is moved from the defining characteristic of the subject to one possible expression of subjectivity. As ambiguous, the subject is also expressed in its immanence. The ambiguity of all embodied subjects now becomes a fluidity that escapes patriarchal, bi-polarized sexed identities.

Defining itself as ambiguous, the subject no longer experiences its immanence as an alienation. Aware of itself as expressing the active intentionalities of the project and the "passive" intentionalities of disclosure, the subject no longer experiences the passivity of the flesh as the threat of objectification. It now experiences its flesh as its other face.

Understanding that there are two voices speaking in *The Second Sex* and that each of these voices speaks for a different concept of the subject, we are able to understand the ways in which the meaning of the term flesh shifts in *The Second Sex*. When it appears in the context of discussions grounded in the definition of the subject as transcendence, it is a synonym for the objectified body—the body dominated by the other—the body that alienates me from my subjectivity by closing me off from my transcendent possibilities. In these discussions, Beauvoir accuses the myth of femininity of reducing women to woman as flesh.

Once Beauvoir defines the subject as ambiguous, her concept of the flesh changes. It is no longer a synonym for the body. Moving closer to Merleau-Ponty, Beauvoir now accords the flesh revelatory powers. Attending to the flesh's powers of disclosure and drawing on her analyses of intentionality, her ethic of generosity, and her understanding of transcendence as risk, Beauvoir, discovers the humanizing reality and ethical meaning of erotic love. Amidst all the discussions of the ways in which humanity, identifying itself as transcendence and equating transcendence with violence, has lived the bodily risk that characterizes the subject as violence, domination, conquest, and war, the few pages of *The Second Sex* dedicated to the analysis of erotic love reveal that of all the risk-taking activities invented by humanity, this is the most revelatory and dangerous.

As your lover I risk my subjectivity, not by daring you to kill or dominate me, but by asking you to accept the gift of my vulnerability as you recognize me as your other. Unlike the subject who pursues the risks of violence, the subject who assumes the risks of the erotic does not sacrifice the value/meaning of recognition to the demands of domination. Unlike the warrior who forgets our need for each other and unlike the patriarchal man who equates need with dependence, the lover who figures the subject as ambiguous recognizes that:

> In both sexes is played out the same drama of the flesh and the spirit, of finitude and transcendence; both are gnawed away by time and laid in wait for by death, they have the same essential need for one another ... [31]

This drama of essential need is not a drama that obliterates otherness. Lovers do not lose themselves in each other. They do not become one. Their giving to and receiving of each other is a concrete and carnal act of mutual risk and recognition.[32] In Beauvoir's words:

> The dimension of the relation of the *other* still exists; but the fact is that alterity has no longer a hostile implication ... [33]

In erotic love we must each assume our carnal condition as we ask to be received as free subjects. Given the myths of patriarchy which equate the flesh with the objectified, dominated subject and which teach women to see themselves as flesh in this degraded sense, erotic love promises to return women to their dignity as subjects. It promises to show men another sense of the flesh and to teach them to accept/experience themselves as flesh by exposing the deceptive privileges accorded to them by their aggressive role and by the "lonely satisfaction of the orgasm."[34] This enterprise, "fraught with difficulty and danger ... often fails."[35] When it succeeds, however:

> The erotic experience is one that most poignantly discloses to human beings the ambiguity of their condition; in it they are aware of themselves as flesh and as spirit, as the other and as the subject.[36]

---

[31] *The Second Sex*, p. 810/*Le Deuxième Sexe* II, p. 499.
[32] *Ibid*, p. 448/II, p. 477.
[33] *Ibid*.
[34] *Ibid.*, p. 450/II, p. 478.
[35] *Ibid.*, pp. 449–450/II, p. 478
[36] *Ibid.*, p. 449/I, p. 478.

This analysis of erotic love breaks new ground. Here the ambiguity of the body is embraced by the subject. The subject, instead of experiencing its flesh as the alienation of immanence, is aware of its flesh as the other it becomes for its lover. That is, flesh is not that which objectifies me, but that through which I express myself as gift. In offering myself as flesh I express the ambiguity of my subjectivity. As gift I am a transcending intentionality. As gifted flesh I allow myself to be taken by your touch where:

> in the midst of carnal fever [men and women are] a consenting, a voluntary gift, an activity; they live out in their several fashions the strange ambiguity of existence made body.[37]

In taking up the myths and mystifications of patriarchy, Beauvoir discovers the ways in which the myth of femininity bifurcates and sexes the ambiguity of the body as it relies on imaginary biologies to justify its positioning women as the inessential other. When she defines the subject as transcendence, Beauvoir charges patriarchy with exaggerating the marks of men's transcendence and of depriving women of their transcending possibilities. When she defines subjectivity as ambiguity, she charges patriarchy with repressing the subjective dimensions of immanence. From this perspective, when patriarchy reduces women to woman by imaging them as the other (of the immanent body) it alienates women from their subjectivity by alienating men and women from the lived meanings of their flesh.

The Inessential Other

A: Generosity
   The dominant voice of *The Second Sex* ascribes to the ontology of the look: our fundamental relation to the other is hostile. When speaking in this voice Beauvoir attempts to

---

[37] *Ibid.*, p. 810/II, p. 499.

explain women's domination by heading straight to the dialectic of violence. She calls man "a being of transcendence and ambition,"[38] describes human consciousness as imperialist, seeking always to exercise its sovereignty in objective fashion;"[39] and speaks of "an original aspiration to dominate the other."[40] In trying to understand woman's complicity with domination, however, Beauvoir uncovers a different ontological dimension of our being, the desire for reciprocity and the value of the bond. She writes:

> Thus woman may fail to lay claim to the status of subject because she lacks definite resources, because she feels the necessary bond that ties her to man regardless of reciprocity, and because she is often very well pleased with her role as the *Other*.[41]

In this sentence, Beauvoir attributes women's status as the inessential other to three sources. Two of these sources are familiar; one is not. The first source is economic and is addressed in Beauvoir's discussions of the independent woman. The third source concerns woman's attitude toward freedom and is addressed in Beauvoir's discussions of bad faith and complicity. The second source, the idea that woman accepts her non-subject status because "she feels the necessary bond that ties her to man regardless of reciprocity," is hardly analyzed. It is the sound of Beauvoir's muted voice. It tells us that where man forfeits the requirements of reciprocity in the exercise of his transcendence, woman forfeits the requirements of reciprocity in the name of the bond. Beauvoir does not approve of either forfeiture. She condemns both women and men for allowing it to occur. But in searching for an ontology of transcendence without domination, Beauvoir indicates that something more complex than Sartrean bad faith is at work when woman relinquishes her claim to subjectivity.

---

[38] *Ibid.*, p. 63/I, p. 73.
[39] *Ibid.*, p. 64/I, p. 74.
[40] *Ibid.*
[41] *Ibid.*, pp. xxiv–xxv/I, p. 23.

Without the horizon of *Pyrrhus et Cinéas, The Ethics of Ambiguity* and "Must We Burn Sade?" we might not see what is at stake. Without listening for Beauvoir's muted voice we might miss her crucial insight; for like the one little thing in *The Ethics of Ambiguity* that distinguishes Beauvoir's account of intentionality and guides us to the unique strain of her ethics, this one small phrase in *The Second Sex* alerts us to the distinguishing mark of Beauvoir's critique of patriarchy.

Coming to *The Second Sex* from *Pyrrhus et Cinéas, The Ethics of Ambiguity,* and "Must We Burn Sade?" it is impossible to neglect this reference to women's disregard of the demands of reciprocity. It is impossible to read it without thinking of the generosity that marks the ethical desires of the first intentional moment—the freedom that acts without concern for the pay off. Pondering this phrase, we discover that we misunderstand woman's place in the heterosexual couple if we only understand it in terms of negated subjectivity (understood as transcendence). We see that to adequately understand the meaning of patriarchy we need to explore the ways in which it corrupts women's generosity. Through this exploration we discover the full meaning of Beauvoir's designation of woman as the inessential other.

In arguing for the presence of a muted voice in Beauvoir's work, I am not arguing that the main lines of Beauvoir's thought are interrupted here and there by another way of thinking but that Beauvoir's thought is marked by two lines of thinking and that marking out both lines is important for assessing Beauvoir's place in the philosophical and feminist traditions. The concept of the inessential other is one of the places where the two lines of Beauvoir's thought converge. Reflecting the line of thought that identifies subjectivity with transcendence, the concept of the inessential other critiques the ways in which patriarchy equates transcendence with the values of violence and strips women of their transcending possibilities. Reflecting the line of thought that identifies subjectivity with ambiguity, the concept of the inessential other critiques the ways in which patriarchy represses the fleshed immanent dimensions of subjectivity and forecloses the possibilities of gifted generosities.

There is a radical difference between calling woman the inferior other and calling her the inessential other. Beauvoir is not always helpful in keeping this difference before us; for though she begins by showing us that it is by making woman the inessential other that patriarchy establishes masculine privilege, she often refers to woman as the other. In forgetting to preface every reference to the otherness of woman with the word inessential, Beauvoir risks muting her crucial insight regarding the difference between being the other that every human being is to each human being, and being the inessential other that woman is to man within patriarchy. Her forgetfulness ought not trigger ours.

Beauvoir develops the concept of the inessential other to explain the difference between women and other exploited groups. Other oppressed groups become conscious of their exploitation. They learn to say "we" to each other. They learn to see themselves as allies against a common oppressor. They rebel. Key to patriarchy's endurance is the fact that women do not rebel. Instead of coming together as allies, women ally with their oppressors. Isolated with regard to each other, women bind themselves in their individuality to their men.[42]

Beauvoir appeals to Heidegger's *Mitsein* and Hegel's master-slave dialectic to account for this unique phenomenon. Referencing Hegel and Heidegger, Beauvoir discovers that it is as the inessential other that woman does not, will not, and cannot challenge patriarchy. To clarify: it is as the inessential other who values the bond more than recognition that woman *will not* risk the bond by challenging patriarchy; it is as the inessential other who has been excluded from the dialectic of recognition that woman *cannot* challenge patriarchy; but it is as the inessential other who in her generosity *does not* demand recognition that woman embodies the value of the gift that

---

[42] *Ibid.*, pp. xxii–xxiii/I, pp. 20–21.

challenges patriarchy's values of violence and domination. Though Beauvoir's account of the *Mitsein* and reference to the bond does not convincingly explain *how* woman came to embody the value of generosity; her account of the pervasiveness of patriarchy and of the difference between women and other exploited groups depends on accepting that woman does embody this value.

Given the problematic nature of Beauvoir's position that woman's acceptance of nonrecognition reflects an insight regarding the primordial value of the *Mitsein*, we are left wondering whether woman's generosity might reflect the success of the myth of femininity rather than the presence of a fundamental way of being. In behaving as though there were an original *Mitsein*, are women mystified by the myth of femininity? Beauvoir's answer is ambiguous. On the one hand she will answer yes, for this behavior and acceptance is the source of women's exploitation. On the other hand she will answer no, for this behavior and acceptance speaks to certain phenomenological, existential, and ethical truths. According to Beauvoir, the bond between man and woman is the bond of the primordial *Mitsein*. In this bond, which Beauvoir refers to as the primordial unity of the couple, each is essential to the other; for the *Mitsein* as the heterosexual couple, expresses the common sexual desire and desire for children of both men and women. What we see in patriarchy, however, is that men and women live their fundamental desire for each other differently. Only woman recognizes the fundamental value of the *Mitsein*. Where woman, in recognition of her original desire, defines herself in relationship to the couple, man reformulates his desire and defines himself as the absolute, autonomous subject.

Given Beauvoir's repeated insistence on the singularity of the subject and her consistent, if muted, formulation of the ethical question as the question of generosity and otherness, this talk of a Heideggerian *Mitsein* seems forced and arbitrary. Within the context of Beauvoir's thought, the "we" is a (utopian?) hope, not something originally given. Beauvoir's analyses of the ambiguous subject and its erotic expressions, however, invite us to return to this idea of the *Mitsein* and rethink its role in Beauvoir's thought. Keeping these analyses in mind, we see that in identifying the *Mitsein* with the heterosexual couple Beauvoir is not necessarily validating heterosexuality and is not endorsing the patriarchal couple. Her claim that the couple constitutes an original *Mitsein* refers to the ways in which the erotic reveals the intersubjective realities of subjectivity. In identifying the couple as the original *Mitsein*, in identifying woman as recognizing the significance of this *Mitsein* when she forgoes the demands of recognition for the value of the bond, and in identifying woman as the inessential other, Beauvoir may be seen as formulating the question of *The Second Sex*: How does/did patriarchy transform the couple from the original site of the erotic expression of the subject into the place of woman's exploitation?[43]

Beauvoir's allusion to the *Mitsein* is brief, complex, and troublesome. It appears to undermine any appeal to Hegel's master-slave dialectic; for against the master-slave dialectic which would link women's otherness to an historical event, the idea of an original *Mitsein* refers to an ontological or biological fact. As an ontological fact it contests Beauvoir's subjective point of departure. As a biological fact, it carries no force in a phenomenological analysis. Tracing women's inessential otherness to the biological procreative couple is as misguided as tracing men's patriarchal dominance to the biological penis. Rendering the historical account of women's status as woman suspect and only appearing to validate the biological justification of patriarchy, the *Mitsein* reference makes two points. One, it reenforces the idea that woman is a myth unsupported by the materialities of history or nature. Two, in refusing to attribute women's status to an inferiority that would account for either her historical subjugation or biological insufficiency, it directs us to the difference between women as inferior others and woman as the inessential other.

---

[43] *Ibid.*, p. xxiii/I, p. 21.

In distinguishing between women's position as the inferior other and woman's status as the inessential other, Beauvoir argues that though women are regarded as inferior to men, it is their position as the inessential, not the inferior other that upholds the structure of patriarchy. The myth of femininity works on two levels. On the surface it situates women as inferior to men. Here it appeals to the ideal of the neutral subject and images men but not women as realizing the ideal. If we are taken in by the myth at this level and if we object to the position of women as inferior, we will organize our projects of liberation around the issue of equality. We will either claim that women are equal to men or insist that they be given the opportunities to become men's equal. Taking this route we miss the point of patriarchy. There is, Beauvoir insists, no neutral subject here; the norm is man.[44] The lie of the patriarchal neutral subject would have us believe that there is a neutral standard against which women and men are measured and according to which women are found lacking. The truth of the patriarchal subject is that the standard is man; and against this standard women cannot measure up.

As soon as we see that the standard is sexed, the game is over. Preventing us from seeing this is the key to patriarchy's power. Movements grounded in demands for equality lead to dead ends. They play into patriarchy's hand by accepting the reality of the neutral standard. It is time, Beauvoir says, to take a different approach.[45] Beauvoir's concept of the inessential other constitutes a fresh start. By exposing the lie of the patriarchal neutral subject it reveals the deeper workings of the myth of femininity. By refusing to equate women's liberation from the status of the inessential other with woman's entry into the domain of the patriarchal subject, Beauvoir indicates that the transformation of patriarchy requires a transformation of the concept of the subject. As neutral (universally accessible) it cannot be identified with the penis, violence, or domination.

---

[44] *Ibid.*, p. xviii/I, p. 27.
[45] *Ibid.*, pp. xxx–xxxi/I, pp. 30–31.

It must be able to accommodate the different ways in which distinctly sexed bodies live their transcendence and ambiguity.

According to Beauvoir, the patriarchal subject is analogous to the Hegelian master. Like the Hegelian master who succeeds in hiding his need of the slave by oppressing him, the patriarchal man succeeds in hiding his desire (need) for woman by exploiting her. Hegel's account of the master-slave relationship depends on the prior phenomenology of the demands of self-consciousness and the fight to the death. It shows us how equals, those who share the same value system and simultaneously demand absolute recognition, become unequal when one recognizes the impossibility of this demand and submits to the authority of the other. It shows us that the emergent inequality of the master and slave is the mark of two different value systems; for according to Hegel's dialectic, authoritarian subjects become slaves not because they are weak or inferior but because they determine that the value of life takes precedence over the value of absolute subjectivity.

Dismissing the explanatory value of the idea of women's inferiority, we are able to see why Beauvoir references Hegel's master-slave dialectic rather than Sartre's look to account for woman's inessential otherness. Sartre's look parallels Hegel's master-slave dialectic to the extent that both accounts of inter-subjectivity tie the demand for recognition to a contest between equally demanding authoritarian subjects. Beauvoir, however, indicates that women and men have never confronted each other in this way. Woman is not the one who is divested of the right to look. She is not the one who has lost the fight to the death. She is the one who has never had the right to look or to fight. If we try to account for this phenomenon in terms of rights, neither Sartre's nor Hegel's accounts of intersubjectivity are helpful. If, however, we approach the issue from the perspective of values, Hegel's master-slave dialectic offers some help; for Hegel teaches us that the difference between the master and slave is not a matter of rights but of values. Though woman was never man's dialectical equal and never confronted man as the slave once confronted the master, woman stands to man as the Hegelian slave stands to the Hegelian master insofar as both embody the value of the bond and both reject the ethic of violence. Aligned with the Hegelian slave, who aligns recognition with life rather than with death, woman represents the hope of humanity.

Seeing woman as recognizing the *Mitsein* of the couple and as expressing the alternative value of the generous subject who does not demand reciprocity, and seeing woman as analogous to the Hegelian slave who values life more than authority, we see the danger of giving the myth of femininity too much power. To portray woman as so mystified as to have no sense of herself may be too extreme. Like Hegel's slave, whose submission expresses the will to an other value rather than an absence of will, and like the *Mitsein* subject, whose acceptance of nonrecognition reflects the value of the bond rather than the flight of bad faith, woman may not be as abject as she appears. She too may be buying time. She too may be protecting another value.

It is true that we are dealing with brief references. But it is also true that in coming to *The Second Sex* with our ears philosophically tuned, we know that these references are packed with ethical and existential significance. This allusion to the bond and reciprocity catches our attention in part because it speaks to the irony, if not the tragedy, of woman's condition within patriarchy. In *The Ethics of Ambiguity*, recognition of our bond with others was the sign of genuine freedom; in *The Second Sex*, it is the mark of woman's exploitation. Noting this discrepancy we note the power of the serious man. We recognize patriarchy as a codification of seriousness and we see that generosity cannot be lived within a serious social/political structure without becoming a trap—an ally of the powers of subjugation. From this perspective, the story of *The Second Sex*, as an account of the genealogy of patriarchy, is the story of what happens when generosity and concern for/awareness of the meaning of the bond is transformed from an existential insight demanded of all of us into a codified sexed position called mother and wife, and only required of some of us. From this perspective, *The Second Sex* continues, with concrete historical specificity, the discussion of the perversions of freedom begun in *The Ethics of Ambiguity*.

The patriarchal perversions are unique in that woman as the inessential other is not quite reduced to a thing. Her generosity and concern for the bond simultaneously mark her freedom and subjugation. What should be a sign of her transcendence becomes a sign of her alienation. Instead of recognizing woman's signification of the bond as a sign of her value, patriarchy signs woman as the one who acquires value only by bonding with men.[46] Within patriarchy woman does not choose the generosity of the bond. She is required to participate in the laws of bonding. According to the codes of patriarchy, she is required to subordinate herself to the requirements of the heterosexual couple. Once required, however, the generosity of nonrecognition is mutilated. Within the context of patriarchy, the generosity of nonrecognition becomes the ground of an ethics of exploitation. Given this context, Beauvoir determines that the route of liberation lies in the project and its expressions of transcendent subjectivity. She puts the ethic of the bond of the *Mitsein* aside for an ethic grounded in the ties of recognition. The ethic of the we-project is presented as an antidote to the mutilated ethic of generosity.

Given that the ethic of generosity which is rejected is a perversion of the real thing and given that once the question of ethics is sexed, desire can neither be confined to nor exhausted within the space of the project, the question of the relationship between the ethic of spontaneous generosity and the ethic of the project remains. The question of the bond/couple is one of the places where this question presents itself. Though Beauvoir does not take up the questions of the couple and generosity again until the end of the second volume—that she returns to it again (that she must return to it again?) indicates,

---

[46] bell hooks. *Feminist Theory From Margin To Center* (Boston: South End Press, 1984), p. 43.

perhaps, that the privileging of the project that dominates *The Second Sex* is a strategic rather than an absolute privileging. That is, perhaps this privileging of the project speaks for what must be done now in the face of patriarchy's perversions rather than for an absolute ethical position. Eliminating patriarchy is what *The Second Sex* is about. If it succeeds in its aim, its success would force us to reconsider the meanings of generous, erotic, and excessive subjectivity and would allow us to reconsider the relationship between the subject defined as transcendence and the subject defined as ambiguous.

If we look at the places where the issues of generosity, the bond, and the erotic are raised rather than the amount of space dedicated to them, we see that the suggestion in *Pyrrhus et Cinéas* that generosity be taken as the model of ethical action is still at work. We see that the problems *Pyrrhus et Cinéas* and *The Ethics of Ambiguity* identified regarding the project still trouble Beauvoir and that the model of generosity, now eroticized, still presents itself as an antidote to the desires of mastery that infect the project and to the absence of intimacy that characterizes it.

Given the text of *The Second Sex*, we cannot determine how Beauvoir understood the relationship between her project ethic of liberation and her erotic ethic of generosity. For though *The Second Sex* gives us an account of the moral possibilities of the erotic, it does not discuss the ways in which these possibilities intersect with the ethic of the project. In inviting us to explore these possibilities and intersections, *The Second Sex* establishes Beauvoir's legacy to us. It may be seen as setting out the terms of a will that are not always clear.

B: Reciprocity

Beauvoir does not attempt to resolve the tension between the Heideggerian ontology of the *Mitsein* and the Hegelian dialectic of recognition. The *Mitsein* has a place in the line of thought that characterizes Beauvoir's muted voice. However, given that within the context of patriarchy an appeal to the *Mitsein* ultimately strengthens patriarchy's myth of the feminine, it is not surprising to find Beauvoir pushing the ontology of the *Mitsein* aside and returning to her Cartesian roots. "The fact is," she writes," that every concrete human being is always a singular, separate individual."[47] Given this fact, we begin with our differences from each other. The ethical question concerns the ways in which we negotiate these differences. For Beauvoir the key to this negotiation is the concept of reciprocity. To be moral we must cultivate the desires of reciprocal recognition.

Attending to questions of negotiation and difference, we discover the fundamental immorality of patriarchy. It structures itself on the first recognizable human difference—sex—and codifies an order of non-reciprocal recognition.[48] In accusing patriarchy of exploiting the visibility of sexual difference, Beauvoir accuses it of essentialism. Her references to Hegel and Levi-Strauss bolster this accusation.[49] In appealing to the philosopher and the anthropologist, she shows that though it is true that sexual difference is the first difference that we notice, it is not true that sexual difference grounds the category of otherness. Otherness as a fundamental category of consciousness does not originally refer to sex.[50] Though Levi-Strauss argues that all societies structure themselves around binary oppositions he does not argue that these oppositions must be either sexed or non-reciprocal. Nothing requires that sex be recognized as a non-reciprocal difference. Patriarchy is a product of intentionality not nature. Its perverse demands reflect an incomplete understanding of otherness that is motivated by a refusal of finitude.

Hegel demonstrates that the demands of absolute, non-reciprocal, subjectivity/sovereignty are impossible to sustain at the universal level. Patriarchy localizes the demands of sovereignty. In patriarchy men agree in principle, if not in fact,

---

[47] *Second Sex*, p. xvi/*Deuxième Sexe* I, p. 13.
[48] *Ibid.*, pp. xvii–xviii/I, pp. 14–15.
[49] *Ibid.*, p. xx/I, pp. 17–18.
[50] *Ibid.*, p. xix/I, pp. 16–17.

that among men there is more than one subject, and that the other's subjectivity must be recognized. According to the structures of patriarchy, men also agree in principle and in fact that however it stands among men, between man and woman things are different. When it is a matter between man and woman, patriarchy counsels man that sexual difference justifies the (re)assertion of absolute, non-reciprocal sovereignty. Among men, Beauvoir writes:

> wars, festivities, trading, treaties, contests among tribes, nations, classes tend to deprive the concept of the *Other* of its absolute sense and to make manifest its relativity ... individuals and groups are forced to recognize the reciprocity of their relations.[51]

But between man and woman, Beauvoir tells us, woman is defined as:

> the incidental, the inessential ... He is the Subject, he is the Absolute—she is the Other[52]

Reading these contrasting descriptions of reciprocal and non-reciprocal relationships, we see that the effect of relying on Hegel's account of consciousness rather than on Heidegger's concept of the *Mitsein* is to accept the inevitability of violence. As individual and separate, subjects are originally hostile to each other. As conscious of their subjectivity, human beings assert their sovereignty. Whether this assertion is affirmed in the overt violence of war or in the more subtle aggressions of trade, it is only when this assertion of self meets a contesting assertion of self that the dialectic of reciprocity takes hold. We offer the recognition of reciprocity to the one who threatens our sovereignty. To say that men exist within the dialectic of reciprocity then is not to see men as peaceably inclined to each other. Men exist within the dialectic of reciprocity because they see each other as having the right to violently contest each other's claims of absolute sovereignty.

---

[51] *Ibid.*, p. xx/I, p. 18.
[52] *Ibid.*, p. xix/I, p. 16.

Understanding implications of the appeal to Hegel, we see that Beauvoir will not accept the idea that woman's physical weakness explains her subordinate position to man. Were it a matter of weakness, we would speak of woman as a loser in the struggle for recognition. In calling woman the inessential other, however, Beauvoir is making a more radical point. She is not saying that woman has lost the struggle for recognition. She is insisting that woman has been barred from entering the dialectic of reciprocity. One cannot lose a contest if the right to compete is blocked. It is because she is defined as the non-subject, who by definition cannot contest man's absolute subjectivity, not because she is physically weaker, that woman is not a party to the dialectic of reciprocity. Though the dialectic of reciprocity is a dialectic of aggression, this aggression is not always or only physical. Women's weakness would put her at a disadvantage in some contests but not in all. To appeal to woman's weakness as the source of her subjugation does not, for Beauvoir, ring true. Physically weaker men are recognized as subjects by physically stronger men. It is not the weakness of her body but the meaning of her body that is the issue. Woman is placed outside the dialectic of reciprocity because her body has been given the mark of the non-subject. It is as the embodiment of the inessential other, not as the weaker body that woman is barred from the competitions that establish reciprocity. As the physically weaker subject, woman could challenge man. As the non-subject, however, she cannot threaten his absolute sovereignty.

We must be careful, however, not to overstate the case for the non-subject meanings of woman's inessential otherness. However inessential she may be, woman is still an other—one who may or may not recognize others. The effect of patriarchy's strategy is to circumscribe without annihilating woman's status as a subject, a being who can confer the status of subject on another. As circumscribed, woman's subject granting power will reflect patriarchy's codes. As effective, her recognition will count for something. Though she will not be allowed to engage in the contest for self-recognition, she will be allowed to confirm the subjectivity of those constituted as essential.

Hazel Barnes' description of the relationship between Flaubert and his sister points to the ways in which woman's inessential otherness is essential to patriarchy. Having been barred from the contest for recognition, but retaining the authority to bestow recognition, woman becomes the place where man can explore the possibilities of his subjectivity without risking his status as the subject. Using the image of the mirror, Barnes puts it this way:

> In Caroline, Gustave found an active mirror to reflect his image— one with the docility but not the inertia of the looking glass. With her he could hope to create the particular image that she would objectify and reflect back as being him.[53]

Reflecting on this image returns us to the question of risk. We discover that man as the patriarchal subject wants it all. He wants to be recognized as a subject without facing the risks of being a subject. The myth of femininity, by marking women as woman, transforms this impossible desire into a lived possibility. Turning to woman as a subject, man can receive her recognition. Marking woman as the inessential other, man guarantees that his subjectivity will neither be negated nor contested.

Essential to this patriarchal dialectic of recognition is the claim that woman in recognizing man as subject also recognizes the truth of her inessential otherness; for this is the only way to keep the safe patriarchal dialectic of recognition from becoming the risky Hegelian dialectic. In trying to understand patriarchy's success in fulfilling man's fantasy, Beauvoir returns to the myth of femininity. She now gives us two ways of understanding its power. One refers us to the lie of the neutral subject and the broken promise of adolescence; the other refers

---

[53] Hazel Barnes, *Sartre and Flaubert* (Chicago: University of Chicago Press, 1982), p. 98.

us to the erotic ambiguous subject and the value of generosity. It seems to me that neither of these explanations is sufficient. The first explanation does not help us understand the difference between women and other exploited groups. The second explanation does not clarify why women but not men defend the value of generosity. It is going too far to say that taken together these explanations solve the problem of patriarchy, but it does not go too far to say that, taken together, these explanations make patriarchy more intelligible. For taken together we see that the power of the myth of femininity is not simply a reflection of men's ability to dominate/mystify women but rather an unhappy collusion of the demands of transcendence figured as violence and the desires of ambiguity figured as generosity.

Risking: An Ethic of the Erotic

The Second Sex examines the dynamics of subjectivity, sexuality, society, history, and embodiment. It examines the ways in which patriarchy coagulates sexual differences into systems of otherness that hide our fundamental ambiguity. It suggests that there is an alliance between sex and gender that is exploited by the dynamics of bad faith. Against this exploitive codification of bad faith, Beauvoir discovers the erotic body and through it retrieves the subject's ambiguity. The erotic-ambiguous subject does not experience the fleshed body as alienating. Aware of the dangers of embodiment, the erotic-ambiguous subject discovers that the alienating dimensions of the body do not tell the full story of embodiment; for it discovers that it is as flesh that it can live the meaning of its subjectivity as ambiguity.

The turn to the erotic is a crucial moment in Beauvoir's thought. It pulls together the existential themes of Beauvoir's philosophy, links her to the early feminism of Mary Wollstonecraft, and challenges the hegemony of the ethic of the project.

A feminist ethic (an ethic attentive to the exploitation of women) cannot ignore the question of the body. More specifically, it cannot evade the erotic meanings and possibilities of the sexed body. Attending to these possibilities, Beauvoir's attention turns to Sade. The asexual Hegelian dialectic is sexualized. Turning to Sade, Beauvoir discovers that all attempts to socialize the erotic fail because:

> eroticism implies a claim of the instant against time, the individual against the group; ... it is rebellion against all regulation; it contains a principle hostile to society.[54]

Having been tutored by Sade in the revolutionary possibilities of sexuality, Beauvoir is not taken in by him. She identifies his sexual rebellions as perverse patriarchal expressions of a flight from the flesh.

Learning from Sade to attend to the drama of sexuality, Beauvoir comes to this drama with two ethical insights, one phenomenological-existential, the other feminist. The phenomenological-existential ethical insight concerns the ambiguity of the human condition. The feminist one concerns the meanings which women give/bring to the erotic relationship. Working with these insights, Beauvoir introduces a new complexity into the transcendence-immanence dynamic of ambiguity. She first suggests that an adequate understanding of the erotic requires that it be understood as a relationship of gifted reciprocity and generosity. She then directs us to infuse the meaning of gifted reciprocity and generosity with what until now has been degraded and sexed as woman's feminine experience of the flesh.

In appealing to the humanizing powers of the flesh, Beauvoir takes up Mary Wollstonecraft's feminist call for heterosexual friendship[55] without following her example of

---

[54] *The Second Sex*, p. 212/*Le Deuxième Sexe* I, p. 263.
[55] *Ibid.*, p. 158/I, p. 188.

devaluing the meaning of sexuality. Beauvoir understands that though patriarchy uses sexuality to exploit women, to refuse to value the erotic plays into patriarchy's hands; for it is by marginalizing the gifting generosity of the erotic that patriarchy goes unchallenged in structuring the subject according to the ontology of transcendence, and goes unchecked in aligning the ontology of transcendence with the demands of violence.

Patriarchy would have us believe that our erotic relationships are natural/animal. Beauvoir shows us that the erotic belongs to the realm of the moral. Far from abandoning the drama of the erotic to the other side of our humanity, Beauvoir shows us that the way we live the erotic experience of abandonment in/to the flesh of the other is a defining moment of our being.

To read Beauvoir in this way is not without its dangers. Given the patriarchal legacy of the erotic; the ways in which the body has ensnared woman in her immanence; the ways in which romantic fantasies have anchored the myth of the feminine; and the ways in which woman has been the gift that marks her as available for man's exploitation; we need to consider whether a feminism that allies itself with the erotic is not offering itself as an ally to patriarchy. Further, given Beauvoir's rejection of "difference" feminism's attention to the body, and her commitments to *projects* of liberation, we need to consider whether our attention to the erotic, generosity, and the gift belies Beauvoir's intentions.

Given these dangers we must be careful. We must be careful not to bring ammunition to the enemy and we must be careful not to transform Beauvoir into something she was not. Being careful in these regards means insisting that the erotic relationship engages men's and women's bodies in the same ways. It means exposing the ways in which patriarchy has misread the body. It means getting beyond the idea that the male body bears the marks of transcendence and that the female body is otherwise marked.

Remembering Beauvoir's work on Sade saves us from romanticizing the erotic and from being naive about its safety. This de-mystified understanding of the erotic can be read back into Beauvoir's earlier works with interesting effect. The discussion of generosity of *Pyrrhus et Cinéas,* for example, takes on added meaning. We see that spontaneous acts of generosity are never without risk. Where, in *Pyrrhus et Cinéas,* the generous man risked having his gift reduced to an exchange object, in "Must We Burn Sade?", the risks are more dangerous and concrete. Further, bringing the discussion of the erotic to *The Ethics of Ambiguity*'s analyses of intentionality suggests that the relationship between the intentionality of disclosure and the intentionality of being may be concretized as the relationship between the erotic and the project. We come to understand that without the counterweight of the erotic, the project risks solidifying into the bad faith of the desire to be.

We cannot lift Beauvoir's discussion of the erotic out of its context. Keeping it situated we do not risk repeating the patriarchal mistake of bifurcating the meaning of the body into man and woman. What makes the erotic relationship phenomenologically unique and ethically important is its relationship to the meanings of risk, transcendence, immanence, ambiguity, and the flesh. It is as an erotically desiring embodied being that I risk myself before you in the most dangerous way possible. It is here that you and I are called upon to affirm our subjectivity without repressing the ambiguity of our condition. More than anywhere else, the erotic is the place where the risks of recognition are laid out. It is the place where I am called upon to risk my vulnerability before you and take up your vulnerability in my flesh.

CHAPTER 6

Erotic Generosities

Beauvoir's existential phenomenology challenges the priority of the Cartesian knowing subject. Spontaneity, not thinking, constitutes the original stance of consciousness. As a spontaneous, bodied intentionality, the subject is open to being caught in the ambiguity of its desires. Though her language of transcendence and immanence seems to repeat the errors of Cartesian dualism and seems to encourage patriarchy's degradation of the female body, we discover the difference between Beauvoir's thought and traditional dualisms once we place Beauvoir's discussions of transcendence and immanence within the context of her concept of ambiguity and once we listen for the persistent, though muted voices of her texts.[1] Listening to/for these voices, we discover that the ethic of the project, that ethical stance which privileges transcendence and appears to equate conditions of oppression with the conditions of immanence, is indicative of but one of Beauvoir's moral positions. There is also the ethic of the erotic. This ethic, grounded in Beauvoir's phenomenology of the original intentional desire, acknowledges the paradigm of reciprocity as it points to another moral paradigm—the gift.

---

[1] For a discussion of how the abridged English version of *The Second Sex* invites misunderstandings such as this see Margaret Simons, "The Silencing Of Simone de Beauvoir: Guess What's Missing In *The Second Sex?*," *Women's Studies Newsletter* 6:5,78 (1983), pp. 559–564. For a discussion of the history of the critical analyses of *The Second Sex*, see Jo-Ann Pilardi, "The Changing Critical Fortunes of *The Second Sex*," *History and Theory* 32:1 (1993), pp. 57–73.

Discerning the sounds of Beauvoir's muted voice—the voice that develops the erotic and radical implications of Beauvoir's theses of ambiguity and generosity—I hear the difference between Beauvoir's thought and the thought of Hegel and Sartre, and am struck by the affinity between Beauvoir and Merleau-Ponty. Further, understanding that Beauvoir's muted voice, like her dominant voice, is grounded in the idea of ambiguity, I find that its challenge to the project ethic of transcendence is not an oppositional challenge, but a dynamic one. It is not intended to negate the ethic of the project but to remind us of its limits and dangers.

It is tempting to separate Beauvoir's ethic of the erotic from her ethic of the project by calling one an ethic of personal relationships and the other an ethic of political/social interactions. However, Beauvoir's Sade essay, her observations in *The Second Sex,* and her remarks in various interviews preclude this sort of segregated reading. For though *The Second Sex* emphasizes the *extraordinary* character of the erotic, identifying it as a privileged experience of conflict and revelation and as a dramatic relationship between two individuals, it refuses to isolate the erotic or to limit it to the explicit sexual relationship. The source of this refusal is *The Ethics of Ambiguity*'s account of the original intentional moment. The rationale for this refusal is found in *The Coming of Age.* Reading from *The Ethics of Ambiguity* to *The Coming of Age,* we discover that the category of the erotic links the epistemology of joyful disclosure to the ethics of generous gifting and that as a phenomenological-existential-ethical category, the erotic expresses our basic orientation to the world and the other. This dimension of the erotic is best described in *The Coming of Age.*

The Coming of Age

The project of *The Coming of Age* is similar to that of *The Second Sex.* Like *The Second Sex,* it focuses on a group of people designated as Other; like *The Second Sex* it exposes the mythical status of the "facts" about aging and the aged; and like *The*

Second Sex it indicts society for its dehumanization of those it designates as Other. *The Coming of Age* also emulates *The Second Sex* in its method and scope. It trains a phenomenological lens on biological, psychological, and sociological factors in order to understand the phenomenon of marginalized otherness. In many ways, however, *The Coming of Age* corrects what Beauvoir sees as the flaw of *The Second Sex*. In reflecting on *The Second Sex*, Beauvoir says that were she to write it again she would pay less attention to the abstract issue of consciousness and more attention to the material conditions of scarcity. Though it is impossible to say what a revised version of *The Second Sex* would look like, *The Coming of Age* gives us some idea of how it might read. Where *The Second Sex* speaks of woman, *The Coming of Age* never speaks of the aged. Reminding us that old age is our universal destiny, Beauvoir tells us that its lived meaning is specific to our historical, class, and cultural situations. Where *The Second Sex* identifies the ways in which the myth of woman hides the diversity of women and does not seem to see that the single category of the inessential other may not capture the diverse meanings of women's situations,[2] *The Coming of Age* keeps making the point that if we speak of old age as a universal category we will miss the crucial differences amongst the aged that the myths and images of aging hide. Further, unlike *The Second Sex* which speaks of a single myth of femininity, *The Coming of Age* tells us that the image of the aged differs from time to time and place to place.[3]

What is most interesting about *The Coming of Age* from the point of view of the reading I am pursuing, is that in refocusing her attention to the specifics and diversities of the situation, Beauvoir does not silence her muted voice. Neither does she

---

[2] For a discussion of this issue see Elizabeth V. Spelman, *Inessential Woman* (Boston: Beacon Press, 1988). For a description of a situation in which the category inessential other would not apply to women see Angela Y. Davis, "The Legacy of Slavery: Standards for a New Woman," *Women, Race and Class* (New York: Random House, 1983), pp. 3–29.

[3] Simone de Beauvoir, *The Coming of Age*, trans. Patrick O'Brian (New York: Warner Paperback Library, 1973), p. 57.

center it. It remains as before on the margins of the text, quietly but insistently challenging the exclusive claims of the ethic of the project and quietly but persistently directing us to a phenomenology of the flesh and an ethic of the erotic.

Comparing the status of the aged to that of women as woman, Beauvoir notes that both occupy the position of the Other and that as Other both are subject to the powers of mythical, exploitive biologies. Though *The Coming of Age* pays closer attention to the diversity behind the unifying myths and works with a different conception of otherness, it sounds remarkably similar to *The Second Sex* as it traces the sources of the marginal status of the aged. While *The Second Sex* accused patriarchy of depriving women of their subject status by barring them from the project and devaluating the fleshed experience of the erotic, *The Coming of Age* argues that the non-subject status of the aged can be traced to the fact that they are barred from their project and erotic possibilities. The old man, Beauvoir writes, "looks to active members of the community like one of a different species."[4] Like *The Second Sex*, which attended to the givens of biology without allowing them to determine the meaning of the subject, *The Coming of Age* also gives biology its due. The lack of engagement of the aged, Beauvoir notes, is in part imposed from without and in part comes from within; for as we age, the body is transformed from an instrument that engages the world into a hindrance that makes our access to the world difficult.[5]

Paralleling the analyses of *The Second Sex*, *The Coming of Age's* analyses of the aged speak of the subject mostly in terms of transcendence and the project; but there is in *The Coming of Age*, as there was in *The Second Sex*, another voice to be heard. This voice speaks of the ambiguous subject, of the erotic rather than the instrumental body, and of carnal desire and erotic love. Again the references are brief, but again they reveal that far from being an erratic moment of Beauvoir's

---

[4] *Ibid.*, pp. 322–323.
[5] *Ibid.*, p. 470.

thought, the question of the erotic is present whenever Beauvoir turns to the specific issues of the body, the subject, and the Other.

Reminding us that sex is not reducible to biological or genital functions, Beauvoir tells us that however diminished the genital function of the aged person may be, the old person is still imbued with sexual and erotic intentionalities. Clearer about these intentionalities than before, Beauvoir describes sexuality as:

> an intentionality that the body experiences, lives through, an inten-
> tionality that exists in relation to other bodies and that conforms to
> the general rhythm of life. It takes form in relation to a world
> which it provides with an erotic dimension.[6]

This idea of an erotic dimension of the world is new. It goes beyond the intersubjective ethic of the erotic of *The Second Sex*. There, as here, Beauvoir speaks of the turmoil of the erotic as providing a unique opening to the other; there, as here, Beauvoir identifies carnal love as the most extreme and revealing form of the drama of reciprocity/generosity; and there, as here, the erotic is said to preserve the integrity of the subject as it breaches it. But here and only here, the erotic is accorded transformative powers; for here the reciprocity/generosity of the erotic is said to transform the world into a world of desire and this transformation is said to be tied to the person's integrity.[7]

The erotic, as described by Beauvoir in *The Coming of Age* is a matter of what Merleau-Ponty calls the flesh and what *The Ethics of Ambiguity* identified as the joy of the first intentional moment. According to Beauvoir, in desiring to desire, the aged maintain their commitment to the erotic world and remind us that the emotional warmth of the world is lost when carnal desire disappears.[8] As before, Beauvoir keeps this

---

[6] *Ibid.*, p. 472.
[7] *Ibid.*, pp. 473–474.
[8] *Ibid.*, pp. 474, 521.

attention to the erotic brief, and as before she leaves it to us to ponder its implications. But, consistent with her pattern, each time Beauvoir speaks in her muted voice she extends its meanings and implications. In *Pyrrhus et Cinéas* and *The Ethics of Ambiguity* this voice introduces the ideas of openness, joy, generosity, and the gift. In *The Second Sex* it links openness, joy, generosity, and the gift with the erotic's fleshed ethic of risk and vulnerability. In *The Coming of Age,* Beauvoir comes full circle as she moves the idea of the fleshed erotic back to the idea of an intentionality that imbues the world with warmth.

If we align the thought of the joy of disclosure with the idea of the erotic as disclosing the emotional warmth of the world, we find that the erotic event captures the otherness of being as it makes us at home in the world.[9] As fleshed intentionalities we pursue the disclosure of otherness because we find it joyful. We find the disclosure of otherness joyful because it is part of an emotionally warm/welcoming world. On moving the erotic from its specific intersubjective meanings to broader intentional meanings, *The Coming of Age* returns us to *The Second Sex's* allusion to the bond to suggest that this bond may extend beyond the ties of the couple. In its intersubjective sense, the erotic opens us to the human other. In its intentional sense, the erotic awakens us to the warm face of the otherness of being.

Romance, Marriage, Love

Attending to Beauvoir's muted voice and arguing that this voice directs us to an ethic of the erotic and an ethic of the flesh is, given the history and strategies of patriarchy, risky business, for patriarchy has appealed to the image of the feminine erotic and the myth of romance to reduce women to the inessential other. To make the case that Beauvoir's ethic of the

---

[9] In speaking of the erotic as an event, I am invoking the meaning of event developed in Lyotard's thought. See for example Jean François Lyotard, "The Sign of History," trans. Geoff Bennington in *The Lyotard Reader,* ed. Andrew Benjamin (Cambridge: Basil Blackwell, 1989), pp. 393–411.

erotic is liberating, I must make the case that Beauvoir's erotic is distinct from the patriarchal erotic.

Beauvoir's work on Sade makes it clear that she is aware of the risks of the erotic and its propensities for oppression. Her work in *The Second Sex* makes it clear that she is no fan of romance and marriage. *The Coming of Age* and *The Second Sex* indicate that Beauvoir's critique of sadism, her disdain for contemporary myths of love, and her rejection of current marriage arrangements, does not signal her refusal of the possibilities of the erotic and does not mean that she equates patriarchal institutions with the possibilities of the couple.

As Beauvoir's analysis of Sade reveals that sadism is a perversion of the generosity of the erotic and a betrayal of the intimacy of the flesh, the history of romance shows us the ways in which the myth of romantic love supports the patriarchal project of subordination, submission, and oppression by diverting the erotic from its generosities. The history of romance teaches us that erotic domination is not confined to libertine excess and abuse—it can become codified, institutionalized, and rendered respectable. It also teaches us to distinguish reified perversions of eroticism from the liberating possibilities of the erotic.[10]

Libertine bondage and the romanticized couple set the parameters of Beauvoir's portrayal of the erotic. Attending to the libertine, Beauvoir distinguishes the pursuit of autonomous pleasure from eroticism. Attending to the romanticized couple, Beauvoir distinguishes the scripted love of patriarchy from the spontaneous generosity of the erotic. Remembering that Beauvoir's idea of the erotic is linked to her ideas of risk, the gift, reciprocity, and *mutual* vulnerability, we will be saved (perhaps) from conflating her idea of the

---

[10] For an account of this history and its importance for feminism see: Germaine Greer, *The Female Eunuch* (London: Grenada Publishing, 1971); Laurie Langbauer, *Women and Romance: The Consolations of Gender in the English Novel* (Ithaca: Cornell University Press, 1990); Shulameth Firestone, *The Dialectic of Sex* (London: Grenada Publishing, 1972); Juliet Mitchell, *Women, The Longest Revolution* (New York: Pantheon Books, 1966); Willard Gaylin and Ethel Person, ed. *Passionate Attachments: Thinking About Love,* (New York: The Free Press, 1988).

generous erotic with the eroticized idea of woman; we will not make the mistake of accusing Beauvoir of reactivating old sexed fantasies.

Beauvoir's account of love, marriage, the erotic, and liberation in *The Long March* is helpful here. It is difficult to argue that after taking one trip and reading several books Beauvoir was in a position to assess the conditions of China or the role of women in Chinese society. Whether *The Long March* ought to be attributed to Beauvoir's naiveté, arrogance, or faith in her abilities as a phenomenologist-writer is unclear. The issue here, however, is not the psychology at work in Beauvoir's authorship or even the value or accuracy of Beauvoir's account of China, but rather the categories Beauvoir used to interpret what she took to be the status of Chinese women.

Following her admonition to herself regarding the abstractness of *The Second Sex*, Beauvoir focuses her attention on questions of labor and overpopulation. Following Marx's distinction between productive and reproductive labor, Beauvoir argues that China confined women to reproductive household labor because, given its "surplus" population, it did not need women's productive labor. Further, accepting the judgment that productive labor is valued because it is humanizing and that reproductive labor is devalued because it lacks humanizing force, Beauvoir tells us that by confining women to the reproductive sphere, the Chinese could equate their "surplus" population with women. As long as women were confined to work that was viewed as not specifically human, women could be seen as superfluous and treated as pure bodies—expendable and replaceable. Infant girls could be suffocated, drowned, or fed as fodder to the hogs.[11]

In *The Second Sex*, Beauvoir accused the myth of femininity of confining women to the role of the inessential other. In *The Long March*, patriarchal power is tracked to the politics of the family. Tracing patriarchal power to the first emperor Song's edicts of 966 and 977 which required extended families to live

---

[11] Simone de Beauvoir, *La Longue Marche* (Paris: Gallimard, 1969), p. 128.

under the same roof and which gave the father authority to arrange marriages, Beauvoir links China's exploitation of women to its strategy of repressing erotic desire.[12] *The Second Sex*'s charge that patriarchy violates women's and men's subjectivity is repeated here. Its claim that reclaiming the meaning of the erotic is essential for reclaiming the intersubjective possibilities of women and men is also reiterated; for according to *The Long March*, freeing the children from the desire of the father is crucial to the project of liberation.

Read from the perspective of *The Long March*'s celebration of marriages grounded in love, *The Second Sex*'s condemnation of marriage can be read as an attack on patriarchy's subversion of the promise of love. *The Long March* argues that liberating the children to/for their desire dethrones the literal patriarch. *The Second Sex* argues that to date, the victory that enabled the children to marry for love has only been a victory for the son. The daughter, freed from the authority of her father, remains the subject of and a subject to a desire that is not her own.

While *The Second Sex* and *The Coming of Age* point to the ethical dimensions of the erotic without directly pointing to the liberating and revolutionary possibilities of the erotic, *The Long March* links the erotic directly to the politics of revolution and liberation. It does not, however, address the question of the relationship between the repression of the erotic and the designation of women as surplus labor. It does not ask whether Chinese men would have consented to the shortage of women (a consequence of infanticide and the abuse and neglect of girl children) with its consequence of enforced male celibacy if they understood that in being deprived of the couple relationship they were being robbed of a fundamental dimension of their humanity. Here, as in her other works, Beauvoir identifies the possibilities of a line of inquiry directed by the erotic without pursuing it.

Reading *The Long March*'s account of desire alongside *The Second Sex*'s accounts of marriage, love, and the couple, we

---

[12] *Ibid.*, p. 124.

discover that though Beauvoir does not buy the fantasies of romantic love, she acknowledges the desires that fuel them. In attacking the fantasies she does not dismiss the desires. Though the dreams of the woman in love may be said to reflect the bad faith of a subject refusing to assume her freedom, they may also be said to reflect the legitimate, but betrayed, desires of the erotic subject.

According to Beauvoir, the error of the woman who pursues the romantic myth of love and marriage is that she looks to another to justify her life instead of assuming the task for herself.[13] Clearly a case of bad faith—or is it? Beauvoir suggests that we might wish to reconsider our facile condemnation. Bad faith, Beauvoir reminds us, is often, and especially for women, tied to the dynamics of the look. It is as the inessential other that the woman in love believes that her existence can be justified by her lover, and it is as the inessential other that the woman in love pursues an ecstatic union with her beloved where, with all boundaries dissolved, she becomes one with the man of her dreams. The woman who believes this is no abstract free subject abdicating her freedom. This woman is a concrete subject pursuing what every human subject pursues—transcendence. Love allows her to become, through the other, what she cannot, given the conditions of patriarchy, become for herself—an essential subject. It is by being loved by a necessary being that woman tries to justify herself. The justification fails. However much patriarchy may try to convince her that she is a being-for-others, woman, insofar as she is an ambiguous subject, can never become a pure being-for-the-other.

In following patriarchy's call to become essential by subordinating herself to the essential other, woman contributes to her self-mutilation.[14] This mutilation is not, as Sartre would have it, an act of bad faith and is not, as Freud claims, a characteristic of the female psyche but is rather an attempt to survive

---

[13] *The Second Sex*, p. 585/*Le Deuxieme Sexe*, vol. II, p. 200.
[14] *Ibid.*, p. 722/II, pp. 389–390.

the indignities of patriarchy. "For woman," Beauvoir writes, "love is a supreme effort to survive by accepting the dependence to which she is condemned."[15]

In attending to women fixed on the fantasy of love, Beauvoir discovers that by constructing women as woman, patriarchy appeals to the experience of being-for-others in order to inflate it. It takes this partial experience of subjectivity, and tells women that their unique identity resides in their ability to transform this particular aspect of subjectivity into the totality of their being. As constituted by patriarchy, woman is the being whose being-for-herself is collapsed into her being-for-others.[16] Insisting that the ambiguity of women and men is inalienable, Beauvoir insists that a woman's being-for-herself can neither be negated nor absorbed within her being-for-others.

Patriarchy relies on its myth of romantic love to camouflage the sleight of hand by which women's desire for transcendence is figured as fulfilled in their being-for-others. In consuming romantic fantasies women play into patriarchy's deal. The fantasy, however, may end up threatening the dealer's hand. For if it works to keep women in their place, it does so by appealing to their desires of transcendence. The time may come when women recognize the conflict between their desire to be recognized as a transcending subject and patriarchy's desire to reserve subjectivity for men. The time may come when women recognize the contradiction in equating their being-for-themselves with their being-for-the-other. The time may come when women decide that subordinating themselves to the prince, however charming he may be, is not the way to express one's desire to be essential.

Discovering the ploy of the romantic myth may help women see the contradictions in their current path to subjectivity. For once the goal of love is seen as patriarchal marriage, it becomes difficult to sustain the promise of romance.

---

[15] *Ibid.*, p. 742/II, pp. 414–415.
[16] *Ibid.*

Existing as the being-for-the-other of her husband, a woman's vicarious sense of being essential is eroded by the repetition and routine of married life. She discovers that though he needs clean shirts, doing the laundry neither validates her subjectivity nor identifies her with the subject whose collar is neatly starched.

Beauvoir may be identified with those feminists who attack the institution of patriarchal marriage as perverted. She may be aligned with those who insist that patriarchal marriage will remain perverted until women have equal access to professional lives. She may be seen as sympathetic to those who insist that for marriage to become viable we must reconsider the ways in which the responsibilities for maintaining the life of the home are divided. She should not, however, be confused with those who reject marriage altogether. That she rejected marriage for herself is common knowledge. We should not, however, be too quick to presume that her personal refusal of marriage or her feminist critique of patriarchal marriage signals her condemnation of marriage *per se*.

Marriage is not, from Beauvoir's perspective, a static institution. It is not what it used to be and not what it is capable of being. It is, at present, in a period of transition. And if in this period of transition we need to understand its history in order to escape its perversions, we also need to understand its possibilities. Glimpsing these possibilities and calling on her definition of subjectivity as ambiguity, Beauvoir writes:

> ... every human existence involves immanence and transcendence at the same time; to go forward each existence must be maintained, for it to expand into the future it must integrate the past and while intercommunicating with others it should find self confirmation. These two elements—maintenance and progression—are implied in any human activity and for man marriage permits precisely a happy synthesis of the two.[17]

---

[17] *Ibid.*, p. 480/II, p. 15.

The question is whether marriage can do for women what it now does for men. Or, more precisely put, the question is whether marriage can do for both sexes what it now does only for one.

Beauvoir transforms the romantic tradition's question: Are love and marriage compatible? into the question of the couple: Under what circumstances can human beings form couples that express the possibilities of their ambiguity? She, like the advocates of romance, values love, and she, like the advocates of romance, insists that only love can sustain the couple. Beauvoir's vision of love, however, bears little resemblance to the romanticized vision of lovers transported out of themselves under the influence of some mysterious force. Love, for Beauvoir, is a uniquely human phenomenon. It is an experience and expression of our fleshed ambiguity and transcendence.

The challenge of love, so far a challenge rarely met and barely, if ever sustained, is to save this expression of fleshed ambiguity and transcendence from collapsing into the imperialist transcendence of the look. Marriage, romanticized as the fulfillment of love, has, until now, betrayed love. It has undermined the fleshed transcendent desires of love by calling on the erotic event to justify a set of obligations.[18] Contrasting love with the current state of marriage Beauvoir writes:

> The delight the lovers give and take in mutual recognition of their freedom is what lends strength and dignity to physical passion; under these circumstances nothing they do is degrading since nothing is a matter of submission, everything is a matter of willing generosity. Marriage is obscene in principle insofar as it transforms into rights and duties those mutual relations which should be founded on a spontaneous urge; it gives an instrumental and therefore degrading character to the two bodies in dooming them to know each other in their general aspect as bodies not as persons.[19]

---

[18] *Ibid.*, p. 536/II, pp. 128–129.
[19] *Ibid.*, p. 496/II, p. 48.

Love is a unique expression of the embodied subject's desires. As passion it speaks to/for/of our embodiment; as a movement toward another it speaks to/for/of our transcendence; as that which creates the couple it speaks to/for/of the desire to sustain the meaning of the erotic event. This last dimension of love, its creation of the couple, is crucial. For if the spontaneity of love speaks to its unpredictability and openness, and if the passion of love speaks to the sensuous porousness of our flesh, love's couple speaks of generosity. It establishes the boundaries which separate love from other embodied pursuits of pleasure and situates the question of love within the moral domain.

Given Beauvoir's analyses, it is difficult to escape the conclusion that within the structures of patriarchy heterosexual love is either impossible or possible only as an act of defiance. So long as women and men situate themselves within the categories of the essential and inessential other, the requirements of the couple, assuming the risks of one's vulnerability and generously recognizing the other's vulnerability, are impossible to take up or sustain. The woman as inessential other expects something in return when she recognizes the essential other—her identity. The man as essential other risks nothing when he recognizes the inessential otherness of woman.

The conditions of the couple cannot be met within patriarchy because the categories essential and inessential other distort the realities of our being. If we take essential to mean the condition of being a transcendent, free subject, then the error of patriarchy resides in its reserving this condition only for men. If, however, we take essential to mean necessary, then the error of patriarchy resides in its affirming this condition for any human being. For if, given the first definition of essential, it is wrong to deny that women are essential, it is also, given the second definition of essential, wrong to affirm that men are essential. Given the first definition of essential, we are all essential. Given the second definition of essential none of us qualifies. As human, we are free and finite subjects. Our contingency is a crucial mark of our condition. We are simultaneously essential (transcendent subjects) and inessential (neither necessary nor absolute). The power of patriarchy resides in its attention to this truth. Its error and moral failure resides in the ways it distorts this truth by segregating the essential from the inessential realities of our condition according to sex.

Sade's writings and patriarchal romantic fantasies make it clear that patriarchy, instead of clarifying the two meanings of essential and using this clarification to properly situate us *vis-à-vis* each other, has a vested interest in conflating the meaning of essential as transcendent with the meaning of essential as necessary. Sade gives us libertines who as free subjects present themselves as necessary beings. Romance gives us the romantic hero, the idealized man who as free subject can confer necessity on the loved woman by drawing her into his sphere of necessity. Thus patriarchy allows both sexes to recognize the reality of the transcendence and contingency of the human situation as it provides each sex with a bad faith escape from the ambiguity of their condition. As patriarchal, man affirms his transcendence and recognizes the contingency of the human condition by calling it woman. As patriarchal, woman acknowledges her contingency and recognizes the transcendence of the human condition by calling it man.

To undo the meaning of patriarchy we will have to stop the meaning of essential from sliding from an indicator of our humanity (transcendence) to its falsification (absolute/necessary); for the oppressions of patriarchy stem as much from the illusion of essentialness as from the insistence that women are inessential. The conditions of the couple require that men, against the patriarchal myth, be recognized as contingent, and that women, in opposition to patriarchal gendering, be recognized as transcendent. These conditions, if realized, would undo the power of the modern romantic myth. It would no longer be possible for a woman to believe that loving a man would save her from her contingency for she would discover that," An authentic love should assume the contingence of the other, that is to say his lacks, his limitations and his basic gratuitousness."[20]

This discovery is crucial to the possibility of the couple. For once each sees the other as contingent, neither can transform the other into their sole reason for living.[21] Forsaking this illusion allows us each to recognize the other's transcendence without disarming our own. In Beauvoir's words:

> Genuine love ought to be founded on the mutual recognition of two liberties; the lovers would then experience themselves both as self and other: neither would give up transcendence, neither would be mutilated; together they would manifest aims and values in the world. For the one and the other love would be a revelation of self by the gift of self and enrichment of the world.[22]

Agreeing with Sade's condemnations of the hypocrisies of the married couple, articulating feminist criticisms of the romantic marriage, and noting the relationship between liberated desire and social and political liberation, Beauvoir provides a sketch of the erotic couple. Combining the honesty of the arranged marriage, which regards the couple as existing at the intersection of the public and the private, and the sensuality of the romantically envisioned couple, Beauvoir's couple is cognizant of its mediating role and transgressive possibilities. Like the subjects who constitute it, the couple is fundamentally ambiguous. Neither a pure social institution, nor a purely private affair, Beauvoir's erotic couple challenges the neatly drawn distinctions between the public and the private established by the liberal democratic tradition.[23]

In a perfect world the couple would not need to protect itself from the ways in which the social world institutionalizes

---

[20] *Ibid.*, p. 726/II, p. 394.
[21] *Ibid.*, p. 536/II, pp. 128–129.
[22] *Ibid.*, p. 741/II, p. 413.
[23] For a discussion and critique of this legacy of the liberal social contract tradition see Carole Pateman, *The Disorder of Women* (Stanford: Stanford University Press, 1989).

humanity. In an oppressive world the couple finds itself condemned to death. In our world, a patriarchal world in transition, the couple is a site of resistance and transformation. It sustains itself by rejecting the categories of patriarchy and expresses itself by extending its lived critique of patriarchy into the social and political arena.

Given its essential relationship to the possibility of generosity, the issue of love is moral. Given Beauvoir's descriptions of love, we see that it is as fleshed and sensual that the question of love is an ethical question. Given Beauvoir's analysis of the relationship between love and the couple, we see that love is a moral relationship with social and political fall outs. Taken together, Beauvoir's discussions of love, the erotic, the couple, and patriarchy point us to strategies of resistance that go beyond demands for economic and political equality for women. For though Beauvoir clearly believes that without economic and political equality women will be deprived of their status as subjects, her discussion of passion, the body, and the gift indicate that by themselves, revised economic and political arrangements will not transform patriarchy.

Returning to the early pages of *The Second Sex*, we remember that Beauvoir's case against patriarchy is fundamentally moral. As the inessential other, woman is denied her subjectivity. As the one who is exploited for valuing the bond, woman cannot challenge the patriarchal rule of violence. Beauvoir's stance *vis-à-vis* the violation of woman's subjectivity is clearer than her position regarding the rule of violence. Where the issue is subjectivity, *The Second Sex* is unambiguous: it is immoral to condemn women to the position of the inessential other. When the issue is violence, however, ambiguity prevails. As a Cartesian atheist who cannot resort to proofs of God to relieve us of our solitude, Beauvoir turns to Hegel's formula of recognition to establish the possibility of the "we." This formula privileges violence and this privileging of violence pervades *The Second Sex*'s discussions of transcendence.

But here, as elsewhere, more than one voice speaks. Defined as a risking that refuses the absolute of the given, the subject is defined as an ambiguity as well as a transcendence. Its coming into being is not necessarily linked to violence. As the route to subjectivity is marked by the courage to risk oneself for the meaning/value one brings to the world, the route to intersubjectivity may be marked by risking oneself for the value of the bond rather than by taking up the risks of death. Concretely, this means refusing the privileges of autonomous subjectivity (violently insisting that one's word is law) for the uncertainties of reciprocity (taking the place of the vulnerable subject within the couple). In turning to sexuality, passion, and the couple, Beauvoir's intersubjective directions are distinctly un-Hegelian. Exploring the implications of erotic passion rather than the meanings of the fight to the death, Beauvoir proposes that erotic passion, as unstable, unpredictable, and fleeting, is an event of paradigmatic significance.

The Feminist Erotic

It is important to be clear here. Beauvoir's turn to the erotic is crucial not because it validates the sexed and sexual body and not because it challenges the gender codes of patriarchy, but because it validates the sexed and sexual body and challenges the gender codes of patriarchy in accordance with the criteria of generosity and the gift, and according to the body understood as an ambiguous phenomenological intentionality. We have seen how the appeal to these criteria and this body distinguishes Beauvoir's erotic from the erotic of Sade. If we turn to the erotic of Bataille we discover the ways in which Beauvoir's turn to the erotic disengages her from her Cartesian roots and the influence of Hegel. For in turning to Bataille, whose turn to the erotic is in many ways reminiscent of Beauvoir's, we discover an unsuspected affinity among the Cartesian point of departure, the Hegelian dialectic of death, and the erotic cult of violence. Comparing Beauvoir's erotic to the erotic of Sade and Bataille, we discover the difference between an erotic that takes autonomy as its point of departure and an erotic that begins with the premise of ambiguity. Sade and Bataille approach the issue of autonomy differently. Sade refuses to abandon the myth of autonomy. Bataille, willing to abandon the myth of autonomy, remains tied to the image of autonomy insofar as he is unable to image the breach of autonomy as anything other than a painful cut. It is because Sade and Bataille link the erotic to fantasies of autonomy, that they figure the body as a fortress, autonomous, Lacanian ego-imago, and link the erotic disruption of the self with images of death and destruction. Once we see this fixation on autonomy as a symptom of man's misperception of himself as an essential other, we find it helpful to distinguish between Sade's and Bataille's accounts of the erotic and Beauvoir's, by referring to Beauvoir's erotic as feminist.

Like Beauvoir, Bataille recognizes the fundamental isolation of the subject, and like Beauvoir, he discovers the communicative possibilities of the erotic. He too discovers that it is neither through proofs of God, nor through the experience of the look that we discover the complex reality of our relationship/relatedness to the other and the world. He too discovers that it is through the experience of vulnerability that we escape the boundaries of the self and meet the face of the other/otherness. Between Bataille and Beauvoir we discover the difference between coming to the vulnerability of the erotic from the position of the ambiguous subject and the phenomenological body and coming to it from the enclosed body and the autonomous subject. Beauvoir, seeing the body already existing outside of its imaged limits and figuring the subject as already open toward otherness, sees the risks of the erotic under the sign of generosity and the gift. Erotic woundings occur, but they represent violations, not essential expressions, of the erotic event. Bataille refers to the idea of autonomy as an illusion and identifies the erotic as the force that shatters the illusions of completeness that support myths of autonomy. He tells us, however, that because we come to the erotic from the illusion of autonomy we are destined to experience the erotic as an attack on the integrity of our body and being. The line of his thought goes like this: I originally experience myself as an integral and autonomous whole, enclosed within myself and isolated from others. The erotic experience of vulnerability exposes the lie of my autonomy. Pursuing the wound of my vulnerability, I discover the route to the other. Given this line of thought, the ecstasy of the erotic cannot be severed from the pain of the wound; this pain is the price I must pay to live my desire for the other. Bataille's imagery is compelling: the wound that breaks the integrity of the body is the opening that makes access to the other possible.[24] Communication cannot be severed from annihilation. In Bataille's words:

> Ecstasy is *communication* between terms ... and communication possesses a value the terms didn't have, it annihilates them.[25]
> and
> Attracted to each other, a man and a woman connect through lust. The communication joining them depends on the nakedness of their laceration. Their love signifies that neither can see the being of the other but only a wound and a need to be ruined. No greater desire exists than a wounded person's need for another wound.[26]

Reading Bataille's and Beauvoir's accounts of the erotic against *The Second Sex's* account of gender, we see what happens to the same or similar insight—the idea of the erotic as the mark of my vulnerability and the site of my route to the other—when it is approached from the male myth of autonomy and essential subjectivity and the feminist critique of patriarchy. With Bataille, the Cartesian subject must submit to the Hegelian dialectic of violence or live the isolation of solip-

---

[24] George Bataille, *Guilty*, trans. Bruce Boone (California: The Lapis Press, 1988), p. 27. "The more perfect, the more isolated or confined to ourselves we are. But the wound of incompleteness opens me up. Through what could be called incompleteness, or animal nakedness or the wound, the different separate beings *communicate* ..."
[25] *Ibid.*, p. 30.
[26] *Ibid.*, p. 31.

sistic subjectivity. With Beauvoir, the contesting desires of the intentional, phenomenologically embodied subject make it possible to think of the openness to otherness as a joyful enfolding rather than a painful wound.

What is significant, however, is that despite these differences, both Bataille and Beauvoir are led to the flesh in ways reminiscent of Merleau-Ponty's wild being. Both see that ultimately it is as flesh that we meet the otherness of being. Beauvoir refers to this experience of the flesh as a unique sense of passivity. Bataille speaks of it as an experience of the beyond which:

> begins with a feeling of nakedness. ... Once naked we each open to more than what we are and for the first time we obliterate ourselves in the absence of animal limits. We obliterate ourselves, spreading our legs, our legs opening as widely as possible, to what no longer is us but is something impersonal—a swampy existence of flesh.[27]

The issue between Beauvoir and Bataille does not so much concern the fundamentals of the erotic as the images which are called upon to express them. Bataille, beginning with the male fantasy of the closed virginal body, invokes the image of the wound and appeals to the language of transgression to account for the erotic as an experience that breaks us out of our isolation. Beauvoir begins with the intentional body. This body is already open to the world and the other. As already permeable and penetrable, its vulnerability to the risks of the erotic does not require that it identify its openings as wounds and does not require that it link the pleasures of the flesh to the pain of laceration. Bataille's open wound is Beauvoir's warm opening. Where for Bataille the secret of eroticism is Hegelian—the risk of death that is present once the boundaries of the self are bridged—for Beauvoir the secret of eroticism is Husserlian—the joyful intentionality that brings us to the world and the other—the feminist secret of the bond.

---

[27] George Bataille, *On Nietzsche*, trans. Bruce Boone (New York: Paragon House, 1992), p. 98.

Beauvoir's erotic giftings are neither governed by Hegelian categories of recognition nor controlled by the intentionalities of the project. They are spontaneous abandonments of the demands of the Cartesian subject. As spontaneous, the erotic eludes our grasp. As a spontaneity that is transformative, Beauvoir's erotic challenges patriarchal, romantic, sado-masochistic, and transgressive images of desire. It suggests a vision of the couple where lovers discover that isolation is not a permanent mark of their subjectivity and that revealing their vulnerability does not necessarily expose them to violence.

Bataille's vision of the erotic is one of the most powerful accounts of the ways in which the myth of the autonomous subject determines that the parameters of intersubjectivity will be set by the dialectic of violence. In countering Bataille's vision of the erotic and providing us with a phenomenological subject, Beauvoir's challenge to Bataille and the patriarchal erotic calls on the erotic experience of immanence to provide us with an alternative vision of subjectivity and an alternative understanding of vulnerability. Within Beauvoir's thought this call and this vision are suggestive and provocative. She leaves it to us to work it through.

The Unlikely Ally: Irigaray

It is ironic that Beauvoir's erotic challenge to the patriarchal idea that fleshed immanence is a threat to subjectivity has been taken up by a feminist Beauvoir refused to recognize as an ally—Luce Irigaray. Following a line of analysis uncannily similar to Beauvoir's muted voice, Irigaray notes the way in which touch more than any other sense expresses and allows us to give expression to the ambiguity of our condition. "Touch," Irigaray writes, "is a more subjective intersubjective sense, it lies between the active and the passive."[28] Irigaray, like Beauvoir, pauses to explore this undecidable domain. Like Beauvoir, she discovers that exploring this intersubjective

---

[28] *Sexes and Genealogies*, p. 197.

dimension of subjectivity leads her to the "we" of the couple, and like Beauvoir, Irigaray situates the couple at the juncture between the private and public domains and determines that as so situated, the question of the couple is moral.[29] But where Beauvoir turns to the model of the generous man and the generous mother and to the phenomenon of the gift to explore the moral possibilities of immanence, subjective ambiguity/undecidability, and the couple, Irigaray turns to the pregnant body.

Like Beauvoir, Irigaray recognizes that patriarchy idealizes the pregnant body in order to define woman as mother and confine her to the immanence of the fleshed inessential other. But unlike Beauvoir, who attacks patriarchy's idealizations of the pregnant body by describing the pregnant woman as the plaything of obscure forces of immanence and calling the fetus a parasite, Irigaray rejects the patriarchal idea of pregnancy *per se*. To speak of the pregnant body as the passive instrument of species demands is, according to Irigaray, to be taken in by patriarchal myths. Relying on the research of Hélène Rouch, Irigaray repudiates the passive, parasitic characterizations of pregnancy. The pregnant body, she tells us, is engaged in an active-passive, immanent-transcendent dynamic.

According to Rouch, the biology of pregnancy reveals a complexity that is at odds with the cultural imaginary of the pregnant woman. There is, she tells us:

> a sort of negotiation between the mother's self and the other that is the embryo. ... There has to be a recognition of the other, of the non-self by the mother and therefore an initial reaction from her in order for placental factors to be produced ... It's as if the mother always knew that the embryo (and thus the placenta) was other and that she lets the placenta know this and then produces the factors enabling the maternal organism to accept it as other.[30]

---

[29] *Ibid.*, pp. 132, 145, 153.
[30] Luce Irigaray, *je, tu, nous: Toward a Culture of Difference*, trans. Alison Martin (New York: Routledge, 1993), p. 41.

Iris Young's phenomenology of the lived experience of pregnancy confirms Rouch's biology. Rouch, asking us to see the maternal body's recognition, acceptance, and sustenance of otherness as a "gift of generosity, abundance and plenitude to which nothing is owed,"[31] recalls us to Beauvoir's generous erotic. Young, in showing us the ways in which the pregnant and erotic bodies intersect, shows us that Beauvoir's discussions of the erotic are as potent a weapon for dismantling patriarchal myths of pregnancy as for challenging patriarchal figures of the couple.[32]

Silent on the possibilities of Beauvoir's erotic ethic and perhaps unaware of Young's phenomenological account of pregnancy as an erotic generosity, Irigaray takes up Rouch's account of the pregnant body and places it in the ethical domain. She writes:

> The placental economy is therefore an organized economy ... which respects the one and the other. Unfortunately, our cultures, split off from the natural order ... neglect or fail to recognize the almost ethical character of the fetal relation.[33]

Given Beauvoir's account of generosity and the gift, we discover that Irigaray understates the case. The fetal relation is not *almost* ethical, it is *absolutely* so.

If we accept the ambiguity of our bodies as indicative of the ambiguity of our subjectivity; if we accept Beauvoir's delineation of the ethical relationship; and if we listen to Irigaray, Rouch, and Young, we are challenged to revisit our assumption that to be ethical, activities must be consciously chosen acts of transcendence. As the first prereflective opening of intentionality creates the ground for the reflective moral acts of reciprocity and gifting, the spontaneous generosity of the maternal body is the source of the conscious moral commitment of the mother to the child.

Whether Beauvoir has been taken in by a patriarchal imagery which divests pregnancy of its activity or is over-

---

[31] *Ibid.*, p. 43.
[32] *Throwing Like A Girl*, pp. 160–176.
[33] *je, tu, nous:* p. 41.

reacting to patriarchy's distorting "religion of maternity,"[34] the effect is the same, she misses the radical implications of her affirmations of the erotic body. Depicting the mother as analogous to the woman in love insofar as both live in the joy of their generosity[35] Beauvoir tells us that:

> The child brings joy only to the woman who is capable of disinterestedly desiring the happiness of another, to one who ... seeks to transcend her own existence.[36]

She does not seem to realize that the maternal body has already expressed this desire and that if we take our cue from the body, we discover that as grounded in the body, the mother-child relationship expresses the immanence-transcendence ambiguity of the intersubjective relationship.

In generously sustaining the fetus, the pregnant woman gives it the gift of life. In generously loving her child, the mother allows it to discover its way in the world. Though this generosity is betrayed as soon as the mother identifies her interests with those of the child, maternal generosity cannot be said to be disinterested. It is not as a disinterested subject seeking to transcend my immanence that I offer the gift of love to my child. It is as an engaged mother who feels my child's pain in the pit of my stomach that I encourage this child to become the fullness of her otherness and wait to find her there. Maternal generosity, like the lover's erotic generosity, is the gift one makes of oneself to the other for the sake of the relationship which reveals us to each other in the intimacies of our fleshed being.

In refusing the patriarchal dualities that split the erotic and maternal bodies apart from each other, we do not appeal to the category of the erotic as an excuse for collapsing all distinctions. As erotic, the nursing breast is not experienced in the same way as the breast caressed by a lover. As erotic, the mother-infant/child relationship is not the same as the relationship between lovers. As erotic, however, these relationships

[34] *The Second Sex*, p. 573/*Le Deuxième Sexe II*, p. 181.
[35] *Ibid.*, p. 572/II, p. 181.
[36] *Ibid.*, p. 583/II, p. 196.

express the desires of the erotic. They express the fact that we cannot, as bodied beings, substitute the abstract idea of recognition for the touch that acknowledges us in our fleshed sensuality.

We are, perhaps, still scandalized by Freud's idea of infantile sexuality. This idea, essential to the thought of the man often though of as misogynist, is fundamentally disruptive to the modern patriarchal vision of maternal purity and childhood innocence. Freud's declaration of infantile sexuality is crucial to a feminist theory of the erotic. It tells us that we cannot tack the erotic onto the body after the fact or at a certain developmental date, but that we must view the erotic and the body as coextensive and coexistent. As embodied subjects we are also and necessarily erotic and it is as erotic, that we pursue our desires for the other.

The Oedipus complex is Freud's way of telling the story of the erotic, embodied subject's search for recognition. As Freud tells it, the child begins by demanding that it be recognized as the absolute subject—omnipotent in its abilities to fulfill the mother's desire and impervious to the presence of the father. This demand, based on the infant's misunderstanding of its human condition, cannot be met. It must be given up. The resolution of the Oedipus complex marks the abandonment of the child's misunderstanding. It marks the child's acceptance of its finitude and, in accordance with this acceptance, it marks a reformulation of the child's desire. The child puts aside its absolute demands, exchanges them for the pleasures of reciprocity. In Jessica Benjamin's words:

> The erotic component of infant life is bound up with recognition ...
> the struggle for recognition requires the self to relinquish its claim
> to absoluteness.[37]

The child is no abstract thinker. It does not understand the contradiction in positing itself both as an absolute subject and as the absolute object of the mother's desire. It *experiences* the

---

[37] Jessica Benjamin, *The Bonds of Love* (New York: Pantheon Books, 1988), p. 49.

impossibility of its desire. How we account for this experience is crucial. If, with Freud, we account for it with a castration theory that radically distinguishes the boy's experience of finitude from the girl's, we will end up reinstituting the patriarchal differences unsettled by the thesis of infantile sexuality. We will end up reestablishing the sexual difference as a difference that precludes heterosexual reciprocity. If we appeal to Lacan's modification and speak of boys and girls as experiencing the cut of castration equally and if, with Lacan, we insist on the distinction between having and being the phallus, we will (despite our insistence on the equal cut) have trouble resisting the patriarchal equation phallus equals penis.[38]

To make the case that the erotic propels us toward reciprocal relationships, and to suggest that erotic desire is the ground of the generous moral relationship, we will need to elude the Oedipal trap. Irigaray shows us how this may be done. Instead of directing our attention to the penis, phallus, and father, she directs our attention to birth, the womb, the umbilical cord, and the mother. She tells us that we experience the cut of finitude at birth and that the wound that marks us as human predates all symbolic codings. It is as the body that is not yet sexed that we are cut off from the fetal experience of plenitude. By retrieving this pre-Oedipal experience of the cut that defines us as finite and human, it is possible to retrieve the erotic as the desire that searches for a lost plenitude without being seduced by patriarchal myths of necessary and autonomous subjectivity. Following Kristeva's turn to King Solomon's "Song of Songs" and remembering that the erotic is characterized by risk, we discover the urgency of retrieving the cut of the cord and exposing the politics of phallic symbols and the castration complex. Kristeva reads the "Song of Songs" to speak of bonds of love and an amorous subjugation of reciprocity.[39] In reminding us that the dialogue of the erotic

---

[38] Debra Bergoffen, "Queering the Phallus," *Disseminating Lacan*, ed. David Pettigrew and François Raffoul (New York: State University of New York Press, 1996), pp. 273–291.

[39] Julia Kristeva, *Tales of Love*, trans. Leon Roudiez (New York: Columbia University Press, 1987), pp. 93–94.

is a dialogue of mastery and recognition, Kristeva alerts us to the affinity between the erotic and Hegelian desires for recognition. Sensitive to this affinity, we see how the patriarchal dialectic of domination can overload the fluidity of the erotic. We understand how the erotic master can be seduced into believing that he is the patriarchal absolute subject, and how the erotic submissive lover can be seduced into believing that she is the inessential other of patriarchy.

We are not accustomed to speaking of reciprocity in the context of a dialogue of mastery and submission. We are used to thinking of mastery and submission as precluding dialogue. From Kristeva's point of view this is because we are not experienced in confronting the risks of the erotic outside of sadistic, masochistic, or romantic patriarchal scripts. Coming to the erotic as either essential or inessential subjects, we are unable to explain, imagine, or sustain the fluidity of the risks of the erotic event.

Putting the insights of Kristeva, Young, Irigaray, and Beauvoir together confirms the suspicion that removing the phallus as the universal emblem of desire is crucial to transforming the erotic from a game of domination to the amorous space of the gift. Suspicions are important guides to thinking. They are not, however, effective as strategies of liberation. Irigaray's analysis of the repression that powers the reign of the phallus directs us from suspicion to strategy. As Irigaray tells it, the reign of the phallus hides the secret of the womb. The cut of castration hides a prior cut—the cut of the cord. "When the father or mother threaten Oedipus with scissors or knife," Irigaray writes, "they forget that the cord, already, has been cut and that all that is needed is to take cognizance of that fact."[40]

Irigaray insists that this is no innocent forgetfulness. It is the motivated work of repression intent on murdering the mother so that the father may rule—preserve his desires of omnipotence. The paternal symbolic order severed from the

---

[40] *Sexes and Genealogies*, p. 16.

flesh, the blood, and the body of woman rests on this repression. Within this order, the threat of castration masks the relationship of the penis to the umbilical cord. Instead of offering man a way back to the mother, the penis becomes the horror of the tie to the mother. It threatens man with madness and more if he sees his way back to the mother through it.

Inundated with symbols of castration, we lack symbols for the cut cord and our original loss. Inundated with myths of the law of the father, we are bereft of images for our original bond with the mother. The effect, according to Irigaray, is disastrous, for:

> desire becomes a bottomless pit if the time spent in utero is a taboo issue and if no attempt is made to interpret and come to terms with the losses and scars involved in our separation from that primary home and that first nurse.[41]

Substituting the secondary cut of castration for the primary cut of the cord, we do not confront the wound that can never heal and that we all share. Substituting the law of the father for the body of the mother, we preclude the possibility of heterosexual reciprocity. Were the cut of castration primary, the impossibility of heterosexual reciprocity would be as inevitable as Freud postulated. Seeing the cut of castration as secondary, Irigaray can propose an alternative reading of the Oedipal story—one that holds out the promise of heterosexual reciprocity.

Irigaray's reading of Oedipus rearranges the sexual order from the order of an essential one who speaks and an inessential one who is silent and spoken for, to an order where discourses of otherness discover their possibilities. On Irigaray's reading:

> [Oedipus'] murder of the father means not a desire to take the father's place as rival and competitor, but a desire instead to do away with the one who has artificially severed the bond with the mother in order to take over the power of creating a world, particularly a female one. According to this interpretation, phallic

---

[41] *Ibid.*, pp. 15–16.

erection, far from being all powerful would be the masculine version
of the umbilical cord ... At the very place where there once had
been the cord, then the breast, would appear for the man, the penis
which reconnects, gives life, feeds and recenters the bodies. The
penis evokes something of the life within the womb ... As it softens
and falls it evokes the end, the mourning, the ever open wound ...
a return to the world that allows [men] to become sexual adults
capable of eroticism and reciprocity in the flesh.[42]

Irigaray's theory of repression takes up Beauvoir's analyses
of the relationship between the invitations of biology and the
categories of patriarchy. It resolves Beauvoir's puzzle (how is
it that patriarchy "forgets" the immanence of the flaccid penis
in its valorization of the erect penis?) as it links the issue of the
flacid penis to the issue of the possibility of a reciprocal
heterosexual eroticism—an issue that is crucial to Beauvoir's
feminism.

We do no justice to the thinking of Beauvoir or Irigaray if
we miss the distinctive paths of their thought. But, we do no
justice to the history of feminism if we fail to see that for all
their differences, Beauvoir's and Irigaray's critiques of patriarchy speak to each other, sometimes quite directly. As an
analyst committed to the reality of a dynamic unconscious
and focused on the question of language, Irigaray's priorities
differ from those of Beauvoir, for whom materiality means
economic and political institutions, not words. But if it is the
case that Beauvoir looks to economics to alter the situation of
woman, it is also the case that Beauvoir understands that
economics alone will not transform woman from an inessential
to an essential other. The independent woman will not be
born independent, she will have to become independent.
Prevailing images of women will be crucial to her process of
becoming. Irigaray takes up Beauvoir's thesis of mystification
and runs it in another register. Demystifying woman, Irigaray
tells us, is a matter of reworking the symbolic order. The
fundamental myth of patriarchy is the myth of Oedipus, with

---

[42] *Ibid.*, p. 17.

its spoken crimes of patricide and incest and its unspoken crime of matricide. As Irigaray sees it, the reciprocity Beauvoir calls for and the gifting erotic she hopes for will remain utopian fantasies until and unless patriarchy revisits its Oedipal unconscious, owns up to its crime of matricide and reconnects itself to the maternal body.

Humanist Possibilities—Erotic Legacies

Reading Beauvoir as a phenomenologist-existentialist who speaks in a muted and dominant voice, I have been led to associate Beauvoir with unlikely names. Though Beauvoir offers us the unlikely name Bataille herself, in associating what I have called Beauvoir's feminist ethic of erotic generosity with Kristeva's bond of love and Irigaray's maternal body, I call up names and feminisms that Beauvoir set at a distance. It may be that Beauvoir's legacy of the erotic does not lead in these directions. It may be that in distancing herself from Kristeva and Irigaray, Beauvoir misread the implications of her muted voice or misunderstood the significance of the psychoanalytic and symbolic critiques of patriarchy. Or, it may be that my claim that Beauvoir's muted voice transforms the erotic from a marginal dimension of our being to the site of a paradigmatic ethical event misses the mark. I take some comfort in the company of Michelle Le Doeuff with regard to this last possibility. Where I have appealed to the influences of phenomenology and Merleau-Ponty to make the case that Beauvoir's theories of intentionality and ambiguity establish the ground of an ethic of erotic generosity, Michelle Le Doeuff identifies the erotic as a crucial element in Beauvoir's thought by tracking the tensions between Beauvoir's commitments to existentialism and humanism. Though we come from different directions and are led to different conclusions, we share the same insight: an adequate understanding of Beauvoir requires an attention to the role of the erotic in her thought.

According to Le Doeuff, Beauvoir's feminism is best understood as an attempt to resolve the competing demands of the existential value of freedom and the humanist value of happiness. On the one hand, the issue of woman is the issue of liberation. As Beauvoir will not equate freedom with happiness, she does not, from this existential perspective of freedom and liberation, raise the question of happiness. Beauvoir is not, however, willing to sacrifice happiness to freedom. From my point of view, this unwillingness can be traced to Beauvoir's commitment to the joy of intentionality. From Le Doeuff's perspective, Beauvoir's attention to happiness should be traced to her commitment to humanism. From both points of view, analyses of Beauvoir's attention to freedom/transcendence and happiness/joyful generosity leads to the erotic and to the insight that the erotic is a crucial element of Beauvoir's thought.

Within Beauvoir's thought, the erotic becomes a philosophical category that carries moral weight because as an event the erotic is the site where the demands of freedom and happiness engage each other. According to Le Doeuff, it is in confronting the nexus between freedom and happiness as it appears in the erotic that Beauvoir steps out of the existential field.[43] Given Le Doeuff's perspective, Part IV and the chapter called "The Married Woman" are crucial to *The Second Sex*, for it is here that Beauvoir links the demands of existentialism and humanism by establishing the thesis that freedom is a necessary condition for the happiness of love and sexuality.[44]

Whether we take Le Doeuff's route of humanism or my route of intentionality, we arrive at the same place—the erotic is the point at which Beauvoir's thought exceeds the boundaries of Sartrean existentialism.[45] It is the place where we hear the distinct/distinctive voice of Simone de Beauvoir.

In positing an ethic of the erotic where freedom is identified as the condition of the possibility of the paradigmatic moral act—the gift of passion that reveals us to ourselves and to

---

[43] Michelle Le Doeuff, *Hypparchia's Choice*, trans. Trista Selous (Oxford: Blackwell, 1991), pp. 115–116.
[44] *Ibid.*, p. 113.
[45] *Ibid.*, p. 114.

each other in our joy, our vulnerability, our generosity, and our subjectivity—Beauvoir asks us to reconsider the meanings of intersubjectivity. She asks us to refuse the valorization of violence that marks patriarchy's misreading of transcendence.

Severing the idea of transcendence from the phenomenon of violence, Beauvoir restores transcendence to its original and critical meaning—risk. Instead of allowing the patriarchal validation of violence to pervert the meaning of risk, Beauvoir analyzes the ways in which the meaning of risk is illuminated in the experience of the erotic. In turning to the erotic and the couple sustained by it, Beauvoir's ethic provides us with a paradigm of recognition where generosity and the reciprocity of the gift, rather than violence and the fight to the death, constitute the way in which we acknowledge our need of and relatedness to each other.

This ethic calls on me to see the other as the one who reflects me to myself by showing me the otherness of my being. It does not, however, identify the other as my double. And this, from a Lacanian perspective, is the key to the escape from violence. In recognizing you as the one who is an-other, and in affirming your alteriority, I am able to recognize you as a subject like myself without triggering the aggressivity of the ego that inaugurates the Hegelian war of all against all, and without instituting the master-slave relationship that sustains the patriarchal category of the inessential other.[46]

Beauvoir's ethic of the erotic carries two injunctions. First, I am enjoined to assume/accept the risks of my ambiguity. Second, I am enjoined not to violate the other's vulnerability. Together, these injunctions create the opening for a meeting between others—an opening that we might call the space of generous intersubjectivity. This generosity is feminist insofar as it validates the value that women have protected throughout the patriarchal era—the value of the bond. This generosity is feminist insofar as it refuses to allow the value of the bond

---

[46] Jacques Lacan, *Ecrits*, trans. Alan Sheridan (New York: W. W. Norton, 1977), pp. 8–29.

to be mutilated by the demands of a subject committed to the intersubjectivity of violence and violation. It is feminist insofar as it refuses to allow the value of the bond to become a sacrificial value. It rejects the idea that those who value the bond are obliged to subordinate the demands of reciprocity to the demands of the absolute subject and refuses to relegate those who value the bond to the position of the inessential other.

Beauvoir's ethic as feminist is not only for women. It is an impossible ethic for both men and women who adopt the genderings of patriarchy. An ethic of erotic generosity cannot find a place among those who prefer the securities of inequality to the risks of reciprocity. It is, however, a possible ethic for those men and women who understand that it is neither as men nor as women, but rather as ambiguously fleshed embodied intentionalities that they approach the place of the subject. They understand that this place is an opening not an enclosure. Entering this opening, these men and women do not allow their desires of disclosure to be foreclosed by the demands of their desire to be. Willing to assume the risks of their fleshed ambiguity and recognizing their mutual need of and vulnerability to each other, these men and women do not violate the generosity of the one who offers them the gift of love's fleshed bond.

EPILOGUE

Epilogue

A book dedicated to the un-thought of Beauvoir's work is a paradoxical enterprise. On the one hand, the point of the book is to assert the presence of a thinking that is integral to the body of Beauvoir's philosophy. On the other hand, it recognizes that the thinking it points to is barely acknowledged by Beauvoir herself.

I do not pretend to understand why the category of the erotic, the revised description of intentionality, the paradigm of generosity, and the ethic of the gift remained on the margins of Beauvoir's work. I do hope to have made the case that the category of the erotic, as grounded in Beauvoir's analyses of intentionality, ambiguity, embodiment, and the other, and as the ground of an ethic that calls on us to partake in the risks of recognition according to the rule of the gift rather than the law of the look, is both a stable feature of Beauvoir's thought and a legacy that warrants our attention.

In attending to the phenomenon of the erotic, Beauvoir blurs the distinction between the private and the public, the event and the paradigm, transcendence and immanence, transgression and affirmation, the I and the other. She leads us to suspect that in insisting on these boundaries and in erasing the marks of our ambiguity, patriarchy is intent on maintaining an anti-human social order. She shows us that in teaching us to approach the erotic as a temporary upsurge that only fleetingly disturbs things, and in insisting that the erotic disturbance, as an irrational impulse, ultimately counts for nothing, patriarchy is protecting itself from the fundamental challenge of the erotic event. For once we see that the spontaneous dynamic of the erotic is an event that offers us the paradigms of the gift and generosity, and once we discover the ways in which these paradigms free the meaning of risk from its patriarchal associations with violence and death, we understand that far from being an erratic moment that changes nothing, the erotic is the event that changes everything—or at least could change everything if we gave it the attention it deserves.

Perhaps Beauvoir's persistent references to the erotic and insistent development of its meanings never make it to the center of her thought because she could not break through the taboos on this way of thinking. Or perhaps the ethic of erotic generosities remains on the margins of Beauvoir's thought because she did not believe that this way of thinking could come into its own until the project of liberation was more concretely realized. Whatever Beauvoir's reasons may have been, it seems to me that it is time to break the taboo on this way of thinking and time to say that far from being an unrealistic, naive, or diversionary mode of thought, this way of thinking recognizes the fullness of human desire and the complexity of the ethical question. Further, while I do not believe that thinking through the meanings of the erotic can, by itself, create the conditions of a just society, I do not think that a just community can come into being if the meanings of the erotic are not brought to bear on the realities of social, political, and ethical life.

Beauvoir's muted voice provides us with a gendered phenomenology that speaks of an ethic of erotic generosity. It directs us to reconsider Merleau-Ponty's allusions to wild being and the flesh. It asks us to resituate ourselves *vis-à-vis* the other and to rethink our notions of subjectivity, the bond, and the "we."

As muted, Beauvoir's directives are unmapped openings. It is up to us to chart their territory. Remembering that these directives are part of a thinking that insists on the complexity and ambiguity of the human condition we are reminded that the erotic route to the "we" is ethically dangerous.

The erotic speaks of our desire for the other and of our vulnerability before the other. As erotically desiring subjects we are subjects at risk participating in the drama of otherness. Listening to Beauvoir's muted voice, and taking the erotic event as our cue, we discover ways of playing this drama of risk, recognition, and otherness according to the directives of the generosities of the original intentional moment. We learn that the lures of domination and exploitation can be contested by the ethic of the gift and that we can engage the tensions of our otherness without violating each other's humanity.

BIBLIOGRAPHY

Bibliography

Barnes, Hazel. *Sartre and Flaubert*. Chicago: University of Chicago Press, 1981.

Barthes, Roland. *Sade, Fourier, Loyola*. Trans. Richard Miller. New York: Hill and Wang, 1976.

Baruch, Elaine Hoffman. "The Female Body and the Male Mind." *Dissent*. Vol. 34 (1987): 351–358.

Bataille, George. *Guilty*. Trans. Bruce Boone. California: The Lapis Press, 1988.

_____ . *On Nietzsche*. Trans. Bruce Boone. New York: Paragon House, 1992.

Beauvoir, Simone de. *Pyrrhus et Cinéas*. Paris: Gallimard, 1944.

_____ . *Pour une Morale de l'Ambiguite*. Paris: Gallimard, 1944.

_____ . *The Ethics of Ambiguity*. Trans. Bernard Frechtman. New York: Philosophical Library, 1948.

_____ . *Le Deuxieme Sexe*. Paris: Gallimard, 1949.

_____ . *Faut-il Brûler Sade?* Paris: Gallimard, 1955.

_____ . "Must We Burn Sade?" Trans. Annette Michelson, *The Marquis de Sade*. New York: Grove Press, 1966.

_____ . *La Longue Marche*. Paris: Gallimard, 1969.

_____ . *The Coming of Age*. Trans. Patrick O'Brien. New York: Warner Paperback Library: 1973.

_____ . *The Second Sex*. Trans. H.M. Parshley. New York: Vintage Books, 1974.

_____. "Must We Burn Sade?" Trans. Annette Michelson, *The Marquis de Sade.* New York: Grove Press, 1966.

_____. *The Coming of Age.* Trans. Patrick O'Brien. New York: Warner Paperback Library: 1973.

Benjamin, Jessica. *The Bonds of Love.* New York: Pantheon Books, 1988.

Bergoffen, Debra. "The Look As Bad Faith." *Philosophy Today,* Vol. 36:3 (Fall 1992): 221–227.

_____. "Sartre: From Touch to Truth." *Alaska Quarterly Review,* Vol. 3:1 & 2 (1984): 123-124.

_____. "Queering the Phallus." *Dissemenating Lacan.* Ed. David Pettigrew and François Raffoul. Albany: State University of New York Press, 1995.

Bordo, Susan. *The Flight to Objectivity.* Albany: State University of New York Press, 1987.

Bourdieu, Pierre. *Outline of a Theory of Practice.* Trans. Richard Nice. Cambridge: Cambridge University Press, 1977.

Carter, Angela. *The Sadeian Woman, and the Ideology of Pornography.* New York: Pantheon Books, 1978.

Davis, Angela. *Women, Race and Class.* New York: Random House, 1983.

Desan, Wilfred. *The Tragic Finale: An Essay on the Philosophy of Jean Paul Sartre.* New York: Harper Torchbooks, 1960.

Firestone, Shulamith. *The Dialectic of Sex.* London: Granada Publishing, 1972.

Fries, Amy. "Trafficking in Women and Girls: A Modern Slave Trade." *Choices.* Vol. 3:3, (1994): 1–2.

Fullbrook, Kate and Edward Fullbrook. *Simone de Beauvoir and Jean-Paul Sartre: The Remaking of a Twentieth Century Legend.* New York: Basic Books, 1994.

Gaylin, Willard & Ethel Person, Ed. *Passionate Attachments: Thinking About Love,* New York: The Free Press, 1988.

Green, Marjorie. *Descartes.* Minneapolis: University of Minnesota Press, 1985.

Greer, Germaine. *The Female Eunuch.* London: Grenada Publishing, 1971.

Hoffman, Elaine. "The Female Body and the Male Mind." *Dissent*. No. 34, (Summer 1987): 351-363.

hooks, bell. *Feminist Theory, From Margin to Center*. Boston: South End Press, 1984.

Hunt, Lynn. *Eroticism and the Body Politic*. Baltimore: The Johns Hopkins University Press, 1991.

Husserl, Edmund. *Cartesian Meditations*. Trans. Dorion Cairns. The Hague: Martinus Nijhoff, 1973.

Irigaray, Luce. *Sexes and Genealogies*. Trans. Gillian Gill. New York: Columbia University Press, 1987.

_____. *je, tu, nous: Toward a Culture a Difference*. Trans. Alison Martin. New York: Routledge, 1993.

Jay, Martin. *Downcast Eyes*. Berkeley: University of California Press, 1993.

Kristeve, Julia. *Tales of Love*. Trans. Leon Roudiez. New York: Columbia University Press, 1987.

Kruks, Sonia. *Situation and Human Existence, Freedom, Subjectivity and Society*. London: Unwin Hyman, 1990.

_____. "Simone de Beauvoir: Teaching Sartre About Freedom." *Feminist Interpretations of Simone de Beauvoir*. Ed. Margaret A. Simons. University Park: Pennsylvania State University Press, 1995. pp. 79–96.

Lacan, Jacques. *Ecrits*. Trans. Alan Sheridan. New York: W.W. Norton, 1977.

_____. *The Seminar of Jacques Lacan, Book VII, The Ethics of Psychoanalysis, 1959–1960*. Trans. Dennis Porter. New York: W.W. Norton, 1992.

Langnauer, Laurie. *Women and Romance: The Consolations of Gender in the English Novel*. Ithaca: Cornell University Press, 1990.

Le Brun, Annie. *Sade, A Sudden Abyss*. Trans. Camille Naish. San Francisco: City Light Books, 1990.

Leder, Drew. *The Absent Body*. Chicago: The University of Chicago Press, 1990.

Le Doeuff, Michelle. *Hipparchia's Choice*. Trans. Trista Selous. Oxford: Blackwell, 1991.

Levinas, Emanuel. *Outside the Subject*. Trans. Michael B. Smith. California: Stanford University Press, 1994.

Leder, Drew. *The Absent Body.* Chicago: The University of Chicago Press, 1990.

Le Doeuff, Michelle. *Hipparchia's Choice.* Trans. Trista Selous. Oxford: Blackwell, 1991.

Levinas, Emanuel. *Outside the Subject.* Trans. Michael B. Smith. California: Stanford University Press, 1994.

Ludgren-Gothlin, Eva. "Simone de Beauvoir and Ethics." *History of European Ideas,* Vol. 19:4–6, (1994): 899–903.

Lyotard, Jean-François. "The Sign of History." Trans. Geoff Bennington. *The Lyotard Reader.* Ed. Andrew Benjamin, 393–411. Cambridge: Basil Blackwell, 1989.

McMahon, Joseph. "Where Does Real Life Begin?" *Yale French Studies.* No. 35, (1965): 94–111.

Merleau-Ponty, Maurice. *Signs.* Trans. Richard Mc Cleary. Evanston: Northwestern University Press, 1964.

_____ . *Phenomenology of Perception.* Trans. Colin Smith. London: Routledge & Kegan Paul, 1965.

_____ . *The Visible and the Invisible.* Trans. Alphonso Lingis. Evanston: The Northwestern University Press, 1968.

Mitchell, Juliet. *Women, The Longest Revolution.* New York: Pantheon Books, 1966.

Moi, Toril. "Ambiguity and Alienation in *The Second Sex.*" *Boundary* 2. 19:2, (1992): 96–112.

Pateman, Carole. *The Disorder of Women.* Stanford: Stanford University Press, 1989.

Pettigrew, David and François Raffoul, Ed. *Disseminating Lacan,* Albany: State University of New York Press, 1996.

Pilardi, Jo-Ann. "The Changing Critical Fortunes of *The Second Sex.*" *History and Theory.* Vol. 32:1 (1993): 51–73.

Sade, Marquis de. *Justine, Philosophy in the Bedroom, and Other Writings.* Trans. Richard Seaver and Austryn Wainhouse. New York: Grove Press, Inc. 1965.

_____ . *Juliette.* Trans. Austryn Wainhouse. New York: Grove Press, Inc. 1968.

_____ . *No Exit and Three Other Plays*. Trans. Stuart Gilbert and Lionel Abel. New York: Vintage, 1959.

_____ . *Saint Genet*. Trans. Bernard Frechtman. New York: Pantheon Books, 1963.

Scarry, Elaine. *The Body in Pain*. Oxford: Oxford University Press, 1985.

Schwarzer, Alice. *After The Second Sex: Conversations with Simone de Beauvoir*. New York: Pantheon Books, 1984.

Simons, Margaret A. "Guess What's Missing in *The Second Sex?*" *Women's Studies International Forum*. Vol. 6:5 (1983): 559–564.

_____ . "Sexism and the Philosophical Cannon: On Reading Beauvoir's *Second Sex*." *Journal of the History of Ideas*. Vol. 51 (July/Sept. 1990): 487–504.

_____ . Ed. *Feminist Interpretations of Simone de Beauvoir*. University Park: The Pennsylvania State University Press, 1995.

Spelman, Elizabeth V. *Inessential Woman*. Boston: Beacon Press, 1988.

Stone, Bob. "Simone de Beauvoir and the Existential Basis of Socialism." *Social Text*, Vol. 17 (1987): 123–142.

Yeo, Michael. "Perceiving/Reading the Other: Ethical Dimensions." *Merleau-Ponty : Hermeneutics and Post-modernism*. Ed. Thomas W. Busch & Shaun Gallagher. Albany: State University of New York Press, 1992.

Young, Iris Marion. *Throwing Like a Girl and Other Essays in Feminist Philosophy and Social Theory*. Bloomington: Indiana University Press, 1990.

INDEX

Index

by one's situation, and childhood,
83–84
and Sade, 130
and *The Second Sex*, 157, 159–61,
164, 169

ego, 38, 58
and freedom, 54
and generosity, 65
-imago, 123–25, 203
transcendental, in Husserl, 16
and violence, 56
egoism
ethical, 58
failure of, 13
empiricism, 15
en-soi, 19, 102, 103
enemy
in *The Ethics of Ambiguity*, 89, 100
ontology of, 50
and *Pyrrhus et Cinéas*, 50–51, 60,
62, 67
and Sade, 134–37
epoché, 16, 25, 103
ethics of, 90–98
and Sade, 120–21
equality, 169
erotic, 2, 3, 15–16, 221–23
and Beauvoir's phenomenological
roots, 5–6
definition of, in French dictionaries,
40
dimensions of the world, 189–90
disruption, 203, 221
ethic of, 6–8, 29, 121, 138, 185–218
event, 6, 190, 197, 203, 222
fluidity of, 212
and generosity, 64, 185–218
and humanism, 215–18
and intentionality, 120
love, 161–63
and the maternal body, 209–10
and the myth of femininity, 144–46

and the neutral subject, 160–63
passion, 202
and patriarchy, 110, 191
and perversion, 118–20
as a philosophical category,
11–42, 109
and Sade, 118–21, 127–28, 130, 138
subject, 194
essence
human, 52
universal, 99
essentialism, 132, 151, 174
Ethics of Ambiguity, The (Beauvoir),
4, 75–110, 113, 186, 190
and the erotic as a philosophical
category, 11, 18, 21, 28–30
and erotic risks, 100–104
and the ethics of the epoché,
90–98
history in, 82–85
imagination in, 124
and intentionality, 21, 29–30,
76–82
intimacy in, 70
joy in, 67
and "Merleau-Ponty and Pseudo-
Sartrianism," 18, 21
and *Must We Burn Sade?*, 113, 118,
124, 137
and the Other, 85–90
and perversion, 118
and *Pyrrhus et Cinéas*, 45
and reciprocity, 40
and recognition, 98–100
and the Sartre-Merleau-Ponty
debate, 18
and *The Second Sex*, 113, 142, 171,
173
ethical other, 17, 28–29, 41
ethical will, 90–91
ethics, 2, 6. *See also* morality
and a contingent world, 49
of the epoché, 90–98

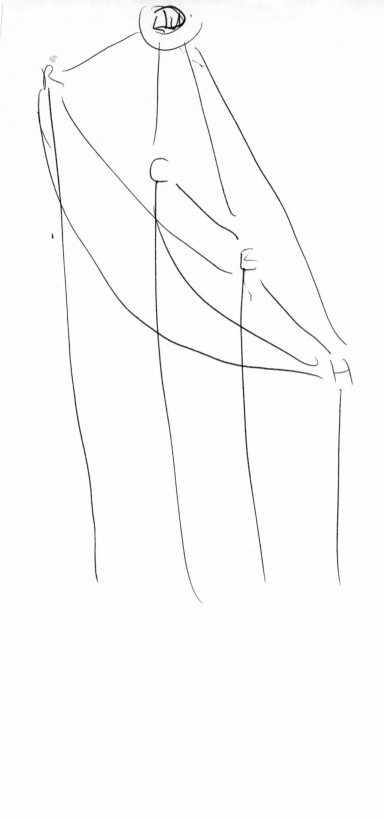